GERMAN EXPRESSIONISM

GERMAN EXPRESSIONISM

Series edited by J. M. Ritchie

SCENES
FROM THE HEROIC LIFE
OF THE MIDDLE CLASSES

Five Plays

CARL STERNHEIM

Translated from the German by

M. A. L. Brown, M. A. McHaffie, J. M. Ritchie, J. D. Stowell

CALDER AND BOYARS · LONDON

First published in Great Britain 1970 by
Calder and Boyars Ltd.,
18 Brewer Street, London W1

© *These translations Calder and Boyars 1970*

All translations taken from Carl Sternheim, *Dramen I* ed. W. Emrich 1963, Hermann Luchterhand Verlag GmbH containing:

> *Bürger Schippel* (Paul Schippel Esq)
> *Die Hose* (The Bloomers)
> *Der Snob* (The Snob)
> *1913* (1913)
> *Das Fossil* (The Fossil)

© Hermann Luchterhand Verlag GmbH in Neuwied/Rhein und Berlin-West 1963

SBN 7145 0026 7 Cloth edition
SBN 7145 0027 5 Paper edition

PRINTED IN GREAT BRITAIN BY
WILLMER BROTHERS LIMITED, BIRKENHEAD

CONTENTS

INTRODUCTION

From 1911 onwards (the date of the appearance of *The Bloomers*)
Sternheim's cycle of satirical comedies *Scenes from the Heroic
Life of the Middle Classes* was prominent on the German stage
and indeed Sternheim became so famous that his plays were
translated into English several times. *The Snob* appeared first
in translation in 1927 in a collection called *Eight European
Plays*, where it was described in the introduction as a masterpiece and it was translated again in 1949 by Eric Bentley. *Die
Marquise von Arcis* was translated into English by Ashley Dukes
as *The Mask of Virtue* and performed in London in 1935. Vivien
Leigh made her West End début on this occasion in the rôle of
Henriette Duquenoy. It was also Eric Bentley's translation of
The Bloomers which reached the London stage in 1963. Sternheim's peculiar linguistic distortions probably proved strange;
however, the *Spectator* critic could quote some parts of this
adaptation with approval:

> 'There are some funny lines, worthy almost of the modern
> accolade of satirical. "May I go to church?", asks the young
> wife at one point. "It's almost an emergency".'

It must be admitted, all the same, that Sternheim has never been
completely successful in English. Indeed few German dramatists
have. Brecht, of course, is now appearing in complete translation,
Dürrenmatt has proved a popular success in recent years. But
even great dramatists like Hofmannsthal are rarely performed
even when their works are available in English. The point remains that Sternheim has been considered to be so significant
for European theatre that connoisseur translators like Bentley
and Ashley Dukes very early made attempts to introduce him
to the English-speaking public. Perhaps Sternheim's comedies,
which depend so much on strictly German imponderables, can
never appeal to a non-German public. Perhaps Sternheim's vision
of the German bourgeois as the source of the modern malaise in

7

the technological world of capitalist enterprise can never be equally significant outside Germany. Perhaps *The Snob* is the only one of his plays which are understandable readily in England or America as an example of how to succeed in society by really trying. Be that as it may in Germany itself at least, Sternheim's reputation is once again approaching the apex reached in the 1920s, when he was widely played and discussed. Authority was never well disposed towards him then, and censorship, official displeasure, wars and exile eventually led to the almost total disappearance of his work into the limbo of the unperformed dramatist, a fate he shared with the whole Expressionist generation. But since the end of the war, many German theatres have successfully played Kaiser, Barlach, Lasker-Schüler and other Expressionists, and Sternheim too has gradually resumed his former place in the permanent theatre repertoire—indeed *Theater Heute* for September 1963 lists so many new Sternheim productions it is able to talk of a 'Sternheim Renaissance.'

So Sternheim has benefited from fashionable interest in satire and from the general re-discovery of the Expressionist generation. The fact that he wrote comedies and not tragedies has also not harmed him in the comedy-starved theatre repertoire of Germany. At the same time his work strangely reflects the effect of present-day political divisions. He is probably little played in East Germany while he is now widely performed in the West. Yet the East German cultural authorities clearly thought at one time that they had in Sternheim an ally in their battle against bourgeois capitalism, for it was the Communist Aufbau-Verlag which brought out the first modern edition of his plays in 1947-8. Unfortunately the East German authorities' reaction to Sternheim is very similar to their reaction to Brecht. They are proud to have him and would like to exploit him but he is *unbequem.* He does not fit. Besides he is an Expressionist! Despite the anti-bourgeois, activist, communist element in Expressionism, it is still rather difficult for East German critics to be positive about any representative of this movement; for them Expressionism tends to come under blanket condemnation as formalistic, abstract, experimental, unrealistic art given to exploiting the absurd and grotesque. Hence the discussion of Sternheim has continued in

8

the West rather than the East—in America where Sternheim's most faithful supporter Wolfgang Paulsen has been working on a Sternheim monograph, and in West Germany, whence have come several searching studies in recent years. The final accolade of academic acceptance lies clearly with the inclusion of Sternheim in Benno von Wiese's *Das Deutsche Drama vom Barock bis zur Gegenwart* (1958) and the appearance of the imposing volumes of Professor Wilhelm Emrich's critical edition of the complete works. As *Theater Heute* again put it: *Sternheim wird Klassiker!* Sternheim has become a classic.

Sternheim then has pulled off that combination rare in the German theatre; he has written successful comedies which have gained academic acclaim. As has been suggested, this acclaim has not been easily come by and study of the plays themselves does much to explain the embarrassment of earlier critics when faced with Sternheim. At first sight it is hard to reconcile the written texts of his plays with the general picture of the hectic world of theatrical experimentation one normally associates with German theatre of the 1920s in general and Expressionist theatre in particular. Yet when they are studied more closely it becomes clear that almost all the modern theatrical developments right through to Brecht are there already *potentially* in Sternheim. First of all one must remember the date: *The Bloomers* (1911), *The Snob* (1913)—this was over fifty years ago! Yet it is remarkable what Sternheim was already doing. He had realised that the naturalistic theatre *à la* Hauptmann was dead. He had realised that its contemporary opposite, the neo-romantic theatre *à la* Hofmannsthal/Hauptmann was also dead, particularly in comedy. And he had realised that the exquisite nuances of symbolism in the theatre were stone dead. These were avenues which the German theatre had already exhaustively explored. Hence in a Sternheim comedy the audience is never invited to 'hunt the symbol,' never supposed to feel that it is being transported onto a higher plane of 'poetic' truth; nor, however, does Sternheim offer his audience a simple realistic picture of bourgeois reality. He had served a long apprenticeship in the theatre and had written eight plays exploring such theatrical possibilities—the realistic, neo-romantic and symbolic genres—before he found

9

his own peculiar form in 1911 with *The Bloomers*, a middle-class comedy. This became a *succès de scandale* and was immediately banned because of the indelicacy of its subject, namely the deliberately banal tale of how at the changing of the guards a lady's drawers fell about her heels practically before the very eyes of a royal personage and the results that ensued in the lady's youthful *ménage*. (This arabesque receives an elegant variation in *The Snob*, the sequel on ambitious snobbery, sentimental ruthlessness and the craven superman). With the comment that Sternheim had found his *form*, an important statement has been made about the nature of his comedies because they are in fact extremely formalistic, deliberately constructed with extreme care to exploit every possible pun, situation, combination of characters, etc. It is for this reason that he was able to construct a comedy a year from now on and sometimes two. These plays were often linked. Characters from earlier plays reappeared in later plays which again made for some facility in construction and the whole collection of middle-class comedies could then be grouped together under the collective title *Scenes from the Heroic Life of the Middle-Classes*. At the same time as these middle-class comedies, however, Sternheim was also writing other (historical) plays based on literary (and generally French) models and these give some indication of his personal tastes: *The Candidate* after the little-known play by Flaubert; *The Charmer* after Maupassant; *The Miser* after Molière; *Marquise von Arcis* after Diderot; *Manon Lescaut* after Prévost. Oscar Wilde was another of the heroes about whom he wrote a play, and so was Casanova. Many of the themes he tackled had already been attempted by contemporary dramatists and the creative process is reminiscent of Brecht's love of adaptations and popular successes. And like Brecht later, Sternheim too was fascinated by American capitalism and gangsterdom. His last works were called *Knockout* and *John Pierpoint Morgan*. *Paul Schippel Esq.*, was even set to music by Dohnanyi as *The Tenor*, a reminder of how close music and drama were in these days in Germany and yet another pointer to Brecht. Altogether Sternheim's total output numbered about thirty plays. Not all of these were of equal quality, nevertheless even disregarding the prose works, novels, short stories, critical essays, etc., he left behind on his death a considerable *oeuvre*.

As for the plays themselves, although he did turn them out remarkably quickly, it must not be thought that these were mere popular pot-boilers. For a start his peculiar theatrical language with its distortion, intentional starkness and avoidance of all metaphor and emotion was clearly not aimed at wide popular appeal. In effect it was this deliberately mannered unpoetic language which disturbed audiences and critics probably more than anything else in Sternheim. His language, like his plays, is constructed. This unnaturally mannered style can be taken as a foretaste of the expressionistic shorthand called 'telegraphese' or 'telegram style'; but much more significant is the force with which this style registers Sternheim's personal reaction against the melodic and psychological subtleties of the Hofmannsthal variety, and more, it is remarkably akin to Brecht's later rejection of the whole bourgeois aesthetic of beauty as the source of art. Sternheim is working towards something entirely different from the old ideal that the aim of art is beauty and the pleasure which beauty imparts. For Sternheim, as for Brecht later, Romanticism was the great error which contemporary man had to combat at all costs, and he does everything in his linguistic power to destroy it. Perhaps now that the language of Gottfried Benn has been accepted alongside that of Rilke as a possible form of literary expression the time is ripe at last for a proper appreciation of Sternheim's deliberately unnatural style. He himself has many affinities with Gottfried Benn and dedicated one of his plays to him, with the significant sub-title, New Objectivity!

The same process of reduction towards extreme precision and hard functionalism which can be observed in Sternheim's treatment of language can also be observed in his treatment of plot. As Sokel has said of Expressionist drama in general, plot as such almost disappears and a more musical 'theme' takes its place. Sternheim simply selects typical situations and permutates them as required by the demands of his play. In Act I of *The Snob* the social climber gets rid of both of his parents. In Act II he gets one of them back. In Act III there is a dazzling reversal of the classic theatrical situation; in the Sternheim comedy the impostor is *not* exposed in the end, on the contrary he rises to even greater heights. Just as there is little plot so too there are no exquisite nuances in the psychological analysis of character, and no need for a long exposition to introduce the main characters and the situation. The characters, in as much as they are characters, describe themselves. For example, Christian, the Snob, tells in a long monologue how he has managed to 'arrive'. Characters like this are *typical* people in *typical* situations—typical, however, not in any crude naturalistic sense of the word. Nothing about the play is really naturalistic or realistic from the mannered language to the general shape of the play itself. The overall effect is one of shock—the shock of recognition. Already Sternheim has begun to exploit the theatrical tricks which Brecht was to exploit so much more extensively, such a short time afterwards, and like Brecht he is not afraid to break through the bonds of realism into drastic and grotesque extremes. The plays are, as has been suggested, unnaturally constructivistic and formalised. The stage settings, for example, are generally constant from act to act: always just one room, and into this one room stream all the right people and always at the right time. It is like a parody of the well-made play—'la pièce bien faite'—and this is exactly what it is: parody! A parody of the Ibsen drama of domestic interior, or the French society play or the Oscar Wilde variety of the conversation piece. Parody is the medium of nearly all modern literature of the Twenties, parody that often comes dangerously close to plagiarism. It is the medium of Brecht, a deliberate and conscious exploitation of all the technical possibilities to hand permitting of no restriction or limitation of scope from mere realism. This may be Expressionism but it is the cold side of Expressionism. Instead of the chaotic, poetic kind of Expressionist play Sternheim presents plays which are almost geometrically constructed, and pared down to the absolutely bare essentials. And all the unrealistic effects banished by the naturalistic school of drama are re-introduced, as, for example, long monologues and asides. Altogether the effect is of actors *acting*. Audiences are never asked to believe that they are watching something real happening now before their very eyes. It is thereby possible to perform the plays in two main styles, either with the exaggerated overstatement of melodrama, stressing the deliberate unreality of the whole business, or with the very cool understatement of a brittle Noel Coward manner. Either way the play is the thing and its own curious dynamics must simply be accepted. Either way the result is extremely funny.

But Sternheim is more than just funny. He is the surgeon on the body of the age with a quick scalpel which penetrates through the protecting flesh to the very bone, exploring the servility, the philistinism, the hypocrisy, the empty idealism of the hated bourgeois who loves to wrap up even the most sordid negotiation in an aura of idealistic romanticism. This is the 'where-is-the-higher-significance-of-all-this-for-me' cry of Theobald in *The Snob*, when in reality as the play demonstrates, money and power are the only things that talk to him. The bourgeois is the hated enemy. Sternheim attempts to destroy him by making him ridiculous and there is no softening of the blow. Again this is a point which has disturbed many critics about Sternheim's plays. Sokel in the introduction to his *Anthology of German Expressionist Drama* has correctly described this essential difference between a Sternheim comedy and a normal comedy.

'There are not in Sternheim's comedies, as there are in Molière's, characters with moderate points of view, representing common sense—i.e. the common ground shared by author and audience. Sternheim fails to supply us with the convenient yardstick by which we can judge, while feeling comfortably above them, the comic characters as eccentrics. In Sternheim it is not the characters but the world that has lost its centre. His characters demonstrate a process that defines the whole of bourgeois society, and that might be called a quiet pandemonium of cold-blooded, insidious inhumanity'.

All the characters are hateful or unsympathetic.

Sternheim saw himself as the German Molière and his *Snob* is the German Tartuffe, but now there is no king's messenger in the last scene to save the situation. Instead Christian goes on from strength to strength, climbing higher and higher in soc-

13

iety. Theobald, the Count, Christian, even Marianne and Sybil —they all have the same will to power, the same egotism. And when one looks at the other plays this is all there seems to be on the surface: Nietzsche and Darwin. Nietzsche's will to power and the idea of the superman; Darwin's survival of the fittest by adaptation to circumstance and the struggle for existence, the very phrases are exploited even in the starkly reduced text of a play like the *Snob*, though there is absolutely no philosophising except for purposes of ridicule. The result of all this is an almost Brechtian alienation. On the one hand the bourgeois is exposed as a mere climber with the will to power who is prepared even to suppress his own parents to get on in the world. On the other hand the emptiness of the struggle is revealed, a world without values is exposed. On the one hand we despise the snob for what he is doing; on the other hand we almost admire this superman for the enormous vitality, the *élan vital* he deploys in the doing of it. Here again we are very close to the Brechtian character like Mack the Knife, the bourgeois villain of immaculate appearance and enormous crimes and close to Sternheim himself, though Sternheim is perhaps even more like his eponymous hero Oscar Wilde. This again is in a powerful modern tradition. We are nowadays too prone perhaps to think of the artist as the social outcast, the outsider, the tramp with his dustbin perspective of society, thereby overlooking the strong trend in the opposite direction. Some modern artists have attempted to be insiders. They do not need to sink to the lower depths to look at society from below—they write from the top, dress in blindingly white linen like Baudelaire or Oscar Wilde, or the clinical cloak of a Gottfried Benn and cast a cold, contemptuous aristocratic gaze *down* on the middle classes. The modern artist can be a dandy like Sternheim; a German Noel Coward, only much more savage. This is again something that many critics have not been able to forgive Sternheim—the fact that he was so rich and lived in a castle with a butler, valet and servants to look after him even while they admit that it was this same wealth which gave him his extraordinary insight into the capitalistic money manipulations of his age. Yet Sternheim is an almost classical example of the dandy, that problem figure of the modern age whom Otto Mann had described as follows:

> 'The dandy tends to appear in periods of transition when democracy is not yet all-powerful, when the aristocracy is only just beginning to waver and decline. In the confusion of such times it is possible for many disgusted, *déclassé* men of leisure who are still full of originality or strength to seize upon the plan of establishing a new kind of aristocracy which will not be so easily destroyed because it shall be built on the finest, and most indestructible of qualities, on those divine gifts which cannot be achieved by mere hard work or money. The dandy is the last explosion of heroism in the ages of decline.'

This is the real source of Sternheim's heroic battle against the forces of his age, for he is like his own hero Christian the Snob, immaculate, clear-headed, calculating, rational, logical, but at the same time a wild man with a devouring fire in his guts. Sternheim cannot be dismissed as a sardonic rationalist or cynic, there is plenty that he feels strongly about, only this turns to hate expressed in cold language and strict form. He is a man with a mission but once again a mission which has been misunderstood—Sternheim believes quite simply that every man has somewhere within him a self all his own, and it is up to him to realise this self regardless of the various social, political, religious and other pressures of modern society which restrict this. He must have moral and civil courage, the courage of his own vices. The individual must accept his own peculiarities for good or evil and live them to the full. Only in this way can humanity be saved from the dead hand of uniformity and the capacity of man to produce infinitely new forms of humanity preserved. Hence there is no moral or spiritual ideal guiding the conduct of the individual, Sternheim is prepared to accept any 'so-called' vices provided they are the true expression of the self, the only question is which methods the individual must employ to escape the normalising, standardising pressure of society and this generally is the *mask* with which he conceals the true self until he is sufficiently powerful to live out his real life.

From this the reason for the embarrassment of Communist

critics when dealing with Sternheim becomes apparent. It is true that Sternheim was a bitter enemy of the bourgeoisie; it is true that he claimed that all great art must be political and that he wielded his pen for extreme left-wing journals, apparently convinced of the energy of the Russian working class movement and the proletariat as compared with the decadence and debility of the Western middle classes. Yet where does he really stand? Mittenzwei, the Communist critic, sees him between conservative and progressive, mystic and rationalist, idealist and realist, between Nietzsche and Marx. And this is a fair description. Sternheim is essentially non-aligned. His criticism of the bourgeoisie is devastating yet he has no simple solution for society. He is an intellectual afflicted like Gottfried Benn with the curse of 'progressive cerebration' and the longing for escape. This escape he seeks like Gottfried Benn in a kind of primitive vitalism. Hence he is at the same time the destroyer of idealistic platitudes and the admirer of the American capitalist go-better.

His solution to the problems of the age is a form of extreme individualism. But this is an extremely private solution and explains the communist disquiet—formalism is bad enough, but such subjectivism is unforgivable. And yet it is perhaps this same subjectivism so typical of the expressionist generation which is the source of Sternheim's strength today. With ferocity and single-mindedness he exposes the problem of the individual in society—like Brecht he offers no simple solution and like Brecht he is very, very funny. In this way he is more than a mere social critic or satirist exposing the sins and excesses of the philistines, he is the true expressionist visionary. It has been simple for some critics to see in Sternheim's heroes the shadows of the cold-blood mediocrities of the future Hitler regime. But he goes more deeply even than this. His aim was to strike through appearances to the heart of the matter, to reveal the true nature of man. His art is 'the purest image possible for a shattering age like his own', his mission not the 'rebirth of society' but the 'rebirth of man'. Sternheim is not dated, for steeped though he is in the characteristics of the German world of a particular period this vision raises his art above the limitation of time and place. No-one will go to Sternheim for comfort as they would go to Goethe or Hölderlin, yet he remains a great artist—a literary figure, a theatrical figure of stature.

As has been stressed on many occasions, the *juste milieu*, the term Sternheim adopted for the mentality of middle class conformism, can be found in all his works, no matter what their setting or century. For this volume, however, only those plays directly concerned with the middle-classes in Germany at the turn of the century have been included, namely *Paul Schippel Esq.*, *The Bloomers*, *The Snob*, 1913, *The Fossil*. The only exclusion from the six plays which Emrich lists as strictly belonging to *Scenes from the Heroic Life of the Middle Classes* is *Die Kassette* (*The Money Box*), which is available in English in Sokel's *Anthology of Expressionist Drama*.

The title of the first play in the present selection, *Bürger Schippel*, already offers difficulties for the translator. For Paul Schippel, the 'hero' only becomes a 'Bürger' at the end of the play. *Citizen Schippel*, with its echoes of Citizen Kane on the one hand and the French Revolution on the other, is not quite appropriate, and 'bourgeois' is never an adequate translation for the German 'Bürger'. In an attempt to indicate Schippel's rise to middle-class status the compromise solution *Paul Schippel Esq* was eventually arrived at. This play was to be one of Sternheim's greatest successes and it is for this reason that it appears slightly out of chronological order in the present selection of five plays. The following four form a fairly coherent tetralogy concerned with the rising fortunes of the Maske family. Schippel himself is a Chaplinesque figure in a bowler hat, but at the same time an Expressionistic 'New Man' capable of total transformation. With him there is no question of continuity of character or personality; what he experiences and thereby demonstrates is 'nothing less than a total transformation from one second to the next. A rebirth ...' (I,3). One day he is a rabbit cowering in the cabbage-patch. The next he is aware of such a colossal upsurge of strength, he feels knives growing from his toes and sabres from his teeth. He is a charge of dynamite in the drawing-room. By the end of the play Schippel has demonstrated his

17

truly 'heroic' qualities, firstly by his grand gesture in giving up the girl he has done everything to have in his power; secondly by his heroic bearing at the music festival which he turns into a triumph; and thirdly by his challenge to a duel. A pauper who turns down the 10,000 marks dowry which go with the beautiful girl and then, certain of a miserable pittance, goes on to win the wreath by his unwavering divine singing and finally faces the muzzle of a revolver, has proved himself worthy to the full of 'the higher blessings of the middle classes'.

The Bloomers, the first of what was to be Sternheim's great cycle of middle-class comedies, is also concerned with the quest for the heroic. Who is the hero? Frank Scarron, the Nietzschean stormer of barricades? Or Benjamin Mandelstam, the disciple of Wagner? Scarron's philosophy is quite simple: what is weak and lacking in vitality must give way to what is strong and healthy. Only through the individual blessed with certain energies is the boundless mass of humanity given direction. Might is the supreme delight! With this philosophy Mandelstam agrees, adding merely the Darwinian principles that both he and Scarron are descended from the ape, all men are fundamentally equal, and any man can reach the heights in the struggle for existence. But who turns out to be the real cyclops, the giant? Mandelstam, as Theobald quickly realises, has no marrow, and Scarron's will is sapped. Instead of coming to sweep Louise off her feet as he has promised, he ends up drunk and incapable in the arms of a common prostitute. The 'decisive turning point' in Louise's life is lost. Hence the only people who really get what they want are, first of all, Fräulein Deuter, who is endowed with a 'tremendous lust for life' despite her plain exterior, and Theobald, whom she has quickly identified as the true giant. The heroes are not the great thinkers, poets, painters and musicians. The heroes are the Theobalds who achieve complete freedom within their own sphere, a freedom which is lost if the world pays any particular attention to them. Their insignificance is the cloak under which they can indulge their inclinations, their innermost natures, unhindered. By the end of the play all the so-called spiritual forces are in complete disarray and life lived on the basis of reality is triumphant.

In *The Snob* the off-spring Theobald has been able to afford by exploiting those who sought to exploit him is already grown-up and already leaving his parents far behind. He has assimilated his father's maxim completely. By adopting as his cloak the manners and style of the aristocracy, Christian, the dandy, still remains free and governed exclusively by his own will. In Darwinian terms he has adopted the protective colouring of his new surroundings, not only the clothing, the knot of a tie, but also the 'metaphysical' cloud of a feudal ideology. This he has done the better to arm himself in the fierce jungle warfare of the modern struggle for existence.

> 'The struggle for existence, I've been through all that too, and the turmoil taught me a lot too. Impelled by an insatiable impulse, I waded right through the pap of the commonplace because I had learned that life really only begins when you are through and out the other side. But you see how I got there, how I "arrived", how I tore strips of living flesh from my own body and wore them, twisted into an elegant cravat round my own neck. Little by little I approached that form which the superior being must assume among his peers:' (II, 6).

This is a man, who, as he says himself, knows the cast of his own temperament exactly and creates an image of himself without any thought to the judgment of the gallery. In the end it is he who subjugates the haughty aristocrat Marianne and triumphs completely.

In the last scene of *The Snob* Christian mentions a property in Buchow which he is just acquiring. The next play in the cycle, 1913, introduces him as His Excellency, Baron Christian Maske von Buchow. The *Times Literary Supplement* in its extensive discussion of Sternheim on February 8, 1968, summarised this play as follows:

> 'Here Sternheim presents the spectator with three contrasting specimens of humanity whose unholy and unnatural alliance may well be considered responsible for most of the nefarious recent episodes in German history: the financial magnate

ever seeking new battlefields in the economic world until he feels himself a Napoleon; the ardent nationalist bandying patriotic slogans and blindly following the myth of a leader; and the aestheticising scion of the family too weak to do anything but bury his head in the sand. All these attitudes are taken to the extreme right up to the point where the inevitable collapse brings the game of plot and counter-plot to an ominous and bizarre end.'

Certainly the Sternheim doctrine of faith in oneself, even in one's own weakness, is developed here yet again. One must suppress none of one's secret wishes, accept the intoxication of power. Christian has this power and Sophie has it. Ottilie tries to develop it. Krey the nationalist idealist exercises his own kind of power over the youth of Germany, and even the fop Philipp Ernst has power of a kind—over women. Once again the apparently naturalistic setting (in this case the library at Buchow Castle) turns out to be a jungle in which a fight to the death is to be fought. The world of the spirit is stripped naked and revealed as meaningless. Primitive emotions are bared. Questions of ethics are secondary to the need to satisfy basic hungers. As Brecht would later put it: 'Erst kommt das Fressen, dann kommt die Moral'. The reward for the 'hero' as always in Sternheim is 'vital, untrammeled awareness of living'. The effect of the whole is that of a hectic vision in which the modern capitalistic world is seen staggering blindly into war. The masses are filled with dread and even the initiated quake at the roaring from the mountains of gold amassed over their heads. The individual is brainwashed till he is not aware of any individual value in anything and he consumes and discards feelings, judgments and even himself ...! Sophie, the representative of modern capitalistic enterprises has inherited the basic ingredients for success from her father: total lack of scruples. She expands as he did, with more foresight and business acumen perhaps, but now the awareness of what it is all leading to is lacking. As in *The Snob* (I, 1) Christian balances his books. What comes out is the feeling that the time is ripe for someone or other to destroy brick by brick the society he has helped to create.

1913 left the cycle on the eve of the Great World War. In *The Fossil* the scene moves to the heart of Junker Prussia five years after the war. Sophie and her husband Otto have still important rôles to play in the representative family saga but now the final battle is to be that between feudal Germany and the New Man. Otto the captain of industry and his father, the ex-cavalry general, have not exchanged a word since the confirmation of Germany's defeat by the signing of the Treaty of Versailles. The explosive situation which thereby exists in the family circle is resolved by the return of the aristocratic Ago von Bohna from imprisonment in Russia—as a Communist. Ago is the 'New Man'—instead of standing fast against change he is constantly ready to adapt. Ursula, although brought up in the modern scientific attitude which is the awareness of eternal change, is asked by her father, the fossil, to remain true to the unchanging heritage of the blood. It is with the aristocracy and not the defeated bourgeoisie that the man with the social conscience now engages in life and death struggle. Ago and Ursula are the symbols of the conflict, the decisive battle between communism and feudalism. And as always in Sternheim the outcome is ambivalent. Like Brecht he exposes his audiences to a certain dialectic and like Brecht he leaves them to answer the basic questions for themselves. Indeed it was from seeds such as these (e.g. the Communist chauffeur dallying with the daughter of the house) that Brecht's greatest comedy, *Puntila and his Man Matti*, was to grow. But there is no need to regard Sternheim as a mere forerunner of Brecht. The *Times Literary Supplement* reviewer finished his penetrating survey as follows:

'The comedies of *Aus dem bürgerlichen Heldenleben* and some of the stories with the same background look destined to last, because they are firmly rooted in time and place in what now appears the heyday of the urban middle class in the years immediately preceding the 1914–18 War and yet present types and human foibles which we recognise to be of all time. They live above all through their humour, which surges irrepressibly through every varnish of current ideology that may be laid on them.'
                                                                J.M.R.

RECOMMENDED READING

H. F. Garten:
Modern German Drama (London, 1939)
Walter Gropius ed.:
The Theatre of the Bauhaus (Wesleyan University Press, 1961)
M. Hamburger and C. Middleton eds.:
Modern German Poetry 1910–1960 (London, 1963)
Claude Hill and Ralph Ley:
The Drama of German Expressionism. A German-English Bibliography (University of North Carolina Press, 1960)
Egbert Krispyn:
Style and Society in German Literary Expressionism (University of Florida, 1964)
Hector Maclean:
Expressionism in *Periods in German Literature* ed. J. M. Ritchie (London, 1966)
Paul Raabe:
The Era of German Expressionism in preparation (Calder and Boyars)
J. M. Ritchie:
German Theatre between the Wars and the Genteel Tradition, *Modern Drama*, Feb. 1965; The Expressionist Revival, *Seminar*, Spring 1966.
J. M. Ritchie (ed.): *Seven Expressionist Plays, Kokoschka to Barlach; Vision and Aftermath*, four Expressionist War Plays (Calder and Boyars, 1969)
R. H. Samuel and R. Hinton Thomas:
Expressionism in German Life, Literature and the Theatre, 1910–1924 (Cambridge, 1939)
Walter H. Sokel:
The Writer in Extremis: Expressionism in 20th Century German Literature (Stanford, California)
An Anthology of German Expressionist Drama, a prelude to the absurd (Doubleday Anchor, A 365)
August Strindberg:
Eight Expressionist Plays (Bantam Classics, QC 261)

22

PAUL SCHIPPEL ESQ

A *Comedy*

For Albert Bassermann, actor of genius

Translated by M. A. L. Brown

PAUL SCHIPPEL ESQ

Characters

THE PRINCE
TILMAN HICKETIER, *a goldsmith*
JENNY HICKETIER, *his wife*
THEKLA HICKETIER, *his sister*
HEINRICH KREY, *a civil servant*
ANDREAS WOLKE, *owner of a printing works*
PAUL SCHIPPEL
A DOCTOR
MÜLLER and SCHULTZE

ACT I

SCENE 1

THEKLA: (*very light blonde, enters left.*) You alone, Jenny? What d'you think happened last night? About twelve I heard a noise by the garden fence, and saw a shadow, the silhouette of a man crouching there.

JENNY: Thekla!

THEKLA: I watched for ages and he kept crouching there. He noticed me, never moved. In the end, to make it easier for him I withdrew. He disappeared. Who could it have been?

JENNY: Your current admirer.

THEKLA: Why come and go like a thief at dead of night?

JENNY: Your eyes must have been playing you tricks. You still haven't recovered from Adolf's death.

THEKLA: Don't talk like that about Naumann and me anymore. I was supposed to marry him—the ghastly creature. He was so upright it made me squirm.

JENNY: Now he rests in peace. The men will be back from the funeral directly. Wonder if they sang, 'Gently are they laid to rest' without the deceased in the tenor part?

THEKLA: What a morning! To know for certain he is dust. The joy I felt dispelled my terror at the ghostly figure in the night.

JENNY: You used to have a better opinion of Naumann.

THEKLA: One June evening decided everything. Just the two of us—all alone. I overflowed with happiness, ready to give myself to him as to the universe. Had he but spoken, made a sign. I would have engulfed him. The imbecile said nothing. Just sat goggle eyed.

JENNY: Child!

THEKLA: That did it. I was free again.

JENNY: Don't spoil Tilmann's picture of his friend.

THEKLA: No more than I would his picture of me with a halo. In my brother's eyes we are up on a pedestal for ever as bride and groom. I play the inconsolable with him.

JENNY: It's in his nature to need symbols.

(THEKLA *has removed a gold crown of laurel-leaves from its cushion under a glass-case and placed it on her head laughing.*)

Here you see united his two highest ideals—his sister and the crown they won twice over at the music festival.

JENNY: And which, with Naumann dying on them just before the festival, is now in danger.

THEKLA: In that respect his decease showed some lack of consideration. But there's a good chance of Schippel...

JENNY: There's a dangerous complication where he's concerned. I may not tell you what it is.

THEKLA: I've known for a long time. He's a bastard.

JENNY: You must never have heard that word when Tilmann is in the room.

THEKLA: I haven't even heard of storks when Tilmann is in the room.

JENNY: The men have a horror of the idea. They cannot make up their minds about asking him. In the meantime time flies. The Prince arrived at the castle yesterday. Tilmann only just has himself under control, but Wolke and Krey...

THEKLA: (*laughs.*) Are wild!

JENNY: Scoffer! Men like them are not romantic enough for you.

THEKLA: Both boors compared with Tilmann.

JENNY: Because you won't take the trouble to look at their good points.

THEKLA: If I look at Krey at all he is horror-struck. The bachelor goes in fear of the young unmarried woman.

JENNY: Wolke could be fond of you—always was fond of you.

THEKLA: In that case I'd far rather have Krey! I'd be able to mould him. (*Suddenly.*) Last night's ghost resembled Wolke— same size, same shape. Could that be? Wolke bent on nocturnal romance. (*Laughs tempestuously.*) If so, I might fancy even Wolke. I have never been in such a fever of expectation for my Prince Charming.

JENNY: Child!

(THEKLA *draws* JENNY'S *hands to his bosom.*) My heart has reached its equinox. Summer is about to begin.

SCENE 2

HICKETIER, KREY, WOLKE *appear in frock-coats and top-hats.*

HICKETIER: (*to* THEKLA.) My poor dear sister!

WOLKE: He departed from us, so to speak, in glory, snatched away in the prime of life. A splendid funeral. The singing rather treacly with no tenor. A curious effect. What would you say, Krey?

KREY: (*quietly.*) Hold your tongue!

WOLKE: (*to* THEKLA.) In true appreciation of your sentiments we ... what?

HICKETIER: My dear child.

THEKLA: No more please. (*Exit.*)

HICKETIER: Must have been a bolt from the blue.

WOLKE: Upset her to the roots of her being. Our task must be ... what? He was, taking him all in all, a man.

KREY: Let's not waste time gossiping. Fetch the letter. Hicketier.

HICKETIER: I'll go for it.

JENNY: Have you written to Schippel?

HICKETIER: (*to* JENNY.) Stay with Thekla. She's going through a difficult time.

JENNY: It would take more than that to upset someone like Thekla for long.

(*Exeunt* HICKETIER *and* JENNY.)

WOLKE: Strange is the levity of women. The dead man not cold in the ground and already it would take more than that to upset his intended. She's perhaps looking at other men by now.

KREY: Will you hold your blaspheming tongue!

WOLKE: As though I didn't know.

KREY: What do you mean?

WOLKE: Have you nothing to tell me?

KREY: Watch what you say!

WOLKE: I know what to think.

HICKETIER: (*comes back.*) The typewriter spared me the indignity of actually writing to this pauper in my own hand. A rubber-stamp supplied my signature at the end—no 'respectfully yours' or 'yours faithfully'.

KREY: That could be a mistake. Read it out.

HICKETIER: (*reading.*) Messrs. Hicketier, Krey and Wolke —I've put the names in alphabetical order—would be disposed in the event of your suitability to offer you a probationary period in their male voice quartet. You are requested to present yourself at the address of the undersigned on Monday 13th—that is to-day—about 3 p.m. Hicketier.

WOLKE: Bravo! To the point.

KREY: That's how you bring a dog to heel. The ring of an income tax note.

WOLKE: Is this Schippel much more than a dog in a manner of speaking?

KREY: If he has any back-bone at all, he'll be foaming at the mouth.

HICKETIER: When I wrote it I was boiling with rage at the humiliation of having to make the first move—it was the bloodiest sacrifice of my life.

KREY: I should have been consulted. Being a civil servant I know all there is to know about letter-writing. There are ways and means to be polite even if one is bursting with rage. He might have nothing to do with us after a note like this, and then we're in a mess.

WOLKE: In which case duty will nonetheless have been satisfied by Hicketier.

KREY: Is that enough? In this case success is essential.

WOLKE: What did you want him to write—'We are honoured —yours respectfully' to a mere foundling?

HICKETIER: For him to let the whole town know he can make us sit up and beg?

KREY: Rubbish. If he refuses we can't sing. We lose the crown.

WOLKE: Indeed yes—what?

HICKETIER: (*wiping the sweat from his brow.*) Our position is in truth appalling!

WOLKE: I don't know which way to turn.

KREY: In the opinion of well-qualified judges this fellow's voice is superior to Naumann's. That much is certain. If we have him we'll be able to take on all the quartets in the principality.

WOLKE: And you think?

KREY: I can't imagine any independent person responding to such a brusque invitation.

WOLKE: Goodness gracious!

HICKETIER: Independent person—a wretch who plays the flute? Without influence in all the right places it could be as much as his job is worth.

(*The three sit in separate corners of the room looking helplessly at each other.*)

HICKETIER: (*sheepishly.*) Wolke.

WOLKE: Goodness gracious! Krey, are you suggesting ...?

KREY: 'Present yourself'! Ha!

HICKETIER: If only one of *you* had written. Remember I'm a Hicketier—we've been established here as goldsmiths since the time of the Thirty Years' War.

WOLKE: The Wolkes are no jumped up nobodies either.

KREY: And so it should be left to the civil servant to prostitute himself? If only you had approached me: I have a whole arsenal of meaningless phrases at my command.

HICKETIER: What's to be done?

WOLKE: No question—we cannot forego participation in the festival.

KREY: Give up as men, what so inspired us as boys.

WOLKE: Madness!

HICKETIER: All I owe my ancestors, all we promised to hold sacred on the deathbed of our dear departed friend.

KREY: Then, since the members of the quartet must be born

and resident in the principality, and since no other tenor is to be found, we . . .

HICKETIER: We are utterly at Schippel's mercy.

WOLKE: And in these circumstances you wrote *that* letter, Hicketier? I am sweating blood and water.

HICKETIER: (*desperate.*) My whole being was in a state of total upheaval, but I forced myself to do as much as was humanly possible.

KREY: It wasn't enough for our purposes.

WOLKE: May heaven help us out of this unholy mess, amen.

KREY: (*who has been looking out of the window, suddenly.*) Schippel!

HICKETIER *and* WOLKE: (*simultaneously.*) Ha!

HICKETIER: Summoned for three; it's not one yet. What do you think?

KREY: It could be a bad sign.

WOLKE: What? My knees are knocking, Krey, you have me completely muddled.

KREY: Softy! Pull yourself together!

HICKETIER: Who'll do the talking?

KREY: It's your house and it was your invitation.

WOLKE: Take care. Make allowances for him.

KREY: Be persuasive, but not persuaded.

WOLKE: But don't go too far!

SCENE 3

Enter PAUL SCHIPPEL, *skinny, red hair, about* 30.

SCHIPPEL: Schippel . . . Paul.

HICKETIER: Yes, yes.

SCHIPPEL: You're Hicketier?

HICKETIER: (*flaring up.*) Mr! Mr! if you please.

WOLKE: Pst!

SCHIPPEL: Excuse me!

WOLKE: Wolke, member of the city council and owner of a printing works. (*Bows.*)

KREY: Krey.

HICKETIER: You're . . .

SCHIPPEL: Clarinet-player. You know—a black wood-wind with nickel keys.

WOLKE: (*mimes flute-playing.*) Like this.

SCHIPPEL: (*laughs.*) Excellent imitation. Gentlemen, I'm poor. From the dregs of the people, as they say in your circles. The coat I have on is my entire wardrobe. My playing is only fair to middling.

WOLKE: Fair enough, I'll be bound.

SCHIPPEL: Otherwise I'd be in a good orchestra, not playing in the local café. As a player, I strike a note of despair, my last gasp as you might say. (*Laughs rumbustiously.*)

HICKETIER: I think I should have guessed as much.

SCHIPPEL: No question, you'd have judged my playing too favourably. Respected gentlemen, in a nutshell, my playing is terrible; background noise to go with the beer.

WOLKE: (*laughs uproariously.*) Very good.

SCHIPPEL: Would you like to know what I'm paid. Twenty Marks a week exactly. So it's meat every other time, but the nose-bag mostly—to use a horsey expression.

WOLKE: Very funny!

SCHIPPEL: Sleep in an attic, my comb has teeth missing, my toothbrush has no bristles. Story of my life.

HICKETIER: Revolting details. Your origins are known to us.

SCHIPPEL: You amaze me, Mr. Hicketier.

HICKETIER: A bastard.

(SCHIPPEL *laughs.* HICKETIER *laughs.*)

SCHIPPEL: How the word comes trippingly off your tongue! In these surroundings I should never have got it out at all. But with your assurance you broke the ice. So I needn't beat about the bush: my origins are unknown.

KREY: A little accident.

HICKETIER: Shall we let the matter rest?

WOLKE: In obscurity.

SCHIPPEL: But it's all very relevant, gentlemen, in so far as my meagre talents are relevant. Let's get it quite straight: I'm a bastard, gentlemen. A social phenomenon with which you are presumably making your first acquaintance.

KREY: But one which is fairly widespread, when all's said and done.

WOLKE: Being on the board of an orphanage, I am fully acquainted with it.

SCHIPPEL: A social phenomenon which could be said to have stood the test of time in that ...

HICKETIER: To cut the cackle, are you prepared to sing with us?

SCHIPPEL: Kindly let me finish if you please. I want you to realise once and for all my total insignificance.

KREY: The story of his life.

SCHIPPEL: Has it not struck you that my head is bowed?

HICKETIER: I hadn't studied you closely enough to notice.

SCHIPPEL: For this reason: deep down I don't feel free within myself. And then the luxury of these surroundings. What I'm saying at this moment is being blurted out half-deliriously. I do beg your pardon. I'll pull myself together directly. As a child I used to go down to play in the street with the other children. Quite casually, of course. I got kicked. One girl in particular spat in my face. Ever since I've held my head down, I've got to know the earth much better than the heavens.

WOLKE: That sort of thing doesn't happen nowadays. The foster children entrusted to my care enjoy, all in all,—what?

SCHIPPEL: Too kind. In short, all my life I've been lying in a corner the sun never reached. Then your letter. You understand how my situation is suddenly transformed. Despised, overlooked all the time, greedy for all the things ...

HICKETIER: This summons came as a release from your proletarian agony.

SCHIPPEL: You've hit the nail on the head. Please understand the shattered state in which I stand before you. Nothing less than a total tranformation from one second to the next, a re-birth is in progress as you might say.

HICKETIER: That's all well and good, all very intimate ...

SCHIPPEL: (*walking about the room, steps in front of a picture.*) What a divine picture! Painted in oils I observe.

33

C

HICKETIER: You'll have an audition to-day and we'll decide.

SCHIPPEL: (*lets out a dazzling 'A', prolonging it.*)

KREY: Oho!

HICKETIER: If that is any indication ...

WOLKE: Bravo!

SCHIPPEL: Yes indeed, my dear sirs, indeed, it's going to be great! And by the way I did have a mother, the soul of goodness. (*Takes hold of* HICKETIER *by the coat-button.*)

HICKETIER: Take your hands from my jacket!

SCHIPPEL: (*confused.*) No offence. (*Offers his hand.* HICKETIER *ignores it.*)

SCHIPPEL: Your hand, Mr. Hicketier, your hand.

HICKETIER: Our arrangement will be purely business.

SCHIPPEL: A hand, just give me your hand.

HICKETIER: Purely business.

SCHIPPEL: Why do you refuse me your hand?

WOLKE: Hicketier!

SCHIPPEL: You must shake hands—I simply demand it, and a welcome at all times. I shall expect—here or anywhere else —to take your arm. I shall want to be spoken to, addressed, in the street, in cafés, people's houses. What have you to say?

KREY: Your admission to the quartet precludes all other relationships.

SCHIPPEL: Precludes? Meaning? Not even a handshake, when my voice is good enough for yours? (*He shakes both* KREY'S *hands wildly.*)

HICKETIER: Are you out of your mind, man?

WOLKE: Goodness gracious!

KREY: This really is the limit!

HICKETIER: Enough, my friend. Your brain is over-heated. Clear it of these fancies and as a start grasp one stark fact; you are a nobody. You look to us as your employers for a bare living, so to speak, which we have it in our power to take from you. If your voice suits us, however, we are ready to do something to improve your circumstances, a new frock-coat, other small favours. That's all; for the rest you keep your hands to yourself.

KREY: Amen!

SCHIPPEL: (*Horrified.*) So that's it. Oh! (*bangs his fist on the table.*)

HICKETIER *and* KREY: Sir!

WOLKE: What, what?

SCHIPPEL: (*exit.*) Then that's that, gentlemen!

KREY: (*in consternation.*) What was what?

WOLKE: The fellow refuses, it's all up.

HICKETIER: We're exactly where we were before.

WOLKE: What it adds up to is this: we're finished. He laid down his conditions so to speak, with the utmost caution, positively feminine delicacy in my view. Then Hicketier goes and loses his temper with him and upsets the apple-cart for good.

HICKETIER: The fellow seemed set on tearing down cast-iron barriers.

KREY: Given a suitable sense of social distinctions one could have made certain concessions.

WOLKE: But everything he said was a mass of 'would-you-be-so-kinds' and 'if-you-pleases.'

HICKETIER: The demands for personal contact, for crass intimacy came through loud and clear. (*Beside himself.*) Is the fellow to be slapping me on the back in front of all and sundry? Have you no sense of shame? If we let this ox have a finger, he'll be all over us like ivy. God, the poor do smell! Open the windows.

WOLKE: And his 'A,' old chap? Hasn't it dawned on you yet that that note more or less settles the whole festival problem, practically guarantees us victory.

KREY: Certainly, there was no mistaking that. It was far away superior to Naumann's.

HICKETIER: Even if half my heart were set on it—I couldn't do it. Any more than I would wish the society of the nobility —intimacy with which would be beyond me, horrify me. I like my spheres clearly defined, above and below.

We have just buried Naumann. It seems to me that we must face to-day an even greater grief: the burial of our dearest, our constant dream.

WOLKE: Is there no way out without Schippel?

KREY: None: we know there isn't. Scarcely two weeks till the festival and apart from him no local tenor.

HICKETIER: This character, once he knew us a little better, would be impudent enough to be familiar with our women as well. How could one convey to Thekla that such a mongrel even exists—good God!

WOLKE: Still it does break your heart.

HICKETIER: Please, not another funeral oration. Two on one day is excessive. All right, it's fate. Life has no built-in safety barriers.

(Exit.)

WOLKE: Thekla! That's what's behind it! If it was just himself he would condescend to such company in the end. But Thekla, the defenceless maiden, the high and mighty Miss Hicketier.

KREY: What do you mean?

WOLKE: Can you deny it? As a result of Naumann's death she is no longer protected against that individual—that was the decisive factor.

KREY: So?

WOLKE: I repeat, we are alone—you can tell me.

KREY: Stuff and nonsense.

WOLKE: It's wrong to take male timidity too far.

KREY: God almighty!

WOLKE: You are in love with Thekla. And if Hicketier knew her to be under your protection safely married ...

KREY: What a criminal proposition. Because I haven't got your glibness I have got to put up with this vile play-acting. I don't love her—you do.

WOLKE: It's you who's in love with her.

KREY: She is sheer torture, the very sight of her is odious. To see, to smell her is repellent.

WOLKE: I know you through and through.

KREY: Sodom and Gomorrah! My life is cosy and contented and you ...

WOLKE: You love her! Propose to her! It's an historic moment.

KREY: You love her. I've known it for years.

36

WOLKE: You love her! Even if you were blaring forth your lie from heavenly trumpets I know you love her and I solemnly exhort you: save a precarious situation by surrendering to your own happiness.

KREY: (*hurrying away.*) I'll hang myself!

WOLKE: (*calling after him.*) Would you, you temperamental beast, pig-headed prig! But I won't let you.

(*Outside confused noise is heard. Immediately* KREY *opens the door and appears in the doorway with a deep bow.*)

SCENE 4

Enter the PRINCE, 20, *in uniform. After him* KREY *and* WOLKE

PRINCE: Whose home am I invading? From what I saw ...

KREY: (*with another bow.*) Hicketier's, your Highness.

PRINCE: Fetch a strip of linen, a bowl of water. Send a message to the castle to have a doctor in readiness. (*He sits down in an armchair, opens the torn sleeve of his tunic. Suddenly stares at* WOLKE. KREY *has gone out.* WOLKE *pressing shyly against the wall, with a deep bow.*) Wolke.

PRINCE: What? Damned horse! The sound of a steam engine and he's off like lightning along the road, no holding him. I steered him sharply into the street wall of this house, rubbed against it, braked so to speak. And a plucky lad was able to grab the reins. The brute stopped.

WOLKE: (*beaming.*) Superb!

PRINCE: Brute! I'll keep him on a tight rein in future.

SCENE 5

HICKETIER *and* WOLKE *enter bowing.*

HICKETIER: What an accident ... your Highness.

PRINCE: Water, bandages. A woman would be best.

HICKETIER: My wife rushed off for some at once.

WOLKE: (*with a deep bow.*) Wolke!

37

PRINCE: So I heard. So what? Well, Mr. Hicketier?

HICKETIER: At your service?

PRINCE: Brute! Wound bleeding. Day began badly. Old woman crossed my path, slow raindrops, a grey cloud. (*Smiles to* WOLKE.) Now I understand. Melancholy ...

(*Faints away.*)

KREY: (*leans over him.*) Your Highness! Fainted. (HICKETIER *and* WOLKE *race aimlessly round the room, then towards the door, just as* JENNY *and* THEKLA *enter.*)

SCENE 6

JENNY *is carrying a bowl of water,* THEKLA *bandages.* THEKLA *kneels in front of the prince, takes his arm which is hanging down and begins to clean and bandage it, while* JENNY *is doing everything possible to bring him round.*

PRINCE: Tight rein. What's this? A ministering angel? (THEKLA *finishes her work neatly.*) Kindness itself. Most gracious. My thanks. Charming.

(*The women leave the room.*)

HICKETIER: She is trained in nursing, your Highness.

PRINCE: *Charité* in person, I tell you. Never knew what that meant. A mere word till this moment. Masterly bandaging. *Charmant!* It lost its head. Dangerous brute. (*Rises, reaches for his cap.*) Excuse me, didn't I have a whip? (*To* WOLKE.) Why did you say Wolke?

KREY: His name, your Highness. Owns a printing works.

PRINCE: Aha! Our Wolke! The blue sign in the market-place: all types of printing speedily executed.

WOLKE: At cheapest rates.

PRINCE: Delighted. Where did the ladies go?

HICKETIER: My wife, my sister Thekla.

PRINCE: Thek . . . Dear Mr. Hicketier, you are not unknown to us. At one time you frequently ...

HICKETIER: Your Highness, in my childhood his late Majesty . . .

PRINCE: Yes, yes. I'll come back to that. So this is Mr. Wolke. No illegal pamphlets? Nothing socialist, anarchist?

WOLKE: Out of the question, your Highness.

KREY: Krey. Civil servant, grade two.

PRINCE: The middle-class, the civil service—bravo, gentlemen! The lady who assisted me? Why am I given no chance to express my thanks?

HICKETIER: At once. (Exit.)

PRINCE: (sees the crown.) A crown of laurels? What . . . ?

KREY: Won twice by our male voice quartet.

PRINCE: My father's famous singers. Our very own 'Mastersingers' so to speak. Which reminds me of my sins of omission —in a fortnight, isn't it—and the prize-song is still undecided. (To himself.) Something as amusing as this so close at hand and one is consumed by blackest boredom. (Aloud.) The male voice choir; a cause of major importance and close to the hearts of the people, demands our closest consideration, a worthy weapon against the onslaught of an age without ideals. The German 'Lied' gentlemen! In this regard we shall take extraordinary measures, grace the forthcoming festival with our princely presence. (To himself.) Heavens, what am I saying? (Aloud.) Won twice over by you. I have every hope that once more the victor's crown will be in your grasp. This time above all victory must be yours. (WOLKE and KREY bow.)

SCENE 7

HICKETIER returns with JENNY and THEKLA.

PRINCE: These gentlemen, dear Hicketier, know my views on the prize-song. (Bows to JENNY, kisses her hand.) Most gracious lady! (Bows to THEKLA.) Charité, may heaven watch over you! (Very quietly to her.) Thekla! (Leaves with a salute. All bow deeply. THEKLA sinks into the chair invisible to the others on the stage for the remainder of the scene.)

39

WOLKE: My legs are like water.

HICKETIER: He stood on that very spot.

KREY: (to HICKETIER.) Your roof over the Prince's head!

JENNY: Let us hope his injury heals quickly.

KREY: And the way he spoke—how simple, how affable!

WOLKE: How cordial! 'Our Wolke', his Wolke in a manner of speaking.

HICKETIER: From another, higher sphere.

WOLKE: 'You must be victors at the festival gentlemen. *Charmant.*'

KREY: Did he say that?

His wish, command—no contradicting it. With a piercing look.

WOLKE: Piercingly affable. The German '*Lied*' against anarchy. *Charmant.* You and you alone must gain the victor's crown.

JENNY: (to HICKETIER.) Do come to table now. (*Exit.*)

KREY: What is to be done after that order which must be obeyed?

HICKETIER: It's up to one of you.

WOLKE: (to HICKETIER.) Let's not beat about the bush: you're the man of strength among us. You alone can find ways and means of luring Schippel back without demeaning us in any way.

KREY: As it is a matter now, quite independently of our personal wishes, of honour or dishonour in the eyes of the Prince.

HICKETIER: But...

WOLKE: The Prince! Oh, Hicketier—even if he had not come into it—look me straight in the eye—you could not just have sat back and not done everything in your power to realise our wish.

KREY: You cannot live, unless you can coerce this Schippel.

WOLKE: And you've got the turn of phrase.

HICKETIER: (*after a pause.*) All right! Passions are too far roused. I seize the bull by the horns again; honour and conscience are satisfied.

WOLKE: (*quietly to* HICKETIER.) And I know what's to be done about Thekla.

HICKETIER: (*laughs.*)

WOLKE: Let us solemnly shake hands. In consideration of the importance of the cause. We swear.

(HICKETIER, KREY *and* WOLKE, *close to the footlights, giving each other their hands, simultaneously.*) We swear!

KREY: That was a to do! I'm terribly relieved.

WOLKE: An eventful morning. But 'after battle's heat, comes time of wine and meat.' Powerful chap, Hicketier, eh?

HICKETIER: I've still got to face that creature and prove it. And now to table. (*Exit.*)

KREY: We must have a word privately.

WOLKE: What, what?

KREY: Faker, horse-trader!

WOLKE: My dealings are honest and above board. (*Exeunt.*)

(THEKLA *leaps from the chair to the window which she throws open. She leans out. Suddenly she raises her hand and waves a handkerchief.*)

ACT II

The same room.

SCENE 1

THEKLA *alone. A knock at the window.* THEKLA *flies to the window, half opens it. An arm is seen handing in a letter. She takes it, shuts the window. Looks at the letter.*

THEKLA: This evening about ten he means to ... heavens above!

WOLKE: (*who entered just as* THEKLA *was taking the letter.*) If I might ask whether your brother's back—without being inquisitive.

THELKA: To stop any mystery-mongering on your part—here! (*Hands him the letter.*)

WOLKE: (*not taking it.*) Nothing would induce me, Thekla. Perfectly all right. In keeping with the divine harmony of the universe. Birthday greetings fluttering through the window, to which I add my own. And in any case I knew all about it. My knowledge of human nature uncovered the secret some days before it became obvious. I told the infatuated fellow of his feelings.

THEKLA: You—whom did you tell?

WOLKE: I realise what your tone implies and so permit me to declare myself openly at once. You know that from early childhood I too had a special regard for you. And there's no question this heartfelt regard can never lessen this side of the grave. But then I noticed that Krey . . .

THEKLA: Krey?

WOLKE: That certain air of complete distraction in your presence, that certain particular *je ne sais quoi*, what?

THEKLA: You are saying that Krey and you yourself . . . ?

WOLKE: The very stuff of tragedy. In all honesty and conscience I had to acknowledge Krey's utter superiority to me in every respect and so I withdrew. You may now be suspecting that Krey has commissioned me to say this; but I solemnly swear that I am driven solely by the dictates of my own heart to tell of his unsurpassed manliness, his dignity and worth, his most noble character, loyalty, ambition, his iron will and on the other hand his noble restraint where appropriate, his essential sobriety not only as regards you know what . . .

THEKLA: I always found him pleasant. But you mention sobriety? Has he no imagination?

WOLKE: Krey no imagination? Good heavens, when he has such extravagant ideas! Surely his every movement reflects the silent grandeur of his inner thoughts. Not sober, only timid to such a degree that I fear force may be needed to make him confess his passion. And so, I would ask you, Thekla, . . .

THEKLA: To encourage him? (*To herself.*) Could this joke help me gain my own ends? (*Aloud.*) The things you ask a young girl to do . . .

WOLKE: My motive is friendship. What my renunciation costs me—can be said in one sentence, but for one's heart to grasp it . . .

(*He has taken her hand and kisses it.*)

THELKA: I shall try to be guided by your disclosures. (*Exit laughing silently to herself.*)

WOLKE: What one might call a bull's eye. If he will insist in his foolishness on wrapping up the truth more and more tightly other people will have to unseal his lips by force.

SCENE 2

Enter JENNY.

WOLKE: Is he not back from seeing Schippel?

JENNY: All night long moaning and groaning. He was battling with the spectre in his dreams.

WOLKE: In suffering activity is preferable to mute suppression of one's feelings like Krey's.

JENNY: Is it causing him suffering too?

WOLKE: That and something else. A letter from him to Thekla fluttered in through the window a moment ago.

JENNY: A secret correspondence. You're mad!

WOLKE: You know me, Jenny, to be a person of moderation. I had the epistle in my hands—he loves her.

JENNY: Impossible.

WOLKE: It was there in black and white. Put with such reverence, such purity ...

JENNY: Tilmann will not take it well. How reluctant he was to give her to Naumann, who was far closer to him than Krey.

WOLKE: But his shining virtues! The vehement power of his passion. I beg you in the name of our friendship ...

JENNY: Wait till the business with Schippel is settled. And Thekla herself?

WOLKE: She did not say in so many words, but my knowledge of human nature would be seriously wanting if I did not feel that within her fair form the blue bird of love is about to take wing.

JENNY: If that is so, I promise you every assistance. She talked about a man standing by the fence at night, gazing up at her window.

WOLKE: Krey! Q.E.D.

43

HICKETIER: (*enters.*) Victory! Just as I turn into Windisch Street there is Schippel—he raises his hat unperturbed. And in a few words I talk the matter over and sort things out. He's coming.

JENNY: Thank heavens!

HICKETIER: I would have brought him with me for every hour counts now.

WOLKE: The audition must be to-day.

HICKETIER: He has to let someone know first, but then he's coming straight-away. In the meantime our matter has been occupying him secretly—the Prince's decree about the festival was in the evening paper and he knew it by heart. (*To* JENNY.) You open the door to him; we mustn't let everybody see him coming and going.

(*Exit* JENNY.)

WOLKE: And what I was saying about Thekla still stands.

HICKETIER: I respect your anxiety and can guess your intentions, but postpone it till after the suspense of this crisis is all over. Moreover, Krey was making delicate hints as well.

WOLKE: Never!

HICKETIER: So don't confuse me. To be able to act, I've got to have everything clear cut.

WOLKE: And let us know the outcome of the discussion with Schippel immediately, we're dying to know.

HICKETIER: Immediately. It's Thekla's birthday. Have you seen her?

WOLKE: In a cloud of sorrow at what is lost, a cloud pierced by the flickering rays of new hope.

HICKETIER: How poetic. (WOLKE *gives him his hand and exits.*)

HICKETIER: He is in love with Thekla. (*Takes a gold bangle from his desk and holds it to the light comparing it with the the laurel crown.*) The exact replica of the original. If I were to lose the crown now, I have its twin safe for ever with Thekla. I wonder what she will think of my brainwave?

SCENE 4

Enter THEKLA.

HICKETIER: I was on the point of calling you. Come closer.

THEKLA: What's that?

HICKETIER: Made by my own hands. Guess who for?

THEKLA: For me, who else? Thank you. (*Sits on his lap.*)

HICKETIER: Since the ties that bound you to me as a child will loosen with the passing of time—do you feel what this gift means?

THEKLA: (*her arms round his neck.*) I love you, as I always did.

HICKETIER: And this gold band shall symbolise the love of a brother and sister, the soul of the Hicketiers even when it is lost to view more and more completely. When you are alone, it will remind you.

THEKLA: That's sad and unnecessary. Even without it I shan't forget my childhood origins.

HICKETIER: In our family the women have rarely prospered. The will-power of the Hicketier men turned to whimsy in their women. The closer we are, the more intimate we remain even after your marriage, the more fully you will satisfy your nature and your needs.

THEKLA: Part of me never leaves you, even though I am often passionately drawn to someone else.

HICKETIER: And you feel it must remain so.

THEKLA: Don't be so solemn on my birthday.

HICKETIER: Do as I ask (*Takes her arm.*) Wear it under your sleeve hidden from other people. (*Slips it on under her sleeve.*) Your family home will always be your place of refuge. Here your most secret thoughts are free. Let a hand-shake be your promise to me for ever!

(*They shake hands.*)

45

HICKETIER: And now listen, you rascal; one minute you're the widowed bride the next you have a new admirer in hot pursuit.

THEKLA: I know ...

HICKETIER: With your looks it's only natural that everyone should want you. And with an honourable family name and money to go with it! What are his chances!

THEKLA: (in extreme confusion.) Oh, heavens! (Runs away.)

HICKETIER: Well, well, well. An adorable girl. (Exit on the other side.)

SCENE 5

JENNY brings in SCHIPPEL and exit left. SCHIPPEL: stands in the centre of the room, looking on all sides I still can't take it in. Luxury I've hungered for these thirty years. My days of aimless drifting are over. From one day to the next I've become a name to reckon with. As that fat Hicketier fell asleep last night I wager he was thinking—That Schippel. I'd like to get my hands . . . (Tiptoes about the room.) Red plush furniture! Your owners know I'm here. It's quite in order for me to loll around in you. (Sprawls in an armchair.) Or look through a photograph album at my ease. (Starts leafing through one.) If anyone comes I'll stand up and take my time and say, Hello there! It's alright for me to be here, they invited, very nearly dragged me here. Fine people the lot of them, no shortage of relations and all most respectable. Gold brooches and watch-chains. Fat signet rings. Good afternoon, sir, delighted to make your acquaintance! I'm one of the family, it's up to me what I do or don't do. Mr. Schippel! A little belch, vicar. Permitted among friends after a good meal.

SCENE 6

HICKETIER enters.

HICKETIER: My behaviour yesterday calls for an explanation.

SCHIPPEL: Not at all. What's past is past. To-day everything is different.

HICKETIER: So much the better. With your background we were a little worried that you might not grasp the historical importance of the prize-song—despite fine vocal quality ...

SCHIPPEL: What you say is bitter for me.

HICKETIER: I'm not beating about the bush.

SCHIPPEL: No concessions if we are to arrive at a genuine understanding. But we may be in luck and the song will just be about roaming the countryside or the common or garden variety of love—tumblings in the hay etc., which I am no doubt particularly well qualified to interpret with my—as you put it.

HICKETIER: Where did you learn breathing, phrasing?

SCHIPPEL: From my instrument. My throat opens and closes just like the keys.

HICKETIER: Ever practised in front of the mirror?

SCHIPPEL: Know my throat backwards. The uvula works like a glockenspiel.

HICKETIER: Shall we have a try then?

SCHIPPEL: Place myself entirely in the service of the cause.

HICKETIER: Excellent. Just a word about behaviour in company.

SCHIPPEL: I'm completely in the picture. Keep the brakes on. Gently does it.

HICKETIER: You see in me a man whose nature is firmly rooted. I need to stand on terra firma. In me everything takes time to develop.

SCHIPPEL: Understood. Not like me, shot up in a flash out of nothing, with a head that wobbles on its thin stalk, so to speak. I've got to try and lose a bit of speed. Understood. Mustn't give in, when it comes over me ...

HICKETIER: Gently!

SCHIPPEL: No grabbing—perhaps in anticipation. (Holding out his arms to Hicketier.)

HICKETIER: What's got into you?

SCHIPPEL: (with mesmeric effect.) Or tapping you on the chest, don't flinch. (SCHIPPEL taps him on the chest.) Morning, Hicketier old man!

47

HICKETIER: (*mesmerised.*) How dare you—what do you think you're ...

SCHIPPEL: (*controlling himself.*) Mustn't be so gross. Understand. Keep my distance.

HICKETIER: (*furious.*) Manners! Behave! Or else ...

SCHIPPEL: Enough. I'll sing. With a voice like an angel. Mind's made up. We'll have them all well and truly licked—time?

HICKETIER: This evening at eight.

SCHIPPEL: Agreed. That's all then.

HICKETIER: And assuming that you conduct yourself in future according to my express wishes I shall keep the promise made yesterday and make it worth your while. I'll fetch a little something from the till. (*Exit.*)

SCHIPPEL: Living in the past, you doddering idiot. Yesterday I was still a rabbit cowering in the cabbage-patch. Now with such a colossal upsurge of strength I feel knives growing out of my toes and sabres from my teeth. I'm afraid my company is going to rub you a bit raw and I'm going to have to foul your well-kept parlour.

SCENE 7

THEKLA *crosses from right to left and goes into her room, ignoring* SCHIPPEL'S *bow.* SCHIPPEL: (*imitating her erect walk, crosses the room in the same way stopping in mid-stage.*) Wafting by on a wave of white linen. Marking the gulf between her and me. Let me get a whiff of you, my little dove. (*Walks in* THEKLA's *path sniffing.*) Lovely.

SCENE 8

HICKETIER: (*returns.*) Who went out? (*Gives* SCHIPPEL *a gold coin.*)

SCHIPPEL: (*takes it laughing.*) If only you knew ...

HICKETIER: Was it ...?

SCHIPPEL: A pretty little wagtail. Back a moment sooner and you would have had to introduce me formally.

48

HICKETIER: There will never be any question of that. Where my family is concerned, I live in strictest privacy.

SCHIPPEL: Naturally. Except for ...

HICKETIER: What?

SCHIPPEL: Singing to-night at eight.

HICKETIER: Except for what? Speak out.

SCHIPPEL: Let me keep it to myself. Wild ideas. In your drawing-room I feel like a charge of dynamite. (*Laughs aloud.*) Dynamite is good, isn't it? But I know what's what: leave quickly, wait till outside before I go off. Till this evening. (*Exit.*)

HICKETIER: (*shuddering.*) Except for what—? If you only knew? What?— Thekla went through here. I'm beginning to get goose-pimples already. (*Calls into the room left.*) Jenny!

SCENE 9

Enter JENNY.

HICKETIER: There will be too many men about the house till the music festival. Thekla must leave now and go to her aunt in Naumburg.

JENNY: Krey passed a letter through the window for her to-day.

HICKETIER: Krey? Get her case ready, quickly. Send her to me. (*Exit* JENNY.) Krey as well? She's got even the stupidest old goats in rut, Wolke *and* Krey. A letter through the window. And she didn't mention it earlier when we were so close.

SCENE 10

THEKLA *enters from her room.*

HICKETIER: Give me Krey's letter. (THEKLA *is silent.*)

HICKETIER: Produce the letter.

THEKLA: It's not from him, Tilmann.

HICKETIER: So, from Wolke after all, then. Give it to me. (*Reproachfully.*) Why behind my back?

49

THEKLA: (*looking at him calmly.*) It's not from Wolke.

HICKETIER: Not from Wolke—or Krey—good God! (*Sinks into a chair, leaps up again, exclaims.*) No! No! No! It must not be!

THEKLA: What?

HICKETIER: Child—I'm going crazy. Out with it—it was my own fault. Forgot about you, thinking about the crown. Who from? Thekla? (*They stand close together, looking into each other's eyes.*)

HICKETIER: (*whispers.*) Schippel?

THEKLA: You are crazy! (*And begins to exit.*)

HICKETIER: (*takes hold of her and pulls her towards him.*) Well, who then?

THEKLA: (*defiant.*) My business! (*Runs out slamming the door.*)

HICKETIER: A wolf in the fold. She must leave. But I'll get him whoever he is.

ACT III

Yard and garden at the back of HICKETIER'S *house, bordered on the right by a fence. It is evening.*

SCENE 1

THEKLA *leaning out of an upper storey window.*

PRINCE: (*appears from the right in a black coat. Under her window, pressed hard against the wall.*) Thekla!

THEKLA: It's him!

PRINCE: Groped my way in the dark along the fringe of the wood. The Gentleman of the Bedchamber was one hazard. Worst of all were five or six houses with lights still on which I had to pass. My subjects are not asleep yet. I must have a law passed.

THEKLA: We have a parliament, noble sir.

PRINCE: Since when do young girls know about politics?

THEKLA: These days they receive a wide general education. Know the sciences and can read a railway time-table. But princes who creep up to windows at night only exist in fairy tales nowadays, so they are told.

PRINCE: If anyone catches me, I'll be Haroun-al-Raschid reassuring himself about his people. Would they believe it of me?

THEKLA: People have a melancholy picture of you which goes well with night and a black coat.

PRINCE: Does Thekla think it is my nature to be gloomy?

THEKLA: The monocle worn by the Prince night and day stops her from holding any such view. He wouldn't see without it, he replies. The true man of gloom looks only at the abyss in his own heart.

PRINCE: Women have said that it suits me.

THEKLA: I know fairy-tale princes with a shining sword by their side. And if they appear beneath young girls' windows they are embraced dagger and all. A girl's self-respect demands a dagger.

PRINCE: So I'm more like the legendary Duke of Württemberg who could lay his head unarmed in the lap of any of his subjects. Has Thekla any idea what I ardently desire at this moment?

THEKLA: To be Duke of Württemberg;

PRINCE: Precisely.

THEKLA: Because the call of duty came while you were still a boy you are loved by the people.

PRINCE: Excellent. Are you of the people, Thekla?

THEKLA: Yes.

PRINCE: My subject?

THEKLA: Your subject.

PRINCE: Descend this instant. I'm appearing here like some character in Shakespeare. Have conceived an affection for you and command you in a voice of thunder.

THEKLA: Alas, Shakespeare is *passé*. We have moved three hundred years on now.

PRINCE: How is this sort of thing treated by modern writers then?

THEKLA: To be convincing, parliament must be a party to it, since you are a constitutional prince.

PRINCE: And supposing I were to summon parliament?

THEKLA: What about the Social Democrats?

PRINCE: Only one. Outvoted. All the rest follow me like sheep.

THEKLA: But the assembled legislators would first have to remove my brother and his companions who are barring my path.

PRINCE: Why are they still up?

THEKLA: On most important business. The quartet is being resurrected. In a fortnight the laurel crown awarded by the Prince will be at stake. A new tenor is stepping into the shoes of the previous one who died.

PRINCE: The singing connection will enable me to maintain official contact with your family over the next few weeks. I shall grant your brother an audience tomorrow morning. Shh!

Shadows have been seen moving at the broad, brightly lit window of a ground floor room. Now SCHIPPEL's *silhouette can be recognised at the window.* SCHIPPEL's *voice sings an aria from the 'Merry Wives of Windsor':*
'Hear the skylark's pretty note,
Hearken, hearken, lady fair,
Hearken, hearken, lady fair,
Through the stillness hear it float
Singing true of love so rare.'

Applause within.

PRINCE: Superbly sung. Why is a voice like that not one of the glories of our court theatre?

THEKLA: The singer is a bastard.

PRINCE: This is a Shakespeare play then after all! Bastards are his trademark. Princes and bastards. You can no longer refuse to treat this as an historic occasion. My monocle has vanished as well.

THEKLA: The telegraph poles over there still spoil the atmosphere.

PRINCE: But what can they do in face of a bastard, a prince —and surprise!—a dagger here too. Actually only a hunting-knife, but with a little effort of the imagination ...

THEKLA: Which I'm willing to make.

PRINCE: Only a ladder missing.

THEKLA: Over there in the shed. Wait! Haroun-al-Raschid was never known to climb in.

PRINCE: It's a variant.

THEKLA: And the maiden's honour?

PRINCE: Is covered by the sultan's cloak.

THEKLA: A ladder and a sitting-room—it's not romantic enough.

PRINCE: A sitting-room and a ladder—exactly the middle-class setting I had pictured.

(HICKETIER, inside, has gone up to the window, thrown open the curtains, and looks out into the darkness. Further back in the room SCHIPPEL, KREY and WOLKE can be seen round the piano.)

THEKLA: Madness. I daren't risk it. I had the most upsetting scene with my brother. The letter was discovered. In the end, to put his mind at rest, I told my sister-in-law a lie, namely, that the letter contained the prince's thanks for the assistance given him yesterday. I've to leave early tomorrow all the same. He's afraid.

PRINCE: Of whom?

THEKLA: Who but you?

PRINCE: Did it make you unhappy? (HICKETIER has disappeared from the window.)

THEKLA: I love Tilmann. The hardest thing for me is to see him worry.

PRINCE: Then I am intruder on a scene of peace and quiet. Leading an angel into deception.

THEKLA: Since yesterday every breath I draw is sinful. Imagine, a prince! A melancholy young hero! My brother and I have been singing folk-songs for so long in which a prince constantly appears that I was his before he ever appeared in reality.

PRINCE: Does he match your expectations?

THEKLA: Completely.

PRINCE: That is a confession, Thekla.

THEKLA: Was meant to be. Would I be speaking to you at night from the window if it were otherwise?

PRINCE: Trust me?

53

THEKLA: Utterly.

PRINCE: Listen—tomorrow I'll meet you at the hunting lodge by the bridle-path.

THEKLA: I have to leave here. It's impossible.

PRINCE: You mustn't. Not tomorrow. Not till you've seen me again. Between six and seven in the morning no-one in the house will miss you. I'll ride up the bridle-path wearing my green hunting coat, the hat with the oak-leaves, and a hunting-knife in my belt—is that romantic enough? If you like, I'll pin on a decoration—the little gold crown given me by the emperor—my gentle cousin and my liege.

THEKLA: And how shall I come?

PRINCE: I imagine you in plain cotton. Don't dress up, come to me as one of your own class. You are divinely perfect, just as you are.

THEKLA: (hums.)

'Her little neck all white and eyes so bright,

Her yellow locks so fair,

Her body soft as down and whiter far . . .'

PRINCE: When I am with you I feel alien to the sentiment of these songs, and the whole business with your brother and the competition for the crown, such a laudable middle-class aspiration, moves me deeply. The material of these songs is there to be found in our woods and our small towns, overpowering in its vitality.

THEKLA: These songs are born here with us and belong to us all our lives. The region we live in has the most beautiful songs. All in the anthologies.

PRINCE: And hence the prince of the region is in duty bound to cherish them.

THEKLA: I'll teach you all there is to know about them.

PRINCE: And tomorrow we'll set the finest of them for the competition.

The quartet inside sings a chorus from 'Der Freischütz'. HICK-ETIER *can be seen in the middle with baton.*

'The joy of the hunter on earth all surpasses,

The fountain of pleasure for him doth abound,

Through wood and through flood where the stag flits and
                                                  passes,
He flies in pursuit while the horns gently sound.
Oh, this is a pleasure that princes might envy
For health and for manhood the chief of delights.—'

(*The* PRINCE *stretches up both hands.* THEKLA *stretches down
hers.*)

PRINCE: That princes might envy, the chief of delights.

THE QUARTET: 'Mid echoes replying when day-light is dying
            To rest and the wine-cup labour invites.'

THEKLA: The ladder, fetch the ladder quickly. (PRINCE *brings
the ladder.*)

THE QUARTET: 'Then hark, follow hark, follow hark, follow
hark.'

THEKLA: Look away! I'm coming down. (*She does so hurriedly.
The* PRINCE *catches and embraces her.*)

THE QUARTET: 'Follow hark, follow hark, follow hark, follow
hark.'

THEKLA: Take the ladder away! (PRINCE *carries it to the
side.*)

THEKLA: Where shall we go? Behind the carriage. If anyone
comes, we'll be hidden.

PRINCE: (*embraces* THEKLA.) You are the perfect picture,
beloved. Your dress, your pinafore—everything just as it should
be.

THEKLA: And pleasing of body too.

PRINCE: Of eye.

THEKLA: And hair.

PRINCE: And lips. (*Kisses her.*)

PRINCE: Your answer?

THEKLA: You're too noble, too proud.

PRINCE: Not proud. (PRINCE *moves as though to sink down
beside her.*)

THEKLA: (*holding him.*) Lowering yourself. (*And sinks to the
ground with him.*)

PRINCE: Oh, maiden ...

THEKLA: (*kisses him.*) Darling!

55

PRINCE: What's my name?

THEKLA: Henry IV.

PRINCE: Never mind the number—I hope I'm the first.

THEKLA: The one and only.

(*They have been standing beside the carriage and now disappear behind it into the open shed.*)

SCENE 2

HICKETIER, SCHIPPEL, KREY *and* WOLKE *come out of the house.*

WOLKE: Not to mince matters—phenomenal, eh, Krey? What do you think?

KREY: Good.

WOLKE: Such line, such timbre. You are profoundly shaken, Hicketier.

HICKETIER: It is more than I had expected. The outcome of the competition is no longer in doubt. It's all over, bar the shouting.

WOLKE: And how his voice moulds itself to ours. We never achieved such unity of tone with Naumann. (*To* SCHIPPEL.) You know the fairy-story of the Emperor of China's sweet voiced nightingale. It was the only creature ever to say to him. 'I have seen tears in your eyes'. You can now say the same.

SCHIPPEL: It's true. I did see one. (*Takes him by the coat-button.*)

WOLKE: I am not denying it; your 'E' did bring the odd tear to my eye.

HICKETIER: The male voice, in the upper registers especially, is one of God's greatest miracles. Scarcely anything moves me so much.

WOLKE: A girl's hands are not so tender. (*To* KREY.) Don't be ashamed of your emotion.

KREY: You exaggerate.

HICKETIER: Let us retire with the impression still warm. Goodnight. (*He turns towards the house.*)

KREY: Good-night. (*Walks with* WOLKE *towards the gate of the yard.* SCHIPPEL: (*follows the two, then turns to* HICKE-TIER.) Hey!

HICKETIER: Yes!

SCHIPPEL: (*hesitating.*) Hm ...

WOLKE: What is it?

SCHIPPEL: Nothing really.

WOLKE: Come on. (*Draws* SCHIPPEL *towards the fence.*) With a tenor like that, Krey, it would surely be worthwhile having your composition performed.

KREY: (*to* SCHIPPEL.) It's an outright lie; I never wrote a note.

WOLKE: (*to* SCHIPPEL.) He'll never admit to his own merits. But they must be evident to you by now as well. What was it you wanted from Hicketier?

SCHIPPEL: (*looking at* HICKETIER.) At the moment something most important; but missed my chance again. Ha ha ha!
(SCHIPPEL, KREY, WOLKE *exeunt.*)

HICKETIER: (*stands in the middle of the yard looking up at the window.*) No good-night, no further appearance at all. It will be like this for weeks on end. I was too quick, too violent about the letter. The Prince's thanks for assisting him yesterday. She'll have been listening to our songs. She must be in a state of emotion, her feelings in flux. Love and defiance wrestle with each other in her head and her breast. My child, are you asleep? But in a flash my concern for you was boundless. I was choking for breath. Cannot explain it. If now I break into the turmoil of her soul I will spoil everything. If only I could be near her to listen. (*He hums.*) 'Singing true of love so rare.' Such melody from that proletarian breast! Not cracked or shaky the way the lower classes sing, but aware of the universal harmony of all being. May all the spirits of peace bless you! Your brother, with heart still torn by doubts, only wanted to ... understand me, I beg you, in your dreams. Good-night. (*Kisses his hand towards the window and enters the house.*)

PRINCE: (*appears again beside the carriage.*) Not a soul about now. Will madam come forth from the darkness of our humble

57

abode and once more grace the circle of light with her presence?

THEKLA'S *voice*: I shun the light, the atmosphere, the area. If only this night would never end!

(PRINCE *disappears again.*)

SCENE 3

SCHIPPEL *comes into view beside the fence.*

SCHIPPEL: Look at the way that house spreads itself over the face of the earth! Every square foot we inhabit costs us a fortune; here a carriage standing empty has an acre to itself. (*With raised fist.*) I hate you! You rotten middle class rabble, you stuff your guts with tit-bits and empty your bowels and gorge again till you're full of rich juices and then you pass on to your offspring the hard gloss that comes from well-fed nerves till it infects the whole world. Our strength is exhausted when we've produced one litter, perhaps even before we've had one. No hope of any of our descendants being born with one good thing in his blood—the memory in his blood to smash you lot for good. (*Goes into the yard.*) My limbs are skinny and my clothes are rags; her skirt was stretched fit to burst over fat thighs. (*Again he copies* THEKLA'S *walk. Then he strokes the house-wall.*) No wind'll ever whistle through that, walls about two feet thick. Inside bloated portraits of father and grandfather: Born 1836, died in his eighty-sixth year. I haven't the former, far less the latter ... you slipped out of my grasp just then, old chap. I had wild plans for you, I meant to go the whole hog, my claws were itching for you. Now I'm itching to get at you again, right up, close enough to breathe in your face. I am down here aching for you, you fat boor. Let loose a fine smug bass from your belly; I'm in love with you, your whole way of living, your class. My heart is thumping, my pulse racing. No use trying to sleep in this state. (*Sees the ladder.*) A ladder! I'll risk it. You're far more attractive than a woman, Baron, to a person of no family at all. (*Places the ladder against* THEKLA'S *window, climbs up and looks in.*) Underwear over the chair.

58

My lady's chamber! Wrong one! (*Climbs down in a flash, puts up the ladder again, climbs up and looks in the window.*) It's him! Let all Nature rejoice! Putting his jacket on a hanger and smoothing it out. Untidiness is an offence against the universe. The braces on six firmly sewn buttons, N.B. Schippel. And socks with elastic garters.

HICKETIER: (*opening the window from the inside.*) Are you out of your mind?

SCHIPPEL: Drunk with song. Still all worked up. Don't look so terrified, bourgeois, at a tiny dose of madness.

HICKETIER: You're destroying the good impression you made completely. Go home.

SCHIPPEL: What a strange man you are. Never grasp my intentions. All I wanted, ha, ha, ha . . . all I wanted was to savour my new-found happiness a little. I'm so conscious of it.

HICKETIER: I'm more inclined to think you're not conscious at all. The middle of the night. In the very next room—my sister sleeping! If she were to hear . . . march, double quick. (*Bangs the window shut.*)

SCHIPPEL: (*climbs down the ladder.*) Quite the sergeant-major! If his sister is sleeping . . . (*stands in the middle of the yard again.*) Fat and fair in her white finery! You rogue, you swine! You are trying to trick me. (*Storms up the ladder and bangs his fist against* HICKETIER's *pane.*) Jump to it! Get up from your snug slumbers! The girl in the next room —I want her—yes her.

The PRINCE *with* THEKLA *beside him has come nearer the carriage, moving gingerly so that they remain invisible to those on stage.*

HICKETIER: (*whose face could be seen briefly behind the panes, rushes out of the house, appears on stage, leaps to the foot of the ladder, and hisses up to* SCHIPPEL) What did you say, you scoundrel?

SCHIPPEL: (*turns round on the ladder to face him.*) Your sister! Or you'll need more than a pair of pliers to drag a note out of me!

HICKETIER: (*rushes to the carriage, grabs a whip from the driver's seat. The* PRINCE *and* THEKLA *have retreated behind the*

carriage as he approaches. HICKETIER *sees them, cries out):*
Oh! (*Pulls himself together and staggers towards* SCHIPPEL.)
Did you bark, you cur? You filthy pleb!

SCHIPPEL: (*jumps off the ladder, tears the whip from* HICKETIER,
*presses him bodily against the wall and stands face to face
in front of him. With violent feeling*) Yes, a pleb and smelling like one. And I mean to marry your sister, the stuck-up
bitch. I'll raise my red flag over the lot of you. Yes, drop dead
of shock, you old oaf, waggle your head. You've not heard
the last of it. (*Rushes out through the gate in the fence.*
HICKETIER *stands paralysed. The* PRINCE *conducts* THEKLA
into the house with a princely gesture. Stops in front of
HICKETIER.)

PRINCE: Your sister Thekla, still rather overcome—tomorrow,
naturally ... (*Quickly turns to go.*)

ACT IV

Same place. Early morning.

SCENE 1

HICKETIER *sitting asleep in a bower.*

JENNY: (*appears in the doorway*) I can't bring myself to wake
him. (WOLKE *crosses to her from the fence.*)

JENNY: (*points to* HICKETIER.) Sh!

WOLKE: Good Lord!

JENNY: He has been there all night. I woke this morning to
find him not in bed.

WOLKE: His worries! Schippel!

JENNY: He's in a state of inner torment despite his stiff upper
lip.

WOLKE: For the few days still left before the festival he must
make the effort. The Wolkes have a reputation to keep up as
well. Did you discuss our plan with him?

JENNY: Which one?

WOLKE: The Krey one. I would like to see a joint celebration
of the betrothal and the festival.

JENNY: You're barking up quite the wrong tree. A delicate mention of an illicit nocturnal rendezvous and Krey reacted with brutal coarseness.

WOLKE: Krey all over. He is full of artful wiles and guiles. Love can take forms, my dear, of such perversity your mind would boggle. One has only to think, for instance, of the dancing dervish who dreams that his beloved is the victim of dire perils, of foulest intrigues, simply in order that his courage alone can save her.

JENNY: Disgusting! (HICKETIER *snores in his sleep.*)

WOLKE: Bravo! Then gradually—and here things turn daemonic —he loses touch with the harmless reality of the adored one so completely that he is now quite incapable of appreciating her in her ordinary state of health. Result: catastrophe. Mothers bleat and fathers wail 'midst ruins all around. And why—the dancing dervish. Without wishing to state categorically that Krey is one, he is nonetheless what is known in nature as a phenomenon, namely in the following respect: his intellectual superiority—

JENNY: You consider him so clever! Well I never.

WOLKE: A universal genius, Jenny! Talk to him about the Jews. Such insight! Or take technology, physics, algebra, and watch the pupils of his eyes. The whole mysterious process is there in the way they flicker and narrow to slits.

JENNY: What do you mean?

WOLKE: He has elevated Thekla mentally to the status of paragon of all virtues. A Platonic idea. And now he doesn't dare.

JENNY: And up to a point he is right. She is a Hicketier and a lovely young thing into the bargain.

WOLKE: Delectable beyond compare. Granted. Now listen to my tactics: I bombarded him with arguments, left behind a picture of her, a letter from her, filled his sphere with her spirit, her scent, I—if the expression may be permitted— plagued the life out of him with her. Finally, when the colossus had been brought almost to his knees I blurted out last night that in a state of wild passion she had carved his initials intertwined with hers in the big elm tree in the yard.

JENNY: Wolke!

WOLKE: I did it with my own hands this morning between 5 and 6. Look

(*Shows her the place.*)

JENNY: But—!

WOLKE: I saw Hicketier then already. He was snoring away good and hard. It made me stop and think to see him there at the table. And the odds are now that Krey, before even going to the office, will appear any minute to see for himself.

JENNY: There he is!

WOLKE: (*pulls* JENNY *behind the carriage.*) Get back!

SCENE 2

KREY: (*enters, looks round cautiously and leaps across to the elm tree*) It's true! (*He leans against the trunk and wipes the sweat from his forehead, groaning.*) How ghastly! I'm lost in that case. (*Exit.*)

WOLKE: (*comes out with* JENNY) Tears? That settles it beyond question. Yes my good friend, it was your happiness I wanted. (*Follows him off in a state of emotion.*)

JENNY: (*goes into the bower and sits down opposite* HICKE-TIER.) Dearest heart.

HICKETIER: (*asleep.*) Eh?

JENNY: It's past 8 o'clock.

HICKETIER: (*waking abruptly.*) Thekla?

JENNY: Did you sleep here all night?

HICKETIER: Never closed an eye.

JENNY: Do forget your worries. Once the three of you have the gold crown you can get rid of Schippel.

HICKETIER: It was a nasty dream. Tell me your inmost thoughts.

JENNY: I have none to tell. I'll bring you coffee.

HICKETIER: And Thekla?

JENNY: Must get married.

HICKETIER: Great Heavens!

JENNY: She's the right age. But with her ideas she'll want something special.

HICKETIER: Not a word to anyone, not even to her—Schippel!

JENNY: Thekla!

HICKETIER: Our heads were in the sand. And now it's gone too far. A refusal on my part will guarantee a catastrophe.

JENNY: Thekla Hicketier—Schippel. Over my dead bod ...

HICKETIER: No, I've got a plan. We'll concoct a family-tree for him. That officer, the cashiered one—he's still a bachelor and could have been his father,—he must adopt him. Being without means he must be open to persuasion. I'll back the idea with everything in my power. No questions! You know now. Not another word till the whole matter is settled.

JENNY: I was reproaching *myself*—but *she* was keeping things from us.

HICKETIER: Yes, indeed.

JENNY: Perhaps the Prince could do something on Schippel's account ...

HICKETIER: (*jumps up.*) No crumbs from those in high places! No whining and begging and charity and then in the end embarrassment. A stout heart and we'll see it through alone!

JENNY: May God grant it. (*Exit.*)

SCENE 3

THEKLA *opens her shutters from inside. She opens her arms, not yet fully dressed, to the rays of the sun. The golden bangle can be seen on her upper arm.* HICKETIER *comes out from the bower to the centre of the stage and stands opposite her, silent.* THEKLA *undoes the bangle and throws it to her brother.*

HICKETIER: (*catches it and throws it back. Insistently.*) There is nothing to justify such a gesture. No romantic notions at the moment of decision. There is a communication for you to which I must have an answer: Mr. Schippel asked for your hand yesterday. (THEKLA *cries out softly.*) The doubts which I considered at length are outweighed by practical considerations.

63

THEKLA: (*wildly.*) My brother ...

HICKETIER: No buts. To-day, to-morrow, and for the rest of your life.

THEKLA: My fate!

HICKETIER: Think of your background!

THEKLA: I—oh—my heart ... (*Buries her face in her hands.*)

HICKETIER: (*abruptly.*) The time for dreams is over. Face the facts squarely. Pride, the pride of a Hicketier. Keep a firm grasp of realities or you'll be swept away by your foolish fancies and made to look quite ridiculous.

THEKLA: I'm coming! (*She rushes from the window, appears at once on stage and flies into* HICKETIER's *arms.*) Anything you want. I know how genuinely concerned you are for me.

HICKETIER: You'll be miles away in an hour on the way to your aunt, and you must stay there till I call you back in honour, peace and certainty. Be profuse in your sorrow, abandon yourself to it, let its overwhelming depths single you out above all others, be in no hurry to leave it behind you. But keep it hidden. What the world likes to see is how well one can take it. (*Putting his arm round her shoulders he walks a few paces with her.*) When this day rises up before your soul as a wife, mother and grand-mother your heart must be filled with radiant certainty at the superiority of your gesture. Should I in later life cross your threshold the same smile which now, despite the tears, plays about your lips will remind us who we are, what our family is, and what acts of will we are capable of. God bless you, child. (THEKLA *points into the distance where* SCHIPPEL *comes into view.*)

SCHIPPEL: (*calling out.*) Morning all!

THEKLA: Good morning, Mr. Schippel. (*Exit.*)

SCENE 4

HICKETIER: We were just talking about you.

SCHIPPEL: All I could hear was the voice of my own inner unrest. Since last night I have not moved far from your house.

HICKETIER: Like a hawk circling above its prey.

64

SCHIPPEL: I crept up the hill over there as far as the stream and I could see the lights in that room—(*pointing to* THEKLA's *room.*)—all the time. They never went out. Imagine what I felt!

HICKETIER: What did you feel?

SCHIPPEL: Didn't you already say?

HICKETIER: A hawk.

SCHIPPEL: As a child I used to go down to the street to play with the other children. One girl spat in my face: Thekla Hicketier!

HICKETIER: Ah!

SCHIPPEL: The hate which has been smouldering for two decades flared up uncontrollably last night—burst into flames within me. As the pure waters of the stream roared past me this morning I outroared them with a tone such as I never heard myself produce before and which will now be mine till the music festival, as it alone guarantees me possession of this girl. But I would be depriving myself of half the pleasure of my revenge if I did not disclose to you what dreams I had, what gestures I imagined myself making, how I laid hands on her body.

HICKETIER: Quite the wild wooer. For you are now betrothed, thanks to the girl's acceptance.

SCHIPPEL: I was certain of it when I came on you together a moment ago.

HICKETIER: And the honesty you so constantly display ...

SCHIPPEL: In which you are my equal. You will always be ashamed of my company.

HICKETIER: You're not slow.

SCHIPPEL: Have no fears on that score. My picture of the universe is solid, free from phantasy. But the certainty that you are in my hands completely—because of your vanity about the crown—that I can manipulate you as I please ...

HICKETIER: You see yourself as a kind of god then.

SCHIPPEL: And high time too.

HICKETIER: Your sails billowing in the following wind so to speak.

SCHIPPEL: I've got imagination and plenty of go.

HICKETIER: To use on Thekla.

SCHIPPEL: On your sister, brother-in-law.

HICKETIER: In the belief that I'm quaking.

SCHIPPEL: It seems to be indicated.

HICKETIER: You're moving near to me again. You'll be tapping me on the chest next. Ha ha.

SCHIPPEL: Figuratively speaking, my friend. I don't need to bother about actually doing so any longer.

HICKETIER: You're really straining your twopenny-halfpenny imagination over Thekla. Just because she spat at you once ...

SCHIPPEL: And so the hour will come when we stand face to face in my four walls, man and wife ...

HICKETIER: (laughing loudly.) And then?

SCHIPPEL: I loom up before her for the reckoning, with the words ready to burst from between my teeth.

HICKETIER: And?

SCHIPPEL: I begin ...

HICKETIER: The husband, unleasing all his pent-up injured pride—at my sister.

SCHIPPEL: Who until then had had everything wrapped up in cotton wool. And I, a nobody, who came into being by accident, who grew up in the gutter, I want the untouched middle class maiden and I want her now, I want to take hold of her. (Takes hold of HICKETIER.)

HICKETIER: And?

SCHIPPEL: Is your patrician heart breaking, old fellow?

HICKETIER: (laughing resoundingly.) It's laughing at you, a scrap merchant, thinking you're picking up a jewel. Higher laws will take you down a peg or two: What my kind is prepared to offer you has lost its supreme radiance ... (SCHIPPEL recoils.)

HICKETIER: Lost its first bloom to a better man and remains a thousand times too good for you.

SCHIPPEL: Thekla?

HICKETIER: Is yours.

(Long pause during which SCHIPPEL stands with his face turned away.)

HICKETIER: (business-like.) I owe the newcomer to the family further clarification. And the size of the dowry too ought to be discussed between us in my office. (With a gesture towards the house.) If you please. Then I have in view a means by which the unfortunate obscurity of your birth may be resolved. It involves the unmarried officer who was responsible for this misfortune.

SCHIPPEL: (turns to face him.) I understand.

HICKETIER: Splendid.

SCHIPPEL: Say no more. I know enough ...

HICKETIER: Splendid.

SCHIPPEL: To feel that the idea of manly honour now taking root within me, will not allow me to press my suit further.

HICKETIER: (in consternation.) What?

SCHIPPEL: I think not. I have to reserve my decision.

HICKETIER: (his arms outstretched at him.) Get out, get out!

SCHIPPEL: (coming back.) I feel already we can never be related.

(HICKETIER closes in on him.)

SCHIPPEL: (brushing him off with lordly gesture.) Shouldn't we have a little more humility in our predicament.

SCENE 5

KREY and WOLKE enter.

SCHIPPEL: I mean to sing like a god at the festival.

WOLKE: When I see you without a scarf, I'm always anxious about your throat.

KREY: Lozenges.

SCHIPPEL: Have no fear. I know the weight of my responsibility as a gentleman. (HICKETIER has gone up to the house.)

SCHIPPEL: Good morning! (Exit.)

WOLKE: (to HICKETIER.) Listen to me!

HICKETIER: (in the doorway.) Later. (Exit.)

KREY: (pulls WOLKE to the elm tree.) Swear to it!

WOLKE: I could raise my hand for the oath and it would be

done. But first let me tell you something else I have watched her plucking the petals off saxifrage and snapdragon and dandelion—in short, there's not a flower that grows that she hasn't picked to ask—he loves me—he loves me not—he loves me!

KREY: Swear to it, that she carved the letters. Swear. (*Seizes hold of him.*)

WOLKE: You know marjoram. (KREY *squeezes him so hard that* WOLKE *writhes.*)

WOLKE: Stinging-nettle, I mean.

HICKETIER: Swear. (*Kicks him in the seat.*)

WOLKE: (*running.*) And the last was always—he loves me.

KREY: (*has hold of him again and shakes him, shouting, quite beside himself.*) Your oath! your oath!

WOLKE: What difference would it make? (*Raises his hand to take the oath.*) I swear.

(KREY *falls on to the chair and covers his face with his hand.*)

WOLKE: You foolish creature, with your kind heart caught in the grip of prejudice. Look at me, your friend Wolke, who loves you dearly and cannot bear to see your conscience tortured any longer. And who would like some peace for himself in future.
Krey.

(*With hands raised.*)
Krey.

(*Kneeling before him overcome with emotion.*)
Go and take Thekla.

KREY: (*lifts him up and kisses him.*) I cannot begin to see the forces at work behind all this, or understand the why and the wherefore of it all, when things were so cosy the way they were. But I know hearing the tone of heartfelt emotion in your words that it has to be. Say no more. (*They shake hands.*) Wait here. I'll come back betrothed. (*Enters the house.*)

WOLKE: There he goes, blissful and divinely blessed! How shall I, poor creature, ever be able to compete . . . so to speak?

68

ACT V

Clearing in a wood. Daybreak.

SCENE 1

Enter the PRINCE *on the right.* THEKLA *on the left. They approach each other quickly and take hands.*

PRINCE: My memory of you will be forever sublime since you have granted me this last meeting.

THEKLA: I am betrothed to your Highness' civil servant, Heinrich Krey.

PRINCE: Your brother made the announcement yesterday at the music festival which ended in such triumph for him. Thekla was kept out of my reach by all sorts of tricks and machinations which were an affront to my honour. Instead of the expected opposition I encountered smiles and endless acquiescence, but Thekla herself, who had vanished in the meantime I found again only after the announcement. Who is responsible? Who dares?

THEKLA: Don't ask, it just happened. We had to part. Even if it cost both of our lives—and we're still alive.

PRINCE: (*with a gesture.*) Thekla!

THEKLA: Your Highness cannot mean to seduce me anew. If it were your will I would be yours again. Heaven knows that without you I am just ordinary. But so long as circumstances are not too unfavourable I do have some sense of propriety.

(*The* PRINCE *is about to put his arm round her.*)

THEKLA: I said—a sense of propriety.

PRINCE: Beloved!

THEKLA: (*with a last effort of will, stamping her feet angrily.*) Propriety!

(*The* PRINCE *steps away.* THEKLA *smiles immediately.*)

THEKLA: In these difficult days I have been thinking about you

69

and what my fateful meeting with you meant for me and I have come to see you more clearly than you do yourself. (*She loses her balance. The* PRINCE *puts his arms round her and holds her briefly and chastely.*)

THEKLA: You bring a woman a magical, unforgettable happiness. Slender, warm and as greedy as a child, you convince every woman that she is the first you have ever embraced and that you have earned her devotion. But you accept the wealth of feelings lavished on you unconsciously, with the non-chalance of a hero, and only after many years and many friendships will you really come to know and appreciate the full meaning of womanhood. God grant that my image will still have enough radiance for you then, that I may not be numbered among the unworthy. (*She takes the gold bangle from her bosom and gives it to the* PRINCE. *With tears in her eyes.*) A souvenir of Thekla Hicketier!

(*The* PRINCE *bows low over her hand.*)

THEKLA: Will you escort me back across the fields for the last time, now that I am the bride of Heinrich Krey?
PRINCE: Do you love him?
THEKLA: It will come surely. He has shown great nobility of character.
PRINCE: (*going.*) Promise me that your memory will not one day say of me as well, 'he showed great nobility of character', but rather, 'he brought a woman unforgettable happiness.'
THEKLA: Amen to that, with all my heart. (*Exeunt.*)

SCENE 2

Enter SCHIPPEL *in morning coat and top hat.*

SCHIPPEL: This kind of situation demonstrates the wretchedness of reality better than any entanglements a playwright ever thought up. I spent the night in a state of crazed fear and the sun brought the chill of death, not the golden dawn. First, my great gesture in giving up the girl was nearly the death of me, second, my heroic bearing at the music festival which I turned into a triumph—and then all I got from these scoundrels was a nod—and to crown everything a challenge to a duel. Because I hinted to that stuck-up lover that his ravishing bride had more than likely been having a little affair on the side.

How absurd, to judge myself suddenly by *their* standards in a situation where any others would be more bearable. Festival yesterday, duel to-day. I'm never out of top-hat and tails. But I don't care how cunningly your pit is dug, I'm not going to fall into it. I'll run away! As fast and as far as I can. I'm having no neat holes through my ribs.

It's sheer murder to thrust this role on a harmless mortal who has never held a weapon in his life before. With every appearance of legality. You dogs, what was the point of my one act of heroism, if I'm in no position to tell everybody, 'I turned Thekla Hicketier down flat' tell me that?

Its all up with you, lad. You've messed the whole business up good and proper. I would have given my right arm to stay up there. But I won't have them simply pumping bullets through my belly. There's no doubt I'll be killed, I had ghastly dreams, could see myself with a hole in my stomach the size of a man's fist and my insides dragging along after me.

I had it in my grasp and it's lost; all I've still got is my young life. It's back to my flute and my singing, scrounging for tips, but in bed at night I'll be able to feel that my body is all in one piece, I can say what I like again. I don't need to put brakes on my whole way of life anymore.

One moment of glory when Hicketier was in my grasp. But to think it has come to this—fireworks over a dead body. Not for this little man. Good God! Some blind impulse has brought me to the very spot chosen for me to bite the dust. This is where Krey would have shot me down. But I am about to make a gesture which is astonishingly perverse—or perhaps one should say fundamentally appropriate—I'm evaporating into the nothingness from which I arose. (Exit.)

HICKETIER, KREY *and* WOLKE *appear, all in tails.*

WOLKE: Five minutes to go till seven o'clock. We're first. (*To* KREY.) How do you feel?

HICKETIER: Stop badgering him. He looks composed.

WOLKE: But my hair is standing on end. If only I had not given my blessing to this wretched duel, if only we could have won Schippel round diplomatically and got a guarantee of his future behaviour. I am convinced in the light of his whole manner that he'll wield a fearful blade and let Krey have it clean between the ribs. Anyway I saw our friend here in a dream with no head.

HICKETIER: It seems to me that you are losing yours.

WOLKE: Why isn't the doctor here? (*To* KREY.) Is your heart beating? How's your pulse? (*Feels it.*) I noticed when you took a drink that your tongue was furred. What's to come of it all?

KREY: And things used to be so cosy.

WOLKE: Is it any wonder? He's probably prepared for every bloody eventuality—the pistol hasn't been out of his hand for weeks; but Krey, who even had to have the working of the trigger explained to him, will be an easy prey for such a brigand.

HICKETIER: Don't wreck our picture of this meeting with your cowardice.

WOLKE: Appearances mean nothing to me when the life of the person I hold most dear is at stake.

KREY: (*piteously.*) Be quiet, Wolke.

WOLKE: On the eve of marriage, loving and beloved, in the dawn of his life he has to face a cruel death. Is there not murder afoot here and are you not the guilty party, Hicketier? Did you not remind Krey so emphatically of the injury done to his bride's honour—an injury for which he would never have demanded satisfaction on his own account from one so far below him—when he had already given sufficient proof of his generosity of spirit by letting Thekla's unexplained adventure rest under the veil of love? Did you not make this duel a condition of his receiving Thekla's hand, with the result that something extraordinary had to take place all round to make it possible? Why, why?

(*To* KREY *who is in a state of collapse.*)

Courage, Krey! Because when all is said and done you respect the intrigues of this upstart. Hicketier, for a long time now I have suspected dark designs in your soul—don't interrupt me! All that is left of your pretended superiority is a cardboard dummy. Heaven has sent Schippel to try you.

HICKETIER: A pauper and he turned down the 100,000 Marks which went with a beautiful girl, and then, certain of a miserable pittance from us afterwards, he won the wreath by his unwaveringly divine singing, and now, unaccustomed to any such test but manly as he is, he faces the muzzle of a revolver. It's the least Krey can do not to flinch at such valour.

WOLKE: The likes of us, aware of our natural superiority, have no pretentions to excelling Schippel.

KREY: Be quiet Wolke!

HICKETIER: I must be permitted to put the human quality of the people around me constantly to the test. Don't make Krey unworthy at the decisive moment by your fussing.

WOLKE: Seven o'clock. Not a sign of anyone.

KREY: Maybe he's forgotten.

HICKETIER: Nonsense! (*Takes a few steps to the back of the stage.*)

WOLKE: Two minutes past seven.

KREY: When things were so cosy before! You see the full extent of what you've done to me.

WOLKE: How long are we to wait then?

KREY: I feel faint.

HICKETIER: Could they have missed us?

WOLKE: Krey is about to break down.

HICKETIER: (*to* KREY.) Do tell Wolke he's talking nonsense.

WOLKE: Eight minutes past seven. Are we obliged to wait here till evening?

HICKETIER: They have missed us; it's up to us to find them. (*Exit.*)

73

WOLKE: If only a hurricane or an earthquake would strike!
KREY: In fact, it's my nerves which are on strike. And things used to be so cosy.

(WOLKE *takes* KREY *by the arm and almost drags him away.*)

SCENE 4

After a short interval MÜLLER *and* SCHULTZE *appear from the other side, clad in black, and wave to someone behind them. The* DOCTOR, *holding* SCHIPPEL *by the arm, comes to the front of the stage with him.* SCHIPPEL, *hidden by a bush, remains invisible to those on stage.*

DOCTOR: Pull yourself together! Don't be childish.
SCHIPPEL: (*whispering shakily.*) Let me escape, doctor; if you hadn't caught me just in time I'd be miles away by now. You are a friend of the poor, please let me go!
DOCTOR: Rubbish. The consequences.
SCHIPPEL: I'm a poor devil of no consequence.
DOCTOR: Since the festival the whole town looks up to you.
SCHIPPEL: One of the workers, I assure you. A fortnight ago obscure in a corner. I'll vanish into nothingness, interfere with no-one.

(MÜLLER *and* SCHULTZE *have paced out the area, and put in stakes. They now look at their watches.*)

DOCTOR: For heaven's sake, man, your honour!
SCHIPPEL: Doctor, I haven't got any. I swear. Let go!
DOCTOR: Your opponents will let loose a flood of ridicule over you.
SCHIPPEL: Let them. After all, it's what I want, doctor. I'm begging them to, it'd be heavenly! I am a dog, a carrion, a miserable wretch—admit it.
DOCTOR: Excessive nerves, nothing more.
SCHIPPEL: Not at all. My knees are jelly. Played out. I don't want to die, doctor! Let go. I don't want to die, doctor! I'll collapse at your feet.

SCENE 5

HICKETIER, KREY and WOLKE *come back.*

HICKETIER: There are the gentlemen. (*Everybody bows.*) The places are marked. Take up your positions please.

(*All go to their places.* KREY *and* SCHIPPEL *stand diagonally opposite each other, so that* SCHIPPEL, *at the extreme right, can touch the foot-lights and* KREY *occupies the corner backstage on the left. To the right near* SCHIPPEL, *the* DOCTOR, *to the left two* GENTLEMEN, *to the left of* KREY, HICKETIER, *to the right* WOLKE. MÜLLER *has taken two pistols from a box, loads them, shows them to* WOLKE *and says:*)

MÜLLER: Two bullets in each, double barrelled. Both loaded. (WOLKE *reacts comically. The* DOCTOR *has opened his medical bag.* KREY *is unsteady on his feet.*)

HICKETIER: (*quietly to him.*) Courage!

KREY: (*stammers something like.*) B..lood ...

(SCHIPPEL *unsteady on his feet.*)

HICKETIER: (*quietly to him.*) Courage!

SCHIPPEL: (*stammers something like.*) D..ead ...

(SCHULTZE *has pulled out a handkerchief like a flag.*)

HICKETIER: At the signal on the count of 3—fire!

SCHULTZE *counts:* One—two—three. (*And waves the handkerchief.* KREY *falls. Everyone runs to him and pulls him a few paces off stage.*)

DOCTOR'S *voice:* A graze on the arm. Insignificant.

WOLKE'S *voice:* Praise be.

(SCHIPPEL, *who is standing alone on the stage with his arm outstretched like a marble statue, shoots again. Everyone except* HICKETIER *and* WOLKE *rushes at him.*)

DOCTOR: Are you mad? It's all over, Mr. Krey slightly wounded.

SCHIPPEL: (*mechanically.*) Thank you.

DOCTOR: Will you not meet your opponent as a sign of recon-cilliation?

SCHIPPEL: (*mechanically.*) By all means. (*Lets the* DOCTOR *take him to the back of the stage.*)

WOLKE: (*goes to meet him.*) My gratitude, o noble, noble-spirited man. Wolke will never forget your magnanimity.

HICKETIER: (*comes and says to* MÜLLER *and* SCHULTZE.) Your man's bearing was heroic. The same serene calm and assurance as at the festival.

(MÜLLER *and* SCHULTZE *bow.*)

HICKETIER: What an honour, to act as second to such a shot. MÜLLER *and* SCHULTZE *bow. Exeunt.* SCHIPPEL *comes back.* HICKETIER *steps across to him. The two men exchange a long look. Then* HICKETIER *speaks.*

HICKETIER: Filled with spiteful prejudice and conscious dis-taste for your background I have hitherto refused you entry to our preserves. You have beaten me. I consider it a duty to tell you how much I shall be honoured by your company in future.

(*Holds out both hands.*)

SCHIPPEL: I am very happy.

HICKETIER: To-day's events will have their consequences. The memory of what you have achieved must not be forgotten and you have my assurance that the higher blessings of the middle classes shall be yours to the full. Good-bye, dear Mr. Schippel.

(*Raises his hat formally to him. Exit.*)

SCHIPPEL: (*alone in the full blaze of the sun, buries his face in his hands. Their blessings to the full—too much. (Quietly and happily.) You are one of them, Paul. (Makes a sweeping bow to himself.*)

CURTAIN

THE BLOOMERS

A *Middle-Class Comedy*

Translated by M. A. McHaffie

THE BLOOMERS

Characters

THEOBALD MASKE, *civil servant*
LOUISE MASKE, *his wife*
GERTRUD DEUTER
FRANK SCARRON
BENJAMIN MANDELSTAM, *a barber*
A STRANGER

The Scene throughout is the Maske's living-room
Time: 1900

ACT I

SCENE 1

Enter THEOBALD *and* LOUISE.

THEOBALD: Maddening!

LOUISE: Put the stick away.

THEOBALD: (*strikes her.*) A scandal to be bandied about by the whole district. Frau Maske loses her bloomers!

LOUISE: Ouch! Oh!

THEOBALD: In the street, in public, before the King's very eyes, so to speak. And me a civil servant!

LOUISE: (*screaming.*) Stop!

THEOBALD: Isn't there plenty of time to fasten ribbons, button buttons at home? Excess, dreams, fantasies on the inside, slovenliness and neglect on the outside. That's you.

LOUISE: I'd tied a firm double bow.

THEOBALD: (*laughs scornfully.*) A firm double bow! Good God, listen to this contemptible cackling. Firm—here's a firm double clip on the ear for you. The consequences, the consequences! I don't dare think of them. Dishonoured, deprived of livelihood, hunted out of the service.

LOUISE: Do calm down.

THEOBALD: Furious . . .

LOUISE: You're not to blame.

THEOBALD: I'm to blame for having a wife like you, a slattern like you, a trollop and stargazer. (*Beside himself.*) Where's the real world? (*He grabs her head and strikes it against the table.*) Down here, in the saucepan, on your dustcoated living-room floor and not up there in the sky, do you hear? Is this chair polished? No—filth. Has this cup a handle? Wherever I lay my hand, the world is splitting apart. Crack after crack in an existence like yours. Horrible! O woman, just think! Fate in its providence gave me a post which brings in

700 Taler. (*Shouts.*) 700 Taler. On that we can afford a few rooms, eat well, we're able to buy clothes and heat the place in winter. We can rise to a ticket for a play, good health saves us the expense of doctor and chemist—heaven smiles benignly on our existence. Then up you come with those ways of yours and destroy the blessings we could have in life. Why isn't the fire lit yet? Why is this door open, that one shut? Why not the other way round? Why isn't the clock going? (*He winds it.*) Why do the pots and pans leak? Where's my hat, where did that important file get to, and how can your bloomers fall down, how could they?

LOUISE: You know, you knew me when I was a young girl.

THEOBALD: So?

LOUISE: And you liked me dreamy.

THEOBALD: For a young girl there's nothing better considering the unlimited free time she has. It's her lot, because she's not allowed contact with reality. But you've got that, now the dreaming's over.

LOUISE: Yes.

THEOBALD: Louise, look how deeply affected I am.

LOUISE: I can see you are, dear.

THEOBALD: On the street, in public.

LOUISE: There's just no accounting for it.

THEOBALD: Laughing and leering, urchins, loafers. It'll drive me mad!

LOUISE: You're off again.

THEOBALD: My heart stood still. Hate attracting any kind of attention, as you know. Do I allow you a fashionable frock or hat? Why do you have to dress so unbecomingly? Because your pretty face is much too striking for my modest position, your bosom, your eyes too provocative. If I could only make you grasp the fact that all the trouble in the world comes when two factors forming one entity are incongruous.

LOUISE: Stop; I can't bear it any longer.

THEOBALD: (*loudly.*) Two factors forming one entity, do you understand? My position and your appearance are incongruous.

LOUISE: I can't help it, God made me like this.

THEOBALD: Not God. It's all the fault of a shameless upbringing

81

which waved and rolled your hair and forced out with stays a bosom harmless enough in itself. A plague on all match-making mothers!

LOUISE: My mother was a respectable woman.

THEOBALD: What if I should lose my post!

LOUISE: Why ever should you?

THEOBALD: They say His Majesty wasn't far away. Ye Gods!

LOUISE: Theobald!

THEOBALD: A twitch of his brow, I sink in the dust, never to rise again. Misery, shame and hunger, the end of a life full of toil.

LOUISE: You're torturing me.

THEOBALD: (*his head in his hands.*) Oh, oh—oh.

LOUISE: (*after a pause.*) Will a leg of lamb and green beans be all right?

THEOBALD: In the street, in public. It's lucky there's still no child to share the consequences that threaten us.

LOUISE: I was thinking of raspberries for dessert.

THEOBALD: And His Majesty!

LOUISE: Father writes, he's sending some new wine.

THEOBALD: How many bottles is he going to send?

LOUISE: Fifteen.

THEOBALD: Do we still have some?

LOUISE: Five bottles.

THEOBALD: Hm. Leg of lamb. And properly salted. Woman, demons are active in our soul all the time. If we don't enslave them with the whole power of our will—there's no telling how far they'll go. Raspberries and cream. But where will you get cream from at such short notice?

LOUISE: The Deuter woman will let me have some.

THEOBALD: Do you think so?—Frivolity! yes, yes—(*He sits down in an armchair by the window and takes up a news-paper.*)

(LOUISE *busy at the cooking-stove.*)

THEOBALD: There now—they say the sea-serpent has reappeared in the Indian Ocean.

LOUISE: Good heavens, would you believe it!

THEOBALD: It's in 'The Courier' in black and white.

LOUISE: Dear, dear.

THEOBALD: Thank God the country there is sparsely populated, if at all.

LOUISE: What does an animal like that live on?

THEOBALD: Well—the experts don't agree about that. It must be a dreadful sight. I much prefer being in safe surroundings, in my little town. One should limit oneself strictly to one's own, hold on to it and watch over it. What have I in common with that serpent? Doesn't it at most excite my imagination? What's the point of all that? (*Gets up.*) One has one's little rooms. Everything familiar, gradually acquired, dear and cherished. Is there any need to dread that our clock will spit fire, the bird rush greedily at the dog from its cage? No. Six o'clock will strike, when, as for the last three thousand years, it is six o'clock. That's as it should be. That's how we like it, that's the way we are.

LOUISE: Certainly.

THEOBALD: How could you spoil my day off with excitement like that? Pray that we're left with what we have, and see that the roast is well cooked. I'll just go and find out what kind of talk is going the rounds about this damnable business.

LOUISE: Have you forgiven me?

THEOBALD: When I thought over how well-off we've been till now, God moved me. And remember the tulips need watering. Pray, Louise. (*He goes, through the door he can be seen disappearing down stairs.*)

LOUISE: (*has followed him to the landing and looked after him. Now she calls.*) Fräulein Deuter!

DEUTER: (*from below.*) Is it you, Frau Maske? Good morning.

LOUISE: Have you heard about my accident yet?

DEUTER: (*appears upstairs.*) It can't have been all that serious.

LOUISE: Are you coming in for a moment?

DEUTER: I don't mind if I do.

Enter LOUISE *and Fräulein* DEUTER.

DEUTER: The Kieswetter woman said they were pure linen and looked quite proper and respectable.

LOUISE: That's true—

DEUTER: But fancy having your initials on them in red—nowadays everybody wears white. Anyway hardly anybody noticed the incident, because the King was driving in the neighbourhood and everybody was looking out for him. I suppose your elastic broke?

LOUISE: As I was stretching to see the coachman.
(DEUTER *laughs*.)

LOUISE: A pretty kettle of fish. Suddenly the white showed below my dress. I didn't dare to move.

DEUTER: Your husband beside himself?

LOUISE: Completely. And the usual outburst about our slovenliness.

DEUTER: I hear you looked charming.

LOUISE: Who told you that?

DEUTER: Frau Kieswetter. You must have had some of the gentlemen cricking their necks.

LOUISE: I got out of the affair with decorum. First a careful step out of the elastic, then down like lightening and under my cloak with it.

DEUTER: By tomorrow they'll be saying the whole thing was a well thought out piece of coquettishness.

LOUISE: Evil tongues.

DEUTER: Anyone who looks like you can laugh at the world.

LOUISE: My husband can't stand talk at any price.

DEUTER: Your husband will get used to a lot of things.

LOUISE: Why, Fräulein Deuter?

DEUTER: Because sunshine makes people want to walk in it.

LOUISE: What?

DEUTER: My dear Frau Maske, I don't like your husband at all.

LOUISE: Dear Theobald.

DEUTER: Oh God!

LOUISE: No really!

DEUTER: All right.

LOUISE: But Fräulein Deuter! Could you possibly spare me a little bowl of cream?

DEUTER: For you—always. Isn't it about a year just now since you got married?

LOUISE: A year the day after tomorrow.

DEUTER: And nothing stirring? No prospect of the patter of tiny feet?

LOUISE: Alas.

DEUTER: Surely that can be no accident? If I know my Herr Theobald—

LOUISE: Do be quiet.

DEUTER: You shall have your cream. (Exit.)

SCENE 3

After a moment SCARRON *comes very quickly upstairs from below.* LOUISE *who had remained on the landing, utters a cry.*

SCARRON: Have I startled you? Do you know me?

LOUISE: Whom do you want to see?

SCARRON: I am in the right place.

LOUISE: This is where I—

SCARRON: Who else?

LOUISE: My husband will be back directly.

SCARRON: By then everything must be said.

LOUISE: But sir!

SCARRON: May I utter a metaphor, lady? Bluntly dare a great word? No. Forgive me. I am much too excited, too little master of my soul, which I still had a moment ago, and which has now been torn from me and dances through this hall.

LOUISE: Someone's coming, mustn't see us together.

(SCARRON *disappears upstairs.*)

85

DEUTER *returns with a bowl in her hand*: There! Clothes, above all your underclothes, are extremely important. But a lot can be done with a ribbon, a little bow as well. I could certainly show you a thing or two. And how to please is not always a question of clothes. You have sweet eyes. We'll talk about it another time. Today we'd better not let ourselves be caught, you little coquette. (*She runs downstairs again laughing.*)

SCARRON *appears.*

LOUISE: Is there something you want?

SCARRON: Yes, madam, if you want to know, something did bring me here.

LOUISE: Briefly—?

SCARRON: This morning in the main boulevard at the Tiergarten.

LOUISE: Heavens!

SCARRON: Suddenly enchantment penetrates my every limb. A young lady—

(LOUISE *turns away.*)

SCARRON: I believe in miracles, for months I've been rushing hungrily through the city in search of one, turning a hundred street corners at lightning speed in pursuit, and lo it appears under a limetree. Bathed in sun, brown forged to the light green trunk, beneath eyes filled with confusion a helpless body. A stupid greedy crowd and an enchanting martyrdom. A brilliant joke of the Almighty. Life pulsed through me! What I suffered with you in three minutes until you reached for the ground, diverted my heart from what yesterday I thought I loved and turned it to you. I still don't speak your language, much remains not yet fully understood between us, but how soon I can learn from gesture, glance and word what it pleases you to hear.

(LOUISE *makes a gesture.*)

SCARRON: I know, your way of thinking does not permit such emotional breathlessness, since it is not legitimized by any length of acquaintance. But silence is worship. (*A moment of silence,* SCARRON *sits with closed eyes.*)

LOUISE: Sir!

SCARRON: You don't know who I am?

LOUISE: I think I have seen you.

SCARRON: When?

LOUISE: This morning.

SCARRON: Nowhere else? Are you sure?

LOUISE: Certainly not. I don't go to the sort of places you frequent. My life runs its course within these walls.

(SCARRON *steps close to her.* LOUISE *retreats.*)

SCARRON: Hear my destiny.

LOUISE: I'm frightened.

SCARRON: From today I must desire you with all the strength of my soul. It's such bliss for me to say this, that I do not even ask what you think. Whether you wish me to the devil or ask me back.

LOUISE: Unparalleled boldness. Get up.

SCARRON: So much certainty surged through my limbs that I cannot. Kill me, but let me remain seated.

LOUISE: For Heaven's sake! What if my husband were to come suddenly.

SCARRON: You are truly chestnut-brown. I'll rent the two rooms which you advertise in the window. You are glowing like a chestnut over coals. Let's regard it as settled. The preliminary negotiations have already taken place.

LOUISE: A fine gentleman like you staying with us. Who'll believe that?

SCARRON: As soon as I've gone away again—I promise never to come here except dressed as the simplest of citizens.

LOUISE: You plunge me into deepest confusion.

SCARRON: And you me into confusion as deep as a bottomless pit.

LOUISE: Rent the rooms—

SCARRON: I will.

LOUISE: If he comes—

SCARRON: Simply introduce us.

LOUISE: Herr?

SCARRON: Scarron. Between the first sound of his key in the lock and his entry there are still seconds in which to stand up.

LOUISE: You living here?

SCARRON: Where?

LOUISE: A bedroom, a livingroom, oh God!

SCARRON: These simple words: oh God! They say all there is to say. Why are you trembling?

LOUISE: Please—

SCARRON: I am a church bell. My rope is hanging limp. If you strike me, I shall echo your throat's clear cries. Enough. I'm going. When shall I return?

LOUISE: He must be back soon.

SCARRON: You'll be waiting for me?

(LOUISE *is silent*.)

SCARRON: You'll be waiting for me!

LOUISE: Yes.

(*They are standing in front of the ladder.* SCARRON *rushes out*.)

SCENE 6

LOUISE *climbs the ladder as if in a dream, then Fräulein* DEUTER *enters*.

DEUTER: The door open? Good gracious, what are you doing up there?

LOUISE: The curtains—

DEUTER: Even with the longest arms you won't reach the curtains. By the way, you're losing your you-know-whats—no I'm joking. But the ribbon is hanging down again and you'll

88

trip over it as you climb down. Your really are, as I've long thought, an extremely luscious creature.

LOUISE: Don't make fun of me.

DEUTER: What *do* you believe, you little darling? You've known for a long time that I'm not the sort of neighbour who murders people's reputations. Shall I say boldly what I want from you?

LOUISE: Help me down.

DEUTER: Stay there for a bit. It suits what I'm going to say. I'm endowed with a tremendous lust for life, which my face doesn't match. But you are so visibly favoured in appearance, that all my wishes would be bound to come true if I could hear or see at close quarters what you can have if you want it.

LOUISE: I don't understand.

DEUTER: Do you like me?

LOUISE: Certainly.

DEUTER: You know without more ado that I'll stand by you?

LOUISE: You'll not do me any harm.

DEUTER: What did he want?

LOUISE: Just think!

DEUTER: A nobleman! I'd give ten years of my life. What was the pretext?

LOUISE: There was a real reason. He saw me this morning.

DEUTER: In all your glory?

LOUISE: Yes.

DEUTER: How wonderful! You are a person who gives many people pleasure. He leapt at it like a tiger?

LOUISE: He was very impetuous.

DEUTER: Shook the tree of life and overwhelmed you.

LOUISE: He's renting our rooms.

DEUTER: Splendid! Now I understand your expedition to the heights.

LOUISE: Catch me. (*She jumps down.*)

DEUTER: (*kisses her.*) I'll make such a job of fitting you out that the old Cinderella will still be there on the outside for Herr Theobald. But underneath will be a white dream, with a few brightly coloured bows in memory of this day. At the knee a rose-red one like a barricade. Listen quickly. Six metres of fine cambric will make six. I'll borrow a spanking brand new pair to see how they're made, and I can probably find out a lot by asking. Plus four metres of fine lace edging for the frills.

LOUISE: What are you thinking of! I'm an honest woman.

DEUTER: But he's a hero! A stormer of barricades.

LOUISE: Oh—You're a proper match-maker.

DEUTER: Of course. If one is left outside by oneself in the cold facing a black wall there's nothing better.

LOUISE: What silly ideas. You know yourself my husband will wring his neck if he as much as looks at me.

DEUTER: Such naïveté. A husband can have a dozen eyes. If the wife wants to, she'll throw sand in them all.

LOUISE: I'll decline.

DEUTER: Too late. In your domestic greyness there's already too much longing leaning at the window looking out. Why, dearest girl, hasn't the master of the house used the year he's had. Why hasn't he distended your veins with new life? Why aren't you going round padded out, listening to things stirring inside you? What became of God's blessing in this marriage?

LOUISE: We have to save. We can't afford a child on our salary.

DEUTER: But you've begun to sit in judgment on him for his eternal evasions of duty.

LOUISE: It's only by a hair's breadth that I'm not standing in front of you today a virgin. He wanted me to stay that way.

DEUTER: The barbarian!

LOUISE: 'On 700 Taler'—that was what he kept muttering every day.

DEUTER: Raise your eyes to God on high. Every human being has a right to happiness. Now we can both work to that end with a clear conscience. Give me your hand.

LOUISE: Heaven knows, I agree with you.

DEUTER: Hoho, husband Theobald will have to be quite a fellow now to avert disaster.

LOUISE: For heaven's sake! The lamb!

DEUTER: Who?

LOUISE: The lunch, I mean.

DEUTER: Are you having lamb today like me?

LOUISE: I haven't got it; gone clean out of my mind with all this talking.

DEUTER: Wait. My joint will wander into your pot. With the lamb you must have beans. May I include them?

LOUISE: You angel. What about yourself?

DEUTER: Fried egg. Back in a second. (*She runs out.*)

LOUISE: (*goes to the window and takes down the advertisement. Then she lights a fire in the fireplace, meanwhile humming the Mörike song.*)

Early, when the cocks crow
Before the stars disappear
I must stand by the hearth
Must light the fire.

(*Then she goes to the mirror and looks at herself, goes back to the hearth and goes on humming.*)

DEUTER: (*returns with a pot.*) Onto the stove quickly. It's just about ready. Add a touch of butter, a soupçon of salt.

LOUISE: How much do I owe you?

DEUTER: Listen. I've often wanted to say this to you. Your husband is a machine. If you get in his way you'll be flattened. But since, like all pile-drivers, he announces his coming, it's easy to avoid him. For complete safety, however, I offer my services as signalman waving a red flag. If I lower it he'll stop. That will give you time to hoist your signal mast for an unimpeded journey.

LOUISE: How freely I feel my soul stirring, you've removed my last scruples. Yes, I will get away from all this endless duty, these reins and fetters, that warning finger. Help me escape to freedom!

DEUTER: Only if you take to heart what I advised. You lucky little simpleton. Let your common sense be a reliable manager of the many opportunities you'll have during your husband's working hours between nine and three, then in his free time you fulfil your duty, and things can't go wrong. But get the nobleman to fix his alleged business activities for the time when your husband is at home. In that way you'll prevent their meeting and escape a thousand embarrassments. Enough for now. And may I do that shopping?

LOUISE: But bring roses instead of violets and reckon on eight metres not six.

DEUTER: Theobald will have to be a cyclops to escape his fate. A real giant. Something still on your mind?

LOUISE: Don't condemn me.

DEUTER: I've never been capable of condemning. For me there were always only desires, for each one unfulfilled two new ones to take its place.

LOUISE: It's as if someone had lifted a ton weight off my mind.

DEUTER: As if one were a child again.

LOUISE: And all the doors were still open—

DEUTER: Just a young girl walking along.

LOUISE: Dreaming—

DEUTER: Longing—

LOUISE: No telling what—(*They take each other's hands and dance in a ring.*)

Ring-a-ring of roses
A pocket full of posies
A tishoo, A tishoo
We both fall down.

(*Fräulein* DEUTER *hurries away laughing.*)

LOUISE: Quick! Raspberry, stop hiding. I wonder what his first name is? Two spoonfuls of sugar. He's something out of a different world! I remember a picture: in the foreground a woman lying swathed in a veil, the man bends over her, her feet move apart. Father must give me a present of some shoes. But now to set the table: past three. (*She laughs.*) Hoist the mast.

SCENE 7

THEOBALD *enters with* MANDELSTAM: What disgraceful tom-foolery is this; where's the notice in the window?

LOUISE: The rooms, if you're agreeable, are taken.

THEOBALD: Oho! (to MANDELSTAM.) What do you say to that? But meanwhile don't worry, you have my promise. Admittedly a critical situation. (To LOUISE.) For?

LOUISE: 15 Taler.

THEOBALD: Inclusive?

LOUISE: Without.

THEOBALD: (to MANDELSTAM.) Just think: 15 Taler without.

MANDELSTAM: I don't understand.

THEOBALD: Without coffee. This could literally make one's hair stand on end. If only I hadn't gone out. (to LOUISE.) If only your little pranks hadn't driven me into going. Misfortunes always come in twos, and you see how unfortunate this all turns out to be. (to MANDELSTAM.) Avarice is alien to me, the person of the tenant can sway the balance just as much as the amount involved, but—you're a barber, Herr?

MANDELSTAM: Mandelstam.

THEOBALD: Semite?

MANDELSTAM: Certainly not.

THEOBALD: Turn to the light.

MANDELSTAM: With one M. S—t—a—m.

THEOBALD: I am a German. No question of anti-semitism or anything like that, but the Red Sea between them and me would be best as I see it.

MANDELSTAM: Entirely my opinion.

THEOBALD: (shakes his hand.) Bravo! To business: You were prepared to pay 5 Taler for the smaller room?

MANDELSTAM: With coffee.

THEOBALD: Now here's someone who can use both rooms for 15 Taler. I'll carry out the following manoeuvre: I transform myself into Herr Mandelstam and I ask you, Herr Maske: what do you propose, what must you do in your own and your family's interest?

MANDELSTAM: Your calculations, I can see, favour the other person, but I have your word and I rely on your sense of honour. Being young a disappointment in this respect would come as a bitter blow.

THEOBALD: Friend, whither? Can I, a son of the people which bore a Schiller, be faithless?

93

MANDELSTAM: Are you fond of Schiller?

THEOBALD: Young man, I am naturally not a very good judge.

MANDELSTAM: Wagner, not Schiller, is the man of our epoch.

THEOBALD: To remove your last doubt, I speak one name: Luther.

MANDELSTAM: Good.

LOUISE: Can I serve lunch?

THEOBALD: Eat a bite with us.

MANDELSTAM: Since you ask me, I don't mind if I do.

(*They sit down.*)

THEOBALD: Give me your hand. You seem a good sort and you aren't to blame for the predicament you've created.

MANDELSTAM: I lost my parents at an early age, I live by the labour of my hands.

THEOBALD: But you manage to make ends meet?

MANDELSTAM: I've been with the same employer for three years.

THEOBALD: That's good.

MANDELSTAM: In the evenings, every penny I save, everything for Wagner. I've seen *Lohengrin* three times.

THEOBALD: Good Lord!

MANDELSTAM: It's like being in paradise.

THEOBALD: But good long walks too, stretch your legs. Health.

MANDELSTAM: Health—there I must admit—

THEOBALD: What does that mean? Pass me the beans again—out with it.

MANDELSTAM: What is there to say? You've already guessed. Not that there's any precise illness I could put my finger on.

THEOBALD: But?

MANDELSTAM: My mother was delicate, probably undernourished like me. My father was fond of a glass more than was good for him.

THEOBALD: Good heavens!

MANDELSTAM: Had I been born with a completely healthy body, believe me, I'd have considered rather different prospects for myself in life.

THEOBALD: Do you hear that, Louise?

LOUISE: Yes.

THEOBALD: It's true, health, strength above all else. Feel that thigh, the biceps.

MANDELSTAM: Gigantic.

THEOBALD: My boy, with those I ride life so to speak. I can lift a hundredweight. Believe me, I could lift you into the air with one arm. If anybody comes up against my muscles, he knows about it. We'll have to coddle you a little, poor fellow. How would it be if we were to feed you and look after you?

MANDELSTAM: If it doesn't cost more than I can afford I'd like that.

THEOBALD: What do you think, Louise? Don't you feel sorry for him? What should we charge him?

LOUISE: That can't be worked out in a minute.

THEOBALD: I've no say in this, my boy. That's my wife's business. Discuss it with her, I'll raise no objections. (to LOUISE.) Give me a cigar in honour of the occasion.

LOUISE: You were going to buy some. There's not a single one left.

THEOBALD: Forgotten naturally in all the upset. I'll just run across. Can we expect the other tenant to make do with one big beautiful room?

LOUISE: He's coming at a quarter past three. Speak to him.

THEOBALD: If it was for a longer period, we could buy a screen and make two rooms as it were; a lot could be done with a curtain too. But what if he's not willing?

MANDELSTAM: I have your word.

THEOBALD: Good God, you have your room, Mandelstam of Aryan stock. I'll be back directly. (*Exit. A moment's silence.*)

MANDELSTAM: Excuse me—

LOUISE: I'm surprised you haven't even asked to see the room. It must be very important for you to live in this particular house. Do you work across the road with Master Lämmerhirt?

MANDELSTAM: No. I work in Lindenstrasse.

LOUISE: Fifteeen minutes away. That's strange. Wouldn't it be wiser—?

MANDELSTAM: I have reasons.

LOUISE: Are you shortsighted? You're looking at me as if you were.

MANDELSTAM: Oh, Frau Maske!

LOUISE: What's wrong? You've gone red all over.

MANDELSTAM: Don't think badly of me. If I seem strange.

LOUISE: Your secrets don't concern me.

MANDELSTAM: Since this morning, I have one only, and it would be a release to unburden my soul.

LOUISE: Confide in my husband.

MANDELSTAM: He must be the last to know. His sympathy would suddenly disappear. Nothing dishonourable, something which hardly concerns me, something much more to do with you.

LOUISE: Me? How me? (*She has got up.*)

MANDELSTAM: (*rises.*) Forgive me.

LOUISE: Tell me.

MANDELSTAM: Through no fault of my own—

LOUISE: Please!

MANDELSTAM: I've never been in a situation like this. But, but—I must say it: Your bloomers—

LOUISE: What—?

MANDELSTAM: Today—your—

LOUISE: Quiet!

SCENE 8

THEOBALD: (*comes back.*) The decision?

LOUISE: I want to talk to you about it.

THEOBALD: Good. For the time being you'll move in. Would you like a cigar?

MANDELSTAM: I don't smoke.

THEOBALD: Lungs played out? Have you noticed my chest? Plenty of room for everything in there. Come here, stand in front of me. Arms out-stretched. Trunk bent backwards. Slowly. Lower. Listen, we'll have to have a serious talk about this.

MANDELSTAM: I'm exhausted.

THEOBALD: You're puffing like a bellows.

(*The bell rings.* THEOBALD *goes to the door.*)

LOUISE: (*quickly to* MANDELSTAM.) It was unspeakable of you to come.

MANDELSTAM: Don't scold.

LOUISE: Go away!

SCENE 9

SCARRON: (*enters.*) I had the honour of putting my request to madam.

THEOBALD: My wife has told me you need two rooms. Now sir, the situation has arisen that, without knowing of your offer, I have given the smaller of the rooms to Herr Mandelstam here; who incidentally is of a good German family.

SCARRON: Oh!

LOUISE: Herr Mandelstam was just saying—

MANDELSTAM: Not at all, I'm determined to stay.

THEOBALD: Yes, we know that. There remains the quite plausible possibility that you'll be satisfied with the beautiful big room that's left. It measures $6\frac{1}{2}$ metres by 5. Will you please look at it thoroughly and give us your considered decision. (*He leads him to the door and into the room.*)

LOUISE: (*to* MANDELSTAM.) Your behaviour is unworthy. I shall report it to my husband.

MANDELSTAM: I can't prevent you. But I ask you not to, for otherwise I shall have to draw Herr Maske's attention to the following: what induces the aristocratic Herr Scarron to look for quarters in a house like this, if not—

LOUISE: You know him?

MANDELSTAM: I twice had the honour of dying his hair.

LOUISE: What a slander!

MANDELSTAM: He'll certainly not remember me, but I know all about him.

LOUISE: And what makes you behave like this?

97

MANDELSTAM: This morning I re-read *The Flying Dutchman*. Do you know Senta, Frau Maske? You're as dreamy as she is. I was still reading when I saw you coming with your husband, when you passed only two steps away from where I was lying on the ground. Suddenly—

LOUISE: Only two steps! Disgraceful. But when all's said and done your whole behaviour is no concern of mine. I utterly despise you—that's all.

SCENE 10

THEOBALD *and* SCARRON *come back.*

THEOBALD: Herr Scarron is agreeable. He appreciates the room's merits and will pay 12 Taler. By the way he intends normally to use it for only a few hours during the day.

SCARRON: That is so.

THEOBALD: For something important which he cannot carry out in the uproar of the busy street where he lives.

SCARRON: That is so.

THEOBALD: I was able to assure him that we would exert ourselves to make his stay pleasant. My wife, worthy sir, possesses the skill, tact and civility of a person from the better classes and our deep rooted awareness of a decent background gives us a certain pride; nevertheless we, my wife especially, is not averse to doing favours.

SCARRON: I am very pleased, indeed.

THEOBALD: Finally, to touch on the question of the neighbouring rooms, Herr Mandelstam, who by the way is of good German stock—as I already stated—is kept out of the house all day by his business. So we can divide our whole attention between you, during the day it can be devoted unreservedly to Herr Scarron, for the rest of the time to Herr Mandelstam. Another thing occurs to me: on this side there's an alcove with enough light from a window in our bedroom for Herr Scarron to keep anything there that he doesn't want to take into his room. We'll hang up a little curtain for him, so that we can't look in. And the convenience, gentlemen, on the

98

half-landing. Really now everything's settled beautifully. Here are the keys for the street door and the flat for each of you. Nothing now hinders you from regarding the flat as yours at all times. May I, purely as a matter of form, Herr Scarron, ask you, this work which you intend doing in our house isn't of a subversive nature or likely in any way to contravene law and order? I am a civil servant.

SCARRON: Not at all, sir. I give you my word of honour.

THEOBALD: I accept it and feel as man to man that the word 'honour' still has for you the tremendous significance that it has for every German.

MANDELSTAM: Till tomorrow morning then.

THEOBALD: (to SCARRON.) And the agreement for a year.

SCARRON: Certainly.

THEOBALD: Till tomorrow.

SCARRON: Madam!

THEOBALD: Till tomorrow.

(SCARRON *and* MANDELSTAM *off*.)

LOUISE: That barber is an unpleasant lout.

THEOBALD: Because he doesn't smell of scent like the other one.

LOUISE: He'll bring his disease into the house with him and thousands of nasty things with it.

THEOBALD: He doesn't really have any disease. He's tired, weak, he hasn't any marrow or sap if you like. From living in hostels and among hand to mouth existences. That'll improve. For the rest, my dear Louise, you're to behave quietly today and for the next few days and spare us any of your lip otherwise I'll beat your behind so thoroughly that you'll not be able to speak at all for a long time. Thank God that your slattern-liness today doesn't seem to have had any evil consequences. I hope you're now fully aware of how very lucky you are. And it must have dawned on you when you saw the pitiful figure of that hollow-cheeked barber how important inherited good health is. But also if you take a closer look at the middle-aged gent with his impeccable clothes and well-brushed hair, you'll not fail to see how imperfectly his pretended purpose-fulness masks the fact that his will is sapped. Believe me, my dear, my few words about honour and conscience met a character incapable of such considerations. All the same he has taken a year's lease.

(LOUISE *bursts out sobbing.*)

THEOBALD: (*laughing loudly.*) This is priceless! Why tears, don't you agree he's rather comical? (*He chucks her under the chin.*) Shall I really beat you? Laugh, you silly goose. Go on, laugh. These two inferior specimens of manhood that God has sent into our house have put me in a really good mood again. Wasn't it too funny for words, the way he stood there saying Madam! To my Louise who can't even keep her bloomers up. (LOUISE *sobs more violently.*)

THEOBALD: And then: that is so! That is so! That is so! like a nutcracker. (*He shakes with laughter.*) In the other corner that angel of the soapsuds gasping for breath. Anyone not helpless with laughter here just has no feeling for the divine humour of it all. (*They laugh and weep in unison.*)

ACT II

SCENE 1

THEOBALD: (*comes from the alcove.*) That's the little curtain up then.

MANDELSTAM: (*at the coffee table.*) Why haven't you fixed it on your side.

THEOBALD: He must have the feeling that nobody can stick their nose into his affairs.

MANDELSTAM: As long as he has the same intention there'll be no objection.

THEOBALD: His laconic answers, his reserve towards me allow me to suppose so.

MANDELSTAM: The arrogance of a superior social position.

THEOBALD: Would he move here if that were the case? He could find the quiet room he wants for his work in the house of people better situated than we are.

MANDELSTAM: What's the man really doing?

THEOBALD: Why do you avoid the term gentleman? As far as I could make out from what he said, he wants to write about an experience he feels strongly about.

MANDELSTAM: An affair!

THEOBALD: An experience, he said. Watch this tendency of yours to switch terms. Write about an experience he feels strongly about.

MANDELSTAM: Well, well; an experience!

THEOBALD: If you say it like that, you're missing the point again.

MANDELSTAM: You're very precise.

THEOBALD: Naturally. I have to be. From nine in the morning till three in the afternoon I have official documents in front of me. What if I were imprecise there!

MANDELSTAM: Well yes, people do sometimes just talk. I have to entertain my clients when I'm shaving them, see that they don't notice a cut, the shaved-off end of a moustache. No time for long reflection there, one just throws words about. Main thing is to keep talking.

THEOBALD: So you're a victim of your profession! (*He laughs.*)

MANDELSTAM: An experience! Probably a love-affair.

THEOBALD: Possibly. Don't you have to put in an appearance before eight on Saturdays?

MANDELSTAM: That's the way I work it. The boss doesn't come till then either, and the apprentice deals with the riff-raff.

THEOBALD: Hm. Well at least go for a walk in the early morning. If I were as uncertain of my body as you are, I'd go all out to strengthen it.

MANDELSTAM: Long walks are too strenuous for me.

THEOBALD: At first. I'd like to make you realise your condition really clearly.

MANDELSTAM: Why?

THEOBALD: So that you know what's what.

MANDELSTAM: If my means don't permit adequate attention—what use is the truth?

THEOBALD: Good Heavens, man, what use is self-deception?

MANDELSTAM: Heavens above, in the end everything all around is deception.

THEOBALD: You're a queer fellow, hohoho. A pessimist. Everything deception, downright deception?

MANDELSTAM: Don't laugh. I'll prove it to you.

THEOBALD: (*laughing.*) Good. Where?

MANDELSTAM: Wherever you like, everywhere, everybody.

THEOBALD: (*laughing.*) Yourself?

MANDELSTAM: (*furious.*) Certainly.

THEOBALD: Herr Scarron?

MANDELSTAM: Also.

THEOBALD: (*roaring.*) My wife?

MANDELSTAM: Especially.

THEOBALD: Me?

MANDELSTAM: Surely.

THEOBALD: (*uproariously.*) You're the life and soul of the party, a miracle, good value. And you are not a barber at all really? A baron in disguise maybe, my wife's lover who's wormed his way in?

MANDELSTAM: (*in a towering rage.*) Herr Maske!

THEOBALD: A power house of explosive virility with innards like powderkegs.

SCENE 2

LOUISE *comes from the bedroom.*

THEOBALD: Louise, leave your cooking smells behind. Mandelstam is a baron. Your lover, hohoho, and the world is deception and there's an end to it.

MANDELSTAM: Herr Maske, now I must seriously object—

THEOBALD: Oh no, my dear fellow. What my eyes see is as sure as the fact that you remove people's beards and aren't quite firm in the saddle, that I think of nothing but getting my columns to agree, that Herr Scarron writes love stories and my wife belongs to me. Certainly the only deception is something you dream up. And that comes from your liver or your lungs or your stomach. I won't rest till you've realised it. Are you coming with me?

MANDELSTAM: No thanks. In ten minutes.

THEOBALD: Don't be angry with me. Think your hour will come and you'll convince me? Never, my good chap; but let's not be enemies because of that. Well, I'm going. You don't want to?

MANDELSTAM: No thanks.

THEOBALD: Good. Au revoir. (*Exit.*)

MANDELSTAM: He makes it really easy.

LOUISE: (*looks him up and down.*) He does?—Who for?

MANDELSTAM: He really is most ridiculously credulous.

LOUISE: He knows who he can trust.

MANDELSTAM: He's going to have his eyes opened in no uncertain manner.

LOUISE: About people whom he takes into his house.

MANDELSTAM: My opinion entirely.

LOUISE: Who uses a transparent pretext.

MANDELSTAM: Which a child could see through! Writing a love story far from the noise of the streets!

LOUISE: If you mean to insult me, I'll call my husband back.

MANDELSTAM: Call him: He's still on the stairs. Don't provoke me, I'm still not in complete control of myself. Why does he keep laughing at me, why the contemptuous pity in his voice? What cause have you to despise me? I—I say it freely—I have a feeling for you, which however is far removed from approaching you other than respectfully.

LOUISE: No one will prevent you from doing that.

MANDELSTAM: You yourself. Do you think I'll watch calmly while another man conquers you for himself, bear living through what's in the wind, tolerate it as an accessory? I swear by this table: I'll prevent it with any means I can think of.

LOUISE: When do you have to go to work on Saturdays?

MANDELSTAM: You're underestimating me, Frau Maske. Someone took an oath then. May God be my witness, you shall not attain your goal!

LOUISE: (*slowly.*) You're a child.

MANDELSTAM: I'm a highly-strung human being. Heaven knows.

LOUISE: A real child. Getting excited about nothing, nothing at all.

MANDELSTAM: I won't have people despising me.

LOUISE: Getting quite breathless. Have another cup of coffee. I'll spread you a roll with honey.

MANDELSTAM: When one has no-one in the world.

LOUISE: Help yourself to lots of sugar.

MANDELSTAM: One just has no-one in the world.

LOUISE: That's my father's honey. He has a little house in the country a couple of miles from here.

MANDELSTAM: If one had known one's parents better.

LOUISE: Usually I'm grudging with it.

MANDELSTAM: One is so inanely alone. No roots at all, nothing to lean on, nothing to hold on to.

LOUISE: We'll have to look after you a bit. A lot of it's nerves. Only you're so excitable.

MANDELSTAM: No.

LOUISE: I can't help despising violent natures. Docility and submissiveness are what I like. Good children.

MANDELSTAM: When a person doesn't have a mother, that's his one wish.

LOUISE: Yes, yes—his one wish! I've heard that before.

MANDELSTAM: Frau Maske, I swear by the memory of my dead mother who is looking down on us at this moment: I will never pass beyond any line you draw for me.

LOUISE: Not that I have anything against you.

MANDELSTAM: What I saw yesterday wasn't my fault.

LOUISE: You mustn't mention that ever again! Not a syllable. The way you turned up here scared me, I was afraid of unpleasant altercations with my husband.

MANDELSTAM: As if I wouldn't stand by you to my last breath.

LOUISE: Good—perhaps in the course of time we'll become friends.

MANDELSTAM: And Herr Scarron?

LOUISE: But why should that fop concern me?

MANDELSTAM: Fop certainly. But you could be deceiving me. I haven't enough experience with women, even if I'm not altogether a novice. Truly not.

LOUISE: It's not impossible that he has secret intentions here. But you're forgetting me, assuming an understanding which I find outrageous. Do you take me for so blind as not to see that I'd only be another easy victim for that spoiled Don Juan, which he'd abandon just as quickly as it had occurred to him to seize it? I'd sacrifice my reputation and all the advantages of my position for the desires of another man?

MANDELSTAM: His glances at you made me suppose—

LOUISE: Glances can be presumptious without any encouragement from me.

MANDELSTAM: I will certainly never be presumptious. Undemanding, satisfied with the least thing, a mere sigh.

LOUISE: Good. Let's leave everything to time.

MANDELSTAM: But don't hope to deceive me.

LOUISE: How lightly dressed you are. You shouldn't. Put something on, it's raining.

MANDELSTAM: The way you say that! It makes me healthy and strong in a trice. I don't notice the weather. I'll take off my scarf.

LOUISE: But no! Better prevention than cure.

MANDELSTAM: The way you say that!

LOUISE: Would you like to take some sandwiches to work?

MANDELSTAM: Fancy you thinking of that!

LOUISE: I think it would do you good.

MANDELSTAM: I don't need to eat. I have my heavenly dreams. What's earthly misery to me? Would it be all right with you if we sometimes read *The Flying Dutchman* together in the evenings?

LOUISE: Is it a love story?

MANDELSTAM: The most glorious one of all. Listen to what the Dutchman says about Senta: 'Will she be my angel? When out of the terrible force of the torments which shroud my head in darkness longing drives me towards salvation, I shall have reached my longed for goal.'

LOUISE: Lovely. Go now, or you'll be late.

MANDELSTAM: Then the end: 'Alas, without hope as I am, I yet surrender myself to hope.' And you should just hear it sung. It moves you to the very marrow.

LOUISE: Till lunchtime.

MANDELSTAM: Soon! Soon! Soon! (Exit.)

DEUTER: (*appears immediately.*) Who is that long-winded creature?

LOUISE: A dangerous nosey parker. Yesterday he too saw what nobody should have seen, and he's wormed his way in under the same pretext as our friend. They're dividing the rooms between them.

DEUTER: Imagine!

LOUISE: Worst of all: he hates Herr Scarron and is making conjectures. What do you think? He's just sworn here that he'll never tolerate—

DEUTER: How stupid!

LOUISE: I think he's capable of running to Theobald with the whole story before the least thing has happened. I'm beside myself. When I came in here a little while ago, my husband said to me: Mandelstam—that's the barber's name—is your lover. It was said laughingly, but the creature must have spoken seriously of such possibilities, must at least have steered his remarks in that direction.

DEUTER: How have you behaved towards him up till now?

LOUISE: I've been flattering him, trying to make him feel confident.

DEUTER: Well done.

LOUISE: But—

DEUTER: I'll watch him closely. You see what a good thing it is to have me on your side.

LOUISE: What's that you're holding?

DEUTER: Guess.

LOUISE: Tell me.

DEUTER: The material.

LOUISE: You darling! How fine!

DEUTER: Do you like it?

LOUISE: Gorgeous! Expensive, I suppose?

DEUTER: It's more fashionable than silk.

LOUISE: How soft it must be on the skin.

DEUTER: Not like your nasty twill. Twill on a figure like yours. I'll just measure the waistband, hold up your skirt. 65, let's say 66 centimetres.

LOUISE: Have you got the ribbon yet?

DEUTER: Here it is.

LOUISE: Heavenly. You're my very best friend. And you're willing to do all this for me and you still young enough yourself?

DEUTER: I've honestly given up all hope. Otherwise it's true I'd not have much time to spare for you.

LOUISE: We'll have to pray for you.

DEUTER: Do you think that'll help?

LOUISE: For an objective as important as that, everything must be tried.

DEUTER: What progress you're making!

LOUISE: My mind is made up. Last night was absolutely decisive for me. A sweet dream already.

DEUTER: Tell me.

LOUISE: You poor thing.

DEUTER: No, don't tell me or I'll burst into tears.

LOUISE: We'll find someone for you yet. How would the barber do?

DEUTER: Ugh! If it comes to that, I'd rather have your husband. (*They laugh exuberantly.*)

SCENE 4

SCARRON: (*opens the door from outside and enters.*) What heavenly gaiety. I step from rain into tropical sunshine.

LOUISE: (*softly to* DEUTER.) Stay here!

DEUTER: For a moment, then I must go downstairs.

SCARRON: My doorkey allows me to burst in univited on your gaiety and disrupt it. Go on laughing: if I may and can, I'd like to participate. What were you laughing at?

LOUISE: Fräulein Deuter—

(SCARRON *bows.*)

107

LOUISE: And I were talking about the barber.

SCARRON: Which barber?

LOUISE: Mandelstam, of course.

DEUTER: Frau Maske was saying he was too ugly for her and recommending him to me as a lover.

LOUISE: I said no such thing.

DEUTER: God knows, she recommended him and that was what she meant.

LOUISE: As a joke.

SCARRON: Seriously, it wouldn't do. He's not at all what could be called a man.

DEUTER: All the same, good enough for a spinster who's getting on.

SCARRON: Whom do you mean?

LOUISE: She's fishing for a compliment.

DEUTER: Nothing of the sort, only your verdict on this material, Herr Scarron. What do you say?

SCARRON: Batiste, I suppose. What's it for?

DEUTER: To make some bloomers for this young woman; excuse me: What would you say in your circles—lingerie?

LOUISE: Fräulein Deuter!

DEUTER: You interrupted us while we were taking the measurements.

LOUISE: Fräulein Deuter!

DEUTER: 66 cm, that's what I call slender, eh Herr Doktor.

SCARRON: I oughtn't to have held up such a delicious pastime.

LOUISE: Herr Scarron!

DEUTER: I just need the length still. (*Bends and measures.*) 63 to just below the knee.

LOUISE: That's enough. What are you doing?

SCARRON: Since I blundered into so delicate a situation, may I give some advice? Those ladies interested only in fashion and adornment, who set the tone in all questions of taste, would not perhaps have measured quite as far down as you did, Fräulein Deuter, they would have found the point about two or three centimetres above the knee.

DEUTER: Do help us. I was counting on your being well informed. And does our width of 18 correspond with the latest cut?

108

SCARRON: The bloomers are left as wide as possible at the bottom and made tighter fitting further up.

DEUTER: That leaves one question—

LOUISE: (*rushes to bury her head in her bosom.*) Trude, do be quiet; I'll be eternally angry with you!

SCARRON: (*to* DEUTER.) This is extremely important. Are you the person responsible? Do you arrange everything?

DEUTER: You'd not withhold a compliment if you had the opportunity of admiring the finished article in position.

SCARRON: How do I earn your friendship?

DEUTER: Simply by realising that I'm acting on your behalf!

SCARRON: You seem to wish to be fairy godmother to a happiness that needs a protecting hand even more than any fledgling.

DEUTER: That wants to fly, however—

LOUISE: And doesn't know how?

DEUTER: I'm only half a bird, so to speak, that didn't have the nerve when the time came and was left stranded under the eaves. You can't expect guidance from me.

SCARRON: There's no need.

DEUTER: The nestling, by the way, is bestirring herself. Yesterday I found her already fluttering in intimate contact with the higher regions.

SCARRON: Let us take wing!

DEUTER: A bird of prey is circling on the horizon! Not the fat old owl that's to be feared only by night. A slender hungry cloud that falls on the hiding place with lightning speed.

SCARRON: Who?

DEUTER: A cloud of soapy froth, a froth-beater.

SCARRON: The barber!

LOUISE: He's spying on me! He's watching me, he won't tolerate anything, he told me to my face. I'm very unhappy.

DEUTER: Now that's been said, I'm going. Caution!

SCARRON: Thank you!

DEUTER: I'll do what I can to stop him. (*Exit.*)

SCARRON: Louise:

LOUISE: I'm afraid.

SCARRON: Sit down by the table.

LOUISE: My knees are giving way.

SCARRON: Anyone can come through the door, for I'm not touching you. Opposite you, more than two oceans distant, I am quietly encamped against this mountain slope. Away from life basking in two blue suns. They are sending streams of will towards me, scorching what is near and kindling what is more distant with light, joyous warmth. Your clenched hand has grasped the melting thought and savours it. Your bosom is already seething. I see the muslin heaving. And now you're shedding your leaves from top to root with me, Louise, in one sweet gust, and are felled by fate.

(LOUISE *has buried her head in her arms on the table as if asleep.*)

SCARRON: My life began with father and mother. Brothers and sisters moved meaningfully towards me, and from my father there came almost uninterrupted utterance. What became of them? All that I saw was my mother's arm arched like a pleading shadow above me and I stood suddenly alone in a dreadful tumult that tore the ground and cast the heavens down on me. I had a goal but no paths towards it. Stand up, woman, I'm falling into a false passion. Stay! It's something quite different that I have to say to you. There are glorious women living in the world, Louise. Blonde women, with pale pink moles when they are uncovered, and dark women with down like young eagles, along whose backs a wave ripples when they are roused. Some in rustling clothes and stones which shimmer like their sinuous places. Others in narrow close-fitting garments, cool as their skins. There are blonde ones with down and dark ones with pale pink moles. Submissive brunettes and proud flaxen beauties. The sky is full of stars and the nights full of women. The world is sublimely beautiful—but! (*Grand broken off gesture.*)

(LOUISE *has risen.*)

SCARRON: You are the most beautiful woman I have ever set eyes on. I await the moment when you will unleash a storm which will break over me and demolish my mortal remains, and from the refuge of my madness I shall offer up my empty self tenderly at your feet. (*He has stepped up close to her.*) Look at this hand quickly before you clasp it in your own. God may well have chosen it as His instrument to pour out fine new songs in our tormented land's mother tongue. Have you fully realised: I am passionately in love with you, Louise? There must be no doubt of that.

LOUISE: I am yours.

SCARRON: Of what classical simplicity the gesture! A whole destiny clothes itself in three words. What humanity! If I could succeed in catching its living essence in a book—I should certainly count among the greatest.

LOUISE: (*bending towards him.*) Let me be yours.

SCARRON: Table, pen and ink as close to you as possible: as close as this to such simplicity a masterpiece is inevitable.

LOUISE: Yours!

SCARRON: So be it! To a degree high above both of us. A passion like none ever known spurs me on, happiness can escape me no longer. With the metres vibrating within me I feel my soul take wing. I must capture your image for the whole of mankind before I return to demand the complete reward of your favours. (*Disappears to his room.*)

LOUISE: Why?—(*She goes to* SCARRON's *door and listens. After a few moments she plucks up courage and knocks.*) My God! (*She whispers, listens and approaches the table, from which with a glance at* SCARRON's *door, she picks up* MANDELSTAM's *scarf, which she finally presses to her face. Just then* MANDELSTAM *appears outside the flat door. He can be seen pressing his face against it. Then he opens the door quietly and comes in.*)

SCENE 5

MANDELSTAM: Heavens, my scarf! (*Comes close to* LOUISE.)

LOUISE: What a fright you gave me! Where have you suddenly come from?

MANDELSTAM: Why a fright?

LOUISE: Creeping in like that.

MANDELSTAM: Is that my scarf?

LOUISE: God knows.

MANDELSTAM: (*kisses her.*) Louise!

LOUISE: (*slaps him.*) Impudent fellow!

MANDELSTAM: Forgive me!

(LOUISE *goes to* SCARRON'S *door and knocks loudly.*)

SCARRON'S *voice*: Five minutes more.

(LOUISE *stands in confusion.*)

MANDELSTAM: I implore you. It was an impulse. Never again. I'll kill myself.

(LOUISE *towards her room.* MANDELSTAM *swoons.*)

LOUISE: God! (*Runs to him.*) What's wrong? Water! (*She fetches water and gives him some.*)

MANDELSTAM: How well I feel.

LOUISE: Your chin is bleeding. What's that pointed thing?

MANDELSTAM: That? A drill.

LOUISE: What's it doing in your pocket? It could have wounded you fatally just now.

MANDELSTAM: Why not, if you would have grieved.

LOUISE: Who wouldn't? Such a promising young man. What madness! Come and lie on the sofa for a minute.

MANDELSTAM: (*lying down.*) It will show me at all times what is going on in Herr Scarron's room.

LOUISE: You're going to—

MANDELSTAM: Bore a hole in the wall. I'm mad with jealousy, Louise, I don't know myself any longer. What drove you to that wretch's door? Don't misjudge me. In spite of my weakness, I'll murder him.

LOUISE: What right—!

MANDELSTAM: I love you, Louise.

SCARRON: (*quickly from his room.*) Down to the smallest detail tone, colour, every nuance held fast, recorded, no longer to be wrested from me. I come, all gratitude and love—(*He notices* MANDELSTAM.) Beg pardon!

SCENE 7

THEOBALD: (*comes in quickly.*) Good day, gentlemen. I trust we all have a healthy appetite.

CURTAIN

ACT III

SCENE 1

Everyone is sitting round the table covered with the remains of the evening meal.

THEOBALD: (to MANDELSTAM.) It was hard for your employer to manage this afternoon without you. He said you might have arranged your indisposition for some day other than Saturday.

MANDELSTAM: The first afternoon I've missed in three years.

THEOBALD: He hopes you'll be better by the day after tomorrow at the latest. There's the whole of Sunday between then and now.

MANDELSTAM: Even a dog wants a bit of peace if he doesn't feel *koscher.*

THEOBALD: *Koscher?* Hm. But as you wish. By the way I had a very thorough discussion with a colleague who complains of symptoms similar to yours. He knows the inside of his worn-out body like the salary scale and even operates with Latin names. (*He has got up and goes to the back of the stage.*)

MANDELSTAM: (*follows him eagerly.*) But how, devil take it, could you discuss my case?

SCARRON: (*softly to* LOUISE.) I forbid you to stare at that lout all the time.

LOUISE: I'm honestly sorry for him.

SCARRON: He's a cunning scoundrel, a rogue who deliberately spoiled the afternoon for us by his pretence, and you—

THEOBALD: Primarily it's a matter of the nerves, even if the other organs are naturally also infected, some more, some less. If I understood him properly, you have to imagine every nerve as a fine tube, surrounded by a protective second tube. Now in people who've been weakened this other surrounding tube has been partly rubbed away like bark on trees—isn't that so, Herr Scarron?

SCARRON: More or less, as far as I know.

THEOBALD: Yes. And it's surprising how extraordinarily difficult it is to make good the damage once it's been done.

MANDELSTAM: Where in all the world do you get the idea that my nerves are—It's unheard of, without having examined me more closely.

THEOBALD: Do keep calm. I don't want to upset you. But I think many people must have drawn your attention to the state of your nerves already.

MANDELSTAM: Nobody.

THEOBALD: Then I'll ask the completely impartial observer. How does our friend seem to you, Herr Scarron?

SCARRON: Typical neurasthenic.

MANDELSTAM: Ha!

THEOBALD: You see. Other things naturally contribute as well, as I've already said. With the colleague I mentioned it's his stomach, which has been ruined by years of abuse with completely inadequate nourishment, while in your case I'd hazard a guess it's the lungs.

LOUISE: You mustn't frighten Herr Mandelstam, Theobald.

THEOBALD: Quite the contrary. I'm trying to arm him against a catastrophe, to avert it if possible.

LOUISE: But he denies having any serious illness.

MANDELSTAM: Unreservedly.

THEOBALD: All the better. I regard it simply as my duty.

MANDELSTAM: And I regard it as very ill-considered to tell sensitive people such things. Quite naturally one goes on being preoccupied with them inwardly.

THEOBALD: Even when they don't concern one.

MANDELSTAM: Is there a window open?

THEOBALD: A crack.

MANDELSTAM: May I shut it? (*He does so.*)

LOUISE: Put your scarf on.

MANDELSTAM: Many thanks.

SCARRON: (*to* THEOBALD.) As far as your sick colleague is concerned—I find incomparable satisfaction in this thought: what is weak and lacking in vitality must give way to what is strong and healthy.

LOUISE: The task of the strong should be to support the weak. Our religion teaches that as well.

SCARRON: The religion of past centuries, not ours.

LOUISE: (*hands* MANDELSTAM *a newspaper.*) Read that!

SCARRON: We're far beyond that. We've introduced a healthy breath of air into the stuffy, musty climate of compassion from past centuries.

MANDELSTAM: Where? It's swimming before my eyes.

THEOBALD: (*shows him.*) Down there. They say the sea-serpent has appeared again in the Indian Ocean.

MANDELSTAM: (*furious.*) What has that to do with me?

THEOBALD: It may divert you.

SCARRON: (*to* THEOBALD.) Does the name Nietzsche mean anything to you?

THEOBALD: In what connection?

SCARRON: He teaches the gospel of our time. He shows that it's only through the individual blessed with certain energies that the boundless mass of humanity is given direction. Might is the supreme delight.

THEOBALD: Might is delight I agree. I knew that while I was still at school, when I made others suffer at my hands.

SCARRON: Naturally I don't mean mere brute force. Above all spiritual energies.

THEOBALD: Yes, yes.

MANDELSTAM: I didn't notice till this morning that my room faces north-east.

THEOBALD: One moment. Yes. You're right.

MANDELSTAM: That's naturally extremely disadvantageous, even for the healthiest constitution.

SCARRON: (*to* LOUISE.) The spineless dog must be shown who is master. Tonight I'll risk everything to come to you.

LOUISE: Heaven preserve me!

SCARRON: Who do you take me for? Do you think that creep is a match for me when my mind is made up?

LOUISE: Wait a little!

SCARRON: No!

THEOBALD: (*has opened* MANDELSTAM's *door.*) Put the bed against the wall opposite the window, then you'll be sleeping towards the south-west.

MANDELSTAM: I can feel the draught even on the pillows.

SCARRON: (*to* LOUISE.) This very night you shall be with me in paradise.

THEOBALD: (*to* MANDELSTAM.) Now you're exaggerating.

(MANDELSTAM *goes into his room. He can be seen bustling about there.*)

SCARRON: (*to* THEOBALD.) Have you never heard these theories discussed? Do you read so little?

THEOBALD: Hardly at all. I work for seven hours. After that I'm tired.

SCARRON: That's regrettable. Where do you find the criteria for your thinking?

THEOBALD: People like us think less than you suppose.

SCARRON: All the same you live according to a certain plan.

THEOBALD: Looking after number one, if you like.

SCARRON: That means you eat, sleep, do your office work? And where will that get you?

THEOBALD: To my pension, God willing.

SCARRON: Deplorable. No interest in politics?

THEOBALD: I used to be interested in what Bismarck was up to.

SCARRON: He's been dead a long time.

THEOBALD: Nothing much has happened since.

SCARRON: Any intellectual pursuits?

THEOBALD: My God! For the likes of us there's not much point in that.

SCARRON: Are you aware that Shakespeare lived, do you know your Goethe?

THEOBALD: Goethe—I know the name.

SCARRON: For God's sake!

THEOBALD: You take it too tragically.

SCARRON: A comfortable theory of living.

THEOBALD: What's wrong with comfort? My life span is seventy years. With the mental attitude I've acquired, I can enjoy lots of things in my own way in that time. If I wanted to adopt a higher way of looking at things, your rules, then with my limited talents, I'd scarcely have learned what to do in a hundred years.

LOUISE: But that there shouldn't be compassion any more?

SCARRON: There simply isn't.

LOUISE: If I really feel it—

THEOBALD: Please don't interrupt when we're talking.

MANDELSTAM: (comes back.) I'd like after all to ask Frau Maske for a woollen blanket. I've turned the bed round.

THEOBALD: That was sensible.

LOUISE: You shall have a blanket. (Goes into her room.)

SCARRON: I judge every man quite simply according to the degree of his participation in the spiritual development of the human race. The heroes are the great thinkers, poets, painters and musicians. The layman is significant to the extent that he knows them.

MANDELSTAM: And the great inventors!

SCARRON: Certainly; but only in so far as they make human beings cleverer in communicating the thoughts of the genius more quickly and urgently.

THEOBALD: And what about feeling?

SCARRON: What?

THEOBALD: Didn't I express myself properly? How does the heart fit into all this?

SCARRON: The heart is a muscle, Maske.

(LOUISE *comes back.*)

THEOBALD: Good, but it's a special case. Above all with the women.

LOUISE: (*to* MANDELSTAM.) It's big enough for you to wrap up in.

MANDELSTAM: Many thanks.

SCARRON: Where fundamental issues are involved, don't speak to me with such naïveté. Females, let's say women, are, by God, a precious commodity but when a Shakespeare wrestles for Hamlet's soul, Goethe for insight into a Faust, then woman just doesn't come into it.

MANDELSTAM: Schwarz won't have thought of his wife when he invented printing, nor Newton, nor Edison, nor Zeppelin.

LOUISE: Is that certain?

SCARRON: My oath on it.

MANDELSTAM: I'd like to take my oath on it too.

THEOBALD: Leaving Goethe—and as far as I'm concerned Schwarz too—on one side—all the same—if I may put it this way, women do have a heart.

SCARRON: A muscle, Maske.

THEOBALD: I know. But they live by it and are one half of the earth's population.

SCARRON: Well and good. But you're not a woman and ought to be permeated by the dignity of your manhood. Allowing for all the domestic and intimate bonds that unite you with your wife, there are still moments in which you feel that you are a world apart; where the masculine elements in you over-whelms you completely and fills you with extravagant pride.

MANDELSTAM: Wonderfully said.

LOUISE: Not all men are like you.

SCARRON: Deep down all of them, madam.

MANDELSTAM: Unquestionably.

THEOBALD: I don't know. There is something in it, certainly but I've really always struggled against it.

SCARRON: There we have it! Struggled against—nature.

MANDELSTAM: The devil!

SCARRON: What else makes a man a giant then, the gigantic obelisk of creation that is unconquerable by woman if not the transcendental will to knowledge which the deepest erotic passion cannot paralyse?

MANDELSTAM: Paralyse—glorious!

LOUISE: My husband happens to be differently constituted.

THEOBALD: Louise, for God's sake, spare me your stupid comments. Speaking from personal experience, I can't convince myself that it would have brought me advantages in my marriage if I had strengthened and expressed this feeling of difference.

SCARRON: Personal advantage—you have to ignore that. Since it's indisputable that all progress for humanity depends on the preservation of the pure masculine principle.

LOUISE: Pah!

MANDELSTAM: Who would have thought ten years ago that we'd be flying?

THEOBALD: Above all I'm glad to see you both so unreservedly of one mind. How pleasant to have two lodgers who don't quarrel with each other.

MANDELSTAM: It's just one man standing by another.

SCARRON: By the way, you still owe us the disclosure of your real opinion. Up till now you've just been rejecting ours.

MANDELSTAM: Is Zeppelin perhaps not a hero?

SCARRON: Can we dispense with Plato and Kant?

MANDELSTAM: What would the world be without railway and telephone?

SCARRON: Without his predecessors Goethe would simply be an impossibility. And even if you deny Pontius and Pilate, I hope you'll admit that Goethe counts?

MANDELSTAM: And Wagner. The most sacred possession of mankind.

THEOBALD: (slowly.) That apart, there's so much else as well. Having children and such things—

MANDELSTAM: Always a woman's business!

THEOBALD: Don't attack me so fiercely. Did I for one moment doubt the accuracy of your facts?

MANDELSTAM: Even a God couldn't do that.

THEOBALD: But the two I produce from my experience, that

women have a heart and that children are born, make you angry.

SCARRON: Incredible! These are truisms as firmly established as—

THEOBALD: You were saying?

SCARRON: At the moment no comparison occurs to me. An argument with you is pointless.

THEOBALD: Have another glass of beer. Louise, pour some for Herr Scarron.

SCARRON: Thank you.

THEOBALD: We could go to the Zoo tomorrow. They've got themselves a giraffe.

MANDELSTAM: (*bursts out laughing.*) Giraffes!

THEOBALD: What is there to laugh at about that?

MANDELSTAM: I think my thoughts.

THEOBALD: If I'm to be honest: left to myself, I'd never have hit on the idea of looking at such an animal. I'm really averse to such flamboyancies and eccentricities of nature. But since Herr Scarron is pressing me so hard, I want to do something to educate myself.

(MANDELSTAM *bursts out laughing.*)

THEOBALD: Not so wild, Herr Mandelstam.

SCARRON: My dear fellow, you are pretending to a narrowness of outlook ...

MANDELSTAM: Blinkers on!

THEOBALD: (*to* MANDELSTAM.) Don't dissipate your limited resources.

SCARRON: Should not the presence of a noble young woman at your side inspire you to the highest achievements? To raise yourself up out of your ambience?

THEOBALD: My wife's people are tailors, always have been for generations.

LOUISE: Six brothers fell on the field of honour.

MANDELSTAM: Nowadays nobody would be so stupid as to let himself simply be slaughtered.

THEOBALD: Really, isn't that in tune with the times any more? Patriotism out of date?

MANDELSTAM: If you almost made me ill earlier, now you're

making me well again. In spite of many physical disadvantages, I feel that I'm different and I know there are legions behind me. No, we don't let rubbish of that sort affect us any more; we know what all that junk is worth. Even the highest born is descended from the ape like me and Herr Scarron, all mankind is fundamentally equal, and everyone can reach the heights.

THEOBALD: I agree. If he wants to. But there are some for whom one place is just as good as the next, and above all they like the one they are in. With what birth bestowed on me I am most favourably situated in my place and certain of it to my dying day, provided I don't differ too much from my colleagues throughout the country. Only special efficiency or extraordinary disgrace could deprive me of the security which it guarantees.

SCARRON: Sir, that's frightful. Slave morality!

THEOBALD: (*grinning*.) Not at all. My freedom is lost if the world pays any particular attention to me. My insignificance is the cloak of invisibility under which I can indulge my inclinations, my innermost nature unhindered.

SCARRON: God forbid that your credo is shared by your colleagues.

THEOBALD: I can't judge how my colleagues think. On the other hand, I can certainly guarantee that progressive ideas aren't popular in higher quarters. One of our heads of department tolerated his wife's affair with another man; as he put it in the document he drew up in his defence, he didn't want to curb the woman's natural tendencies, an expression that used to be popular for horses. Today he's pushing an ice-cream cart round the streets.

SCARRON: A martyr. His wife will look up to him.

LOUISE: His wife despises him thoroughly.

SCARRON: You're quite mistaken.

LOUISE: From the depths of her soul.

MANDELSTAM: I doubt that too.

THEOBALD: Let's leave that to the two of them.

MANDELSTAM: I happen to have proof from my own past. I lived with little Frau Frühling—they have the boarding house in Ahornstrasse—and her husband put up with the liaison.

THEOBALD: That her name was Frühling and she lived in Abornstrasse doesn't give the matter any special weight.

LOUISE: (*stands up.*) Good night!

THEOBALD: You're staying till we all go.

MANDELSTAM: Since then she's venerated the man.

THEOBALD: I must drink a schnaps on that. Is anyone coming to 'The Golden Basket' for a quarter of an hour?

SCARRON: I'm more confused than I can express. It's the first time I've encountered such a view of life held with conviction.

THEOBALD: By a little man.

SCARRON: A man nevertheless. I feel you wouldn't abandon it under any circumstance.

THEOBALD: Under none whatsoever. Because I'd simply go under.

SCARRON: It would be some job. At least the attempt should be made.

THEOBALD: Don't give yourself the trouble.

MANDELSTAM: I regard it as quite useless too.

THEOBALD: I might possibly agree over a glass across the road.

SCARRON: Above all be good enough to treat the matter with the same deadly earnest as I do.

THEOBALD: No! If I did that would be the end of my politeness and many of the things said, that I can put up with at the moment, would find an echo dangerous for all of us. So come along.

SCARRON: Even if you start with a theory of unchangeable values—

THEOBALD: Mandelstam, you too. They've got excellent Munich beer.

MANDELSTAM: No thanks, I'm going to bed.

THEOBALD: Each to his own ways. (*He goes off with* SCARRON.)

SCARRON: (*gesticulating vehemently at* THEOBALD's *side.*) Even if you assume with Kant—

(*Both exeunt.*)

MANDELSTAM: After that conversation I must view lots of things with different eyes. To live with that pigheaded numb-skull must be hell—I've met confused ideas in other quarters as well, but obstinacy like that—what a swine. And then that gross familiarity, because I mentioned in passing that I wasn't strong. Beside a creature like that Herr Scarron naturally seems like God, if the comparison is adequate. Furthermore it takes devilish brutality to foist a north-east room on a person whose health one assumes to be completely ruined.

LOUISE: You agreed with Herr Scarron that one mustn't feel compassion for anyone.

MANDELSTAM: Who wants compassion? Decency, fineness of feeling is what I demand, such as, I have to acknowledge, Herr Scarron has shown to the highest degree.

LOUISE: How?

MANDELSTAM: In what he said. Didn't he grip you, didn't you feel that the man possesses a great overflowing heart? Isn't it touching that he's still going to try this late in the evening to pour enlightenment into that birdbrain? It's true his only reward will be the same grin that the master of the house had for me when I reproached him about the room.

LOUISE: But we didn't have a third room.

MANDELSTAM: Then it was your duty to warn me against that one.

LOUISE: You asserted to my face that to be near me you had to insist on having the room under any circumstances.

MANDELSTAM: But if it means certain death for me!

LOUISE: You're exaggerating.

MANDELSTAM: (laughs.) Exaggerating! North-east for people with weak chests—there aren't words to express it. And to add to that, naturally my nerves must rebel at the consciousness of such a fact. The bark of a tree! Rubbed off—one can practically see it scaling off. You in your robust health, cheeks red as roses. (He runs into his room.) Not even double glazing. Without a woolly night-shirt I'll not last out the night, and my only one is at the laundry. (He appears again.) How long do you think it takes to put a weakened organism under the ground? (Disappears into his room again.) Didn't he say himself that his colleague would die within three days. The catch of the window doesn't work either. (Appears again.) What was that bit about the tube? For God's sake, he spoke about a tube, didn't he? Say something.

LOUISE: You said yourself it's got something to do with the nerves.

MANDELSTAM: I'm completely confused. I've a feeling now he spoke about two tubes and its being impossible to mend them again. (*He disappears again and shouts.*) A hole like this ought to be reported to the police. Policemen stand about at every corner, but when it comes to a poor fellow like me they let him rot in a hole like a mad dog. (*He appears again.*) What was it the doctor always did? Wait. Look at my throat! (*He wrenches his mouth open.*)

LOUISE: But I don't know anything about it.

MANDELSTAM: No, like this! (*He throws himself into a chair and crosses his legs.*) Strike my knee, like this, with the flat of your hand. (*And as* LOUISE *does this and his leg jerks, he screams.*) I'm done for! Naturally, one night facing northeast has ruined me completely.

LOUISE: (*disconcerted.*) But—

MANDELSTAM: (*beside himself.*) And you pretend to feel compassion!

LOUISE: (*near to tears.*) But you wanted to be near me at any cost.

MANDELSTAM: (*bellows.*) Near the grave, monstrous! We'll have to talk about this again!

(*He runs into his room, slamming the door shut and locking it from the inside.* LOUISE *stands without moving.*)

SCENE 2

DEUTER *appears outside the glass door.* LOUISE *opens it.*

DEUTER: I met both of them arm in arm outside the door?

LOUISE: Where have you been so late?

DEUTER: At the theatre. A splendid play by Sternheim. I'll tell you about it later. You should have seen him, he was literally radiating.

LOUISE: Who?

DEUTER: Not our giant, though he didn't look too bad beside him. Him, our hero! Exuding an aura of power and masculinity!

LOUISE: Ah!

DEUTER: His appearance made Theobald show up well by comparison, he seemed livelier than ever before. You've been able to be together the whole day! Tell me what happened, what went on? I'm burning to know.

LOUISE: Quiet. Mandelstam is in.

DEUTER: Let me look deep into your eyes. Let me clasp you by both hands, by both arms.

LOUISE: Why do you want to do that, Trude?

DEUTER: To drink the breath of your happiness. He sat on this divan, nearer and nearer to your very being every moment. Finally you were pressed against the back and couldn't evade him, even if you had wanted to. Tell me what he did.

LOUISE: I don't remember.

DEUTER: You rascal, you're robbing me. I want a confession with no omissions. Don't be shy, dear Louise, I've read more than you think, and I dream of such things. Even if I haven't experienced it, I know about it all the same. How did it begin? He put his arms round you?

LOUISE: He sat somewhere in the room.

DEUTER: And you?

LOUISE: At the table.

DEUTER: Then he came to you.

LOUISE: He stayed where he was.

DEUTER: And?

LOUISE: Talked.

DEUTER: What? Can you repeat what he said. Glorious things.

LOUISE: I had a roaring in my ears.

DEUTER: He unleashed himself on you like a thunderstorm. It must be like that, I've read it. And your body goes weak in the presence of the male, your feet refuse to function.

LOUISE: That's what happened to me. For a moment all my senses failed me.

DEUTER: Lucky girl! Then?

LOUISE: He came over to me.

DEUTER: O Louise! And?

LOUISE: Talked.
DEUTER: And?
LOUISE: Said something.
DEUTER: And then?
LOUISE: What?
DEUTER: When he'd said everything?
LOUISE: He went away.
DEUTER: What?
LOUISE: He went away.
DEUTER: What did he do?
LOUISE: He went away.
DEUTER: Called: I love you!
LOUISE: Yes.
DEUTER: And you?
LOUISE: The same.
DEUTER: I am yours!
LOUISE: Yes.
DEUTER: You did too?
LOUISE: From my heart.
DEUTER: At last. And then?
LOUISE: He went away.
DEUTER: Where?
LOUISE: Into his room.
DEUTER: You followed?
LOUISE: No.
DEUTER: Miserable girl!
LOUISE: When he shut the door, I followed, plucked up courage and knocked.
DEUTER: You knocked?
LOUISE: But he didn't open the door.
DEUTER: What? Shut himself in?—Now I have it, Mandelstam was about!
LOUISE: No.
DEUTER: Are you sure? Not near at hand without your seeing him? But he had already noticed him?
LOUISE: Ha!
DEUTER: Think back.
LOUISE: Mandelstam really did come in just afterwards.

DEUTER: Ha!

LOUISE: I'm surprised myself, it has only just occured to me.

DEUTER: You see, O you see! To distort my hero for me! Carried too far in his gestures, he suddenly notices the creeping fox I'd urgently warned him against. At once speech and gesture descend to the everyday, in the fineness of his feeling he departs quickly to spare you, and the greedy eyes of the intriguer see the woman alone as is right and proper. How right I was and how little you're able to understand him. Didn't he use the first opportunity that offered itself later to renew his pledge of love?

LOUISE: Yes, and he showed he was jealous of the barber.

DEUTER: Then the picture I formed of him at a distance was more correct than the one you had when you actually saw him.

LOUISE: But afterwards when the men were talking to each other—

DEUTER: What were they talking about?

LOUISE: Then it was quite hopeless. I went out and had to weep.

DEUTER: You were wrong in thinking like that.

LOUISE: Then what I called loathing of my husband and liking for Herr Scarron was wrong too. If I was misled by the misery that constricted my throat at what he went on to say, then everything in me from the first day of my life has been deception.

DEUTER: You understood him as little in those moments as you understood his earlier consideration. You've not taken in what his intentions are. Listen to me and trust in my deepest conviction: he's preparing the deed that will overwhelm you at one stroke.

LOUISE: I'm plunged in despair, eternally unhappy.

DEUTER: You fainthearted creature, it's not for nothing that he draws your husband away from your side at night, it's not for small stakes that he fascinates him with his vitality and ensnares him deeply in scruples and problems. If you'd been at the theatre with me, you'd be counting on happiness to come any minute. There was a man there who climbed walls, burst down doors and started fires to be near his beloved. We poor creatures are engulfed by the conviction of male power. Foolish girl what are we at? The time we're gossiping away is time stolen from the waiting hero. Goodnight, a kiss. I swear by the bones of all the saints, it will come to pass! Quick, go to bed, quickly, put out all the lights. He'll come. (*She flits out.*)

LOUISE: Could it be? (*She sits for a moment without moving and listens. Then she goes to the window and looks out. Sits down again, stands up and goes into the bedroom, where she lights a candle. Coming back, she begins to undress slowly, her face pressed against the glass door. Steps echo on the staircase. She blows out the candle on the stage and stands trembling. But the sound fades again. She says.*) No! (*Her fingers go on unbuttoning mechanically. Now she approaches* MANDELSTAM'S *door and touches its knob and goes with dragging steps back to the entrance to her bedroom. She stays there, lit up from behind, in chemise and bloomers, combing her hair slowly and repetitively, while at intervals* MANDEL-STAM'S *regular snoring shakes the air.*)

CURTAIN

ACT IV

SCENE 1

THEOBALD: (*calls into the bedroom.*) What a slovenly job you've made of mending my braces again! There's to be no question of my being neglected because of those two.

(LOUISE *enters and pours coffee for him.*)

THEOBALD: Luckily neither of them is here. We won't have to reckon with Scarron at all before midday, praise be. After he'd talked at me like a man in the grip of hallucinations till nearly 2 o'clock in the morning, I had to take him, at his ex-

press desire, tired to death as he was, to his other flat because the bed there was better. I drank five pints and three
glasses of schnaps, and the result was out and out diarrhoea.

LOUISE: He's not coming?

THEOBALD: I don't understand how anyone can sleep as soundly
as you with somebody on the trot all the time. Where's the
honey?

LOUISE: There isn't any more.

THEOBALD: What a terrible way to keep house! Kindly get some
more. Furthermore I don't care to find underclothes of yours
on my chair. You don't give me a chance to stop preaching
at you.

LOUISE: I had another scene with Mandelstam about his room
facing north-east and sank into bed.

THEOBALD: That fellow is completely mad! Where does he get
this idea that north and east are inferior parts of the heavens.
The sun rises in the east, every painter is extremely keen on
rooms facing north, and a miserable barber wants west and
south thrown in for five Taler.

LOUISE: South would in fact be better for his weak chest. And
you were saying, Herr Scarron isn't coming today: how is
that possible?

THEOBALD: Kindly blow your nose, you sound all choked up.
What do you mean, how is that possible? He was tipsy and
won't be feeling at his best today.

LOUISE: Tipsy?

THEOBALD: All right sozzled. At the finish he was a pitiable
sight. The idea that he had to convert me never left him in
spite of his condition. By the end of the evening he was rattling
on at a tremendous pace.

LOUISE: Good heavens!

THEOBALD: That man is a strange ornamental plant in the garden of our Lord. Furthermore he has bad breath.

LOUISE: Theobald! But he had, doesn't he have something heroic
about him sometimes?

THEOBALD: Like someone in a novel, you mean?

LOUISE: Yes, like someone in a novel.

THEOBALD: O, God—look Louise: he's not what you might

call sound. Wouldn't he have to be a great deal more heroic for your taste—to compensate for the lack?

LOUISE: Yes.

THEOBALD: What he's doing has no real purpose. Deep down I think he's already tired of the fad that drove him to work here. I don't care. He's taken the room for a year—in writing.

LOUISE: Will you let me go to church today. It's almost an emergency.

THEOBALD: Of course, my dove. I think it's a very good idea. Last week held great danger for both of us on account of your fallen bloomers. You're only doing your duty if you thank your Maker. Meanwhile I'll ponder the consequences of something I have in mind.

LOUISE: Tell me what it is.

THEOBALD: You're curious. Rightly so. When you come back, Louise: let me think about it for another hour or so. I have a surprise for you.

LOUISE: Yes?

(*She goes into the alcove.*)

THEOBALD: What are you doing?

LOUISE: The curtains have to be put up in our bedroom. As it is, anybody can see in.

THEOBALD: Mind you don't fall off the window sill. (*He follows her. He can be heard inside.*) Mmm, my little wife does have a strapping pair of legs.

SCENE 2

MANDELSTAM: (*comes in, sits down hurriedly at the coffee table, begins to eat greedily. Goes to the alcove to shut the door.*) What! (*As he recognises* THEOBALD.) I beg your pardon!

THEOBALD: (*embarrassed.*) I didn't hear you coming. We're taking the curtains through to our room.

MANDELSTAM: Had breakfast? (*He sits down.*)

THEOBALD: Yes.

(LOUISE *crosses the stage into the bedroom.*)

MANDELSTAM: Good morning, Frau Maske.

THEOBALD: You seem to have slept well.

MANDELSTAM: The agitation you plunged me into overwhelmed me with sleep—I slept really splendidly.

THEOBALD: (*laughs*.) In spite of north-east.

MANDELSTAM: Truly. Although—

THEOBALD: An although?

MANDELSTAM: The bed is good.

THEOBALD: Better than the softest bosom.

MANDELSTAM: Although—

THEOBALD: Do you hear noises from the street?

MANDELSTAM: Not a sound, although—

THEOBALD: The morning sun disturbed you?

MANDELSTAM: There's nothing I like more—but of course—

THEOBALD: Five Taler is too cheap a rent for so many advantages. You have my wife to thank for it.

MANDELSTAM: But you're not to raise it the first chance you get.

THEOBALD: Not for the time being.

MANDELSTAM: That's expressed most ambiguously, one doesn't know where one is at all. It's only fair to fix a definite period.

THEOBALD: Why do you want to tie yourself down?

SCENE 3

LOUISE *enters*.

MANDELSTAM: Don't I get any honey today?

LOUISE: Nowhere in the world do people get honey without paying extra.

MANDELSTAM: I thought it was included.

LOUISE: Then you were wrong. Furthermore the sugar is going to run out very shortly. (*to* THEOBALD.) Au revoir.

(LOUISE *exit*.)

THEOBALD: Why do you want to tie yourself down? If the doctor really finds something really serious and feels that north-

131

east may be harmful for you, you'll be in an embarrassing situation. The bed is certainly good. The mattress is horsehair. You won't find the like on a thoroughbred today.

MANDELSTAM: Indisputably.

THEOBALD: Morning sun and perfect peace and quiet—As it happens, we'd decided shortly before you came to replace the bed with another. Fräulein Deuter, as a matter of fact, a neighbour, had offered us sixty Taler cash for it.

MANDELSTAM: You mustn't ever do that!

THEOBALD: (*has gone into* MANDELSTAM's *room.*) A down quilt like this. And hasn't my wife added a second pillow against my express instructions!

MANDELSTAM: To be brief: for a year. We understand each other, Herr Maske.

THEOBALD: Your ailing condition—

MANDELSTAM: I feel like a giant.

THEOBALD: Prices in this district rise from day to day. After three months the room will easily be worth eight Taler instead of five.

MANDELSTAM: You'll get me so agitated that the benefit of last night will be undone again.

THEOBALD: Six Taler. That's as far as I can go.

MANDELSTAM: I can't.

THEOBALD: You'd better.

MANDELSTAM: Agreed then, to make an end of it, agreed. You with Bismarck and Luther on your lips, I wouldn't have thought this sort of thing of you.

THEOBALD: All settled!

MANDELSTAM: For a year. And let's put it in writing straight away. I'll write: Herr Maske lets Herr Mandelstam a room with breakfast until May 15th.

THEOBALD: Without honey.

MANDELSTAM: For six Taler. The bed in the room must not be replaced by another. Sign it.

THEOBALD: Suppose my wife doesn't like it. She finds you revolting.

MANDELSTAM: But good Lord, we have nothing to do with each other.

THEOBALD: Even so. Since she finds your presence in the house uncongenial. Perhaps she'll feel inhibited.

MANDELSTAM: Not by me. I'll swear it to her with a thousand oaths. She doesn't concern me, let her do as she pleases. Don't drive me on to the street. I admit the bed is good. Think of my miserable condition—be merciful.

THEOBALD: Well then—since you press me. I'm not a monster. (*He writes.*) There it is: Theobald Maske.

MANDELSTAM: Would there be an armchair to spare anywhere?

THEOBALD: I'd better tear it up—my wife—

MANDELSTAM: (*wrenches the sheet of paper from him.*) The devil take your wife!

THEOBALD: Here's to an enjoyable life together then!

MANDELSTAM: It won't be my fault if it's not. (*He looks into his room.*) You'd have had to have seen the bed in the lodgings I was in before. A torture rack. And non-stop noise from all sides. In addition, a little menagerie, oh yes, fleas, bugs, my dear fellow; I made a pattern of them on the wallpaper with pins spelling Richard Wagner. (*He laughs.*) I got a bit carried away against you yesterday evening. It wasn't ill-meant.

THEOBALD: I was extraordinarily pleased. Agreement with Herr Scarron comes before all else. He pays well, we owe him some consideration.

MANDELSTAM: (*his hat on.*) I'll do my bit.

THEOBALD: Where are you off to today?

MANDELSTAM: Out to the pleasure gardens.

THEOBALD: Wouldn't it be better if you used your day off to consult a good doctor?

MANDELSTAM: Not as long as I feel as I do today.

THEOBALD: What's her name then?

MANDELSTAM: Nothing at all yet. The last one—Frieda. She's got a technician now.

THEOBALD: Was she buxom?

MANDELSTAM: Extremely. That's what I look for. There'll be others at the fireworks today. (*Exit.*)

THEOBALD: It only occurred to me in passing to charge him more. Thoroughly weak in the head, stupid fellow. 18 Taler all told. 18 times 12 is 180—216 Taler a year. The flat costs 115. That leaves 110. I earn 700, that makes 810, 811 Taler, and we'll be living rent free. It'll work, it'll work, it can be done. That's fine, excellent!—Who's that?

SCENE 4

DEUTER *is standing outside the door.*

THEOBALD: (*opening the door to her.*) Do come in, Fräulein Deuter. We were just talking about you.

DEUTER: Who?

THEOBALD: A barber and I.

DEUTER: That nasty fellow.

THEOBALD: And he seemed very interested in you.

DEUTER: Stop joking.

THEOBALD: Raised his eyes tenderly and said Trude.

DEUTER: How does he know my first name?

THEOBALD: Who doesn't know it that has the good fortune to be under one roof with you!

DEUTER: You're making fun of me.

THEOBALD: Heaven forbid.

DEUTER: Is your wife here?

THEOBALD: Gone to church.

DEUTER: And Herr Scarron isn't here?

THEOBALD: He found the flowered dress you had on last night quite 'outstanding' and thought up a nice word for you when we got outside.

DEUTER: Which was?

THEOBALD: Give me time. Buttocksome.

DEUTER: What's that mean?

THEOBALD: I can't explain it exactly. But it has something. What are you clasping so warmly to your bosom?

DEUTER: Nothing for you. I find Herr Scarron's word for me rather silly, it doesn't sound at all pleasant.

THEOBALD: I like it and it strikes me as appropriate.

DEUTER: You don't even know what it means—(*She sits down on the sofa.*)

134

THEOBALD: It is suggestive—

DEUTER: Suggestive—!

THEOBALD: Of a picture. One thinks of a pair of round arms, of all sorts of things.

DEUTER: Quite stupid. A woman is either ugly or pretty.

THEOBALD: Bony or buttocksome.

DEUTER: Bony—God, I *am* an old maid.

THEOBALD: (*who has taken the parcel from her and opened it.*) It's bloomers! And such bloomers. Pink silk bows and peek-aboo material. Anyone meaning to wear things like these can only be fishing for compliments if she calls herself an old maid.

DEUTER: Do you think so?

THEOBALD: Old sloops don't hoist silken sails.

DEUTER: To be desirable still.

THEOBALD: In fairy-tales. In real life they spare themselves the useless expense. (*He holds the bloomers spread out in the air.*) The things have chic and if they fit as well as I fancy they must be a sight for sore eyes.

DEUTER: Herr Maske! I don't know you like this.

THEOBALD: You don't know me at all. To some extent I was even uncongenial to you till today, and I let that pass because it suited me. But then yesterday you came in that slinky dress, and today these artful bloomers—

DEUTER: I'm carrying them modestly in my arms to show your wife.

THEOBALD: To complete the picture there should be white stockings to go with these.

DEUTER: Fancy you thinking about such things!

THEOBALD: My dear girl, how do you know my thoughts weren't preoccupied with you long since? It seems to me they were. Since you lead me now into talking like this about those delicate little things, those advantages of yours which, Heavens knows, are there for all to see, aren't as new to me as may have seemed.

DEUTER: If your wife were to know about this!

THEOBALD: She knows nothing. I wouldn't tell her such things because it would worry her. I do such things secretly. Not often, but with pleasure.

DEUTER: We're all human—in the end.

THEOBALD: Not in the end at all. In my case from the age of 14.

DEUTER: I'm 32. It's not so easy for a girl.

THEOBALD: Not all that much more difficult.

DEUTER: My parents were indescribably strict. My father struck me if I was a moment late, and he didn't die till I was 29.

THEOBALD: That's hard.

DEUTER: Then I came to live here; but under the eyes of all the old women in the house—

THEOBALD: Is your flat locked?

DEUTER: I locked it when I came up. Everyone spies in this house.

THEOBALD: Twenty past ten. Now I remember. One evening I happened to look out of our bedroom window just as you—

DEUTER: I'm going. Your wife will be coming back.

THEOBALD: Not for an hour. (*He stands in the open door of the bedroom.*) Look how clearly I can see your room from the place by my bed.

DEUTER: (*goes towards him.*) Really?

(*The door closes behind the two of them.*)

SCENE 5

SCARRON *enters through the flat door after a moment and looks around in search of something. There is a knock at the door.* SCARRON *opens it.*

SCENE 6

STRANGER: They told me downstairs that there's a room to let here.

SCARRON: The occupier isn't here. Perhaps you'll be good enough to come back some other time. As far as I know there isn't a room vacant at the moment.

STRANGER: The agent says there is.

SCARRON: Of course I can't say anything definite.

STRANGER: Are there many children in the house, anyone play the piano—can you give me any information?

SCARRON: No.

STRANGER: Thank you. When will the land-lord be back?

SCARRON: I can't tell you anything about that either.

STRANGER: Good day. (Exit.)

(SCARRON *goes into his room.*)

SCENE 7

THEOBALD: (*looks out of the bedroom.*) Who was that? (*Goes to* SCARRON's *door, listens and runs to the bedroom.*) Come on! Scarron is back.

DEUTER: Do you love me? When shall I see you again? Today again? Tomorrow morning before you go?

THEOBALD: We don't want to overdo things. I'll think over how we'd best manage it. In the end, I think, we'll settle on a fixed day every week, for which I'll make the arrangements.

DEUTER: I'm just to see you one day in seven? What am I to do on the others, since from now on every minute without you will mean an eternity for me?

THEOBALD: Pull yourself together. Otherwise your impatience could be fatal for you. If you're prepared to be contented with a limited number of times, both of us will always be sure of achieving the maximum pleasure.

DEUTER: But—

THEOBALD: Otherwise nothing. And I'd better send my wife down to you if you still want to see her today.

DEUTER: I don't really have anything to see her about.

THEOBALD: All the better. And not a look or a word that might hurt her.

SCARRON: (comes.) Good morning to both of you. An elderly
gentleman with a beard was here just now wanting to rent a
room from you.

THEOBALD: Hallo. So I was right, business is brisk.

DEUTER: I'm just going.

THEOBALD: Should I have sent Mandelstam packing?

DEUTER: Where did I leave my parcel?

SCARRON: (passes her the bloomers wrapped in paper.) Voilà.

DEUTER: Thank you, Herr Scarron. Good morning. (Exit.)

THEOBALD: Feeling better?

SCARRON: Since you left me for dead outside my door you have
a right to that question. But what happened will surprise you
very much. For reasons of some insane theory I felt a necessity
stronger than the feeblest body to wrench myself to my feet
again. And so while you were reeling home—

THEOBALD: I had stomach-ache, apart from that I was fine.

SCARRON: The positiveness of your opinion had in fact taken
hold of me, and in spite of my tiredness I felt the achievements
of years thrown in doubt.

THEOBALD: Surely not, the opinions of a lowly civil servant!

SCARRON: It had in fact become so much of an event for me
that it was important to re-establish the truth of my gospel
immediately.

THEOBALD: In the middle of the night?

SCARRON: And God was gracious. While I was walking to and
fro by a bank of the river with my mind confused and agitated,
I noticed that a shadow was following me.

THEOBALD: Ah!

SCARRON: And as I stopped, a woman loomed up close to me.

THEOBALD: How do you mean loomed up?

SCARRON: Don't interrupt! She stared at me with empty eyes.

THEOBALD: The devil she did!

SCARRON: Living incarnation of concern about God and where
the next meal was coming from, the first moments were a

thrilling exchange with nothing but glances. She entrusted more than a sacrament to me. She opened up and poured body and soul into me and made me the confident of her thousand shames; and—this was fabulous!—understand this: never, never before in my dealings with children or even the Holy Virgin, was purity so intensely near me as with that whore. And at once I saw: the judgement which you had emphatically pronounced earlier about the immutability of all values —that, of course, is the plain sense of your view of life—

THEOBALD: So?

SCARRON: It was invalidated in the presence of that woman. Year after year, strengthened by my inner beliefs in the human race's capability of development, I have ceaselessly made the most stringent demand on the cultivation of my psychological receptivity. She rewarded me for that.

THEOBALD: So?

SCARRON: I followed her to a wretched home, and what I then wrenched from her locked breast by the light of a smoking lamp was, word for word, confession of such a high, new, and as yet unscaled, human greatness, that I sank to my knees in front of the straw mattress.

THEOBALD: She was lying stretched out in the trap already, was she?

SCARRON: And uttered prayers full of the terrible strength of humility. I would not have raised my head if she had trodden on it with her thorn-torn feet.

THEOBALD: Things like that do happen.

SCARRON: My God, how wretched you all are in the presence of such emotion. At all hours she offered her body to the coarseness of men, and with each day she raised herself through her suffering nearer to God the Omniscient.

THEOBALD: These girls always have a heart of gold.

SCARRON: When the morning sun touched us, she found me less than her equal.

THEOBALD: What did you pay?

SCARRON: I don't resent that question. Too many oceans lie between us. What sort of laughter would you burst into if I said to you: I would not have dared to ask her to be my wife.

THEOBALD: (*worried.*) You haven't slept at all? You look really ill.

SCARRON: There is no sleep for me until I have attained such complete clarity about that soul that I can recreate it in poetic form for mankind. Will you believe me, yesterday I intended for a moment to make you, Herr Maske, the hero of a work of art; but today I feel with incomparably stronger force than ever: only psychological depth determines suitability as an artistic object.

THEOBALD: Foreign words are the devil. What, for instance, is psychology?

SCARRON: (*smiles.*) I forget, you poor fellow; it was difficult for you even to follow me?

THEOBALD: There was a lot I didn't understand. You were with a woman last night.

SCARRON: With an angel!

THEOBALD: A fallen one.

SCARRON: You arch philistine!

THEOBALD: And you won't tell me what psychology is?

SCARRON: $\Pi\acute{\alpha}\nu\tau\alpha\ \acute{\rho}\epsilon\tilde{\iota}$. Everything is in flux. And thank God, good and evil too.

THEOBALD: My God, that's dangerous!

SCARRON: It is. But I'll live and die thus. Now you mustn't take it amiss if I tell you that I'm leaving you again.

THEOBALD: But you've got a contract for a year.

SCARRON: I don't want to break it. I'll pay you 12 times 12 Taler equals 150 Taler in advance (*he pays*) and I have no objection to your passing on the pleasant little room. Your personality, however sterling it may be within your own sphere, might have an unfavourable influence on my next artistic task. You understand?

THEOBALD: That's six Taler too many.

SCARRON: Let it pass.

THEOBALD: You're a strange character.

SCARRON I'm a man of action, that's all. I cannot rest without final elucidation, and so I am irresistibly drawn to that woman, to become the most intimate witness of her way of life; God has made it my duty to measure out the last depths of the human condition, and just as I was elevated for a long time, now I must lower myself into the bottomless pit. Unheard of pleasures may await me.

THEOBALD: You rogue.

SCARRON: Don't misunderstand me! Along with measureless torments.

THEOBALD: I know what you mean. One just has to watch not to take too much out of oneself too soon. A certain regularity above all.

SCARRON: Irregularity, man! Or I'll hang myself.

THEOBALD: But even that with a certain regularity.

SCARRON: I hope very soon to send you a book that will astonish you.

THEOBALD: And if you have a well-to-do friend who needs a room, recommend us. First of all, however, I'd sleep for a few hours at all events.

SCARRON: Herr Maske!

THEOBALD: Quite honestly!

SCARRON: God knows—perhaps that's really not such a bad idea. I am beginning to feel a little tired now—well, goodbye!

THEOBALD: You'll find your way here again sometimes, I'm sure.

SCARRON: Where will I get a cab near here? Damned endless stairs!

THEOBALD: (laughs.) Haha, your legs! Have a good sleep!

SCARRON: (meets the stranger at the entrance as he goes out.) This is the gentleman who'd like the room. (Exit.)

STRANGER: The agent told me you must certainly be at home. You have a room to let? I hear.

THEOBALD: True. 12 Taler including breakfast.

STRANGER: That's dear.

THEOBALD: A big room. See for yourself.

THEOBALD: No piano nearby, little children, no sewing-machine, canaries?

THEOBALD: Nothing of that kind.

STRANGER: Do you keep cats or dogs?

THEOBALD: No.

STRANGER: Have you daughters of marriageable age?

THEOBALD: No.

STRANGER: You're married yourself, is your wife young?

THEOBALD: Yes.

STRANGER: Flighty?

THEOBALD: That would be the devil.

STRANGER: Then you're constantly on guard?

THEOBALD: Certainly. And the convenience on the half-landing.

STRANGER: I will not permit any personal relationship. The maid has to knock three times before coming in. Instead of coffee, I drink tea which I'll provide. I suffer from constipation, but that's my affair.

THEOBALD: Entirely yours.

STRANGER: In these circumstances, I'll try it for a probationary period of a month. I can give notice on the 15th. My name is Stengelhöh and I am engaged in academic studies.

THEOBALD: Agreed.

STRANGER: The maid has to enter the room in modest clothing, not ragged and revealing. My things will be here in an hour. Good morning.

THEOBALD: Good morning, Herr Stengelhöh.

(*Exit the* STRANGER.)

THEOBALD: I'll take out 'Joseph before Potiphar,' and hang 'Boa Constrictor in Conflict with Lion' in there. (*He carries a picture from his bedroom to* SCARRON's *old room.*)

SCENE 9

LOUISE *enters.*

THEOBALD: Did you meet Herr Stengelhöh on the stairs, man with a beard?

LOUISE: I think so.

THEOBALD: He's our new lodger. Business is irresistibly on the move. He drinks tea, which he's going to provide and is engaged in academic studies.

LOUISE: Scarron?

THEOBALD: Yes, about Scarron. I've seen through him. He's had enough of us and has disappeared for good after paying a year's rent in advance. He sent you his kind regards. There are other things I could tell you about him, but God protect my wife from such ridiculous ranting. He was a poltroon, a buffoon smelling of violets. Mandelstam, on the other hand, is staying for a year, and I'll train him to shave me for nothing. Has church made you feel any better?

LOUISE: Our great Holy Catholic Church, Theobald!

THEOBALD: Yes, yes,—certainly not an empty illusion.

LOUISE: We're a year married today.

THEOBALD: How time passes!

LOUISE: What do you want me to cook for you?

THEOBALD: I happen to know that you've got a tasty roast of pork up your sleeve.

LOUISE: I'll do it with sauerkraut.

THEOBALD: And put a little onion on it. But now I'll produce my big secret too. Those two people, who erupted into our house, have at last put us in the position to—to what, Louise?

LOUISE: I don't know.

THEOBALD: Can't you guess. (*Softly.*) Now I can take the responsibility of starting a family. What do you say?

(LOUISE *begins cooking in silence.*)

THEOBALD: Cook it in butter! Stengelhöh is very odd. He doesn't want any personal contact with us. He asked if you were flighty; he suffers from constipation. (*He walks about the room.*) The clock as usual isn't wound up, despite what I keep saying. The flowers need water. (*He waters them.*) The Deuter woman was here about an hour ago, wanted to show you some bloomers she's made herself. Have a look sometime how they use a kind of stud-fastener these days instead of ribbons. With those fasteners that damned business in the street that caused us so much trouble couldn't have happened at all. Given your notorious slovenliness, the outlay of a few coppers will perhaps save us a lot of trouble. (*He sits down at the window and picks up a newspaper.*) There are curious things behind the wallpapers of life, as it were. I still have

143

stomach-ache. No more of those departures from routine. Stud-fasteners—sometimes mankind does come up with some really nice and straightforward invention. They say the sea-serpent has turned up in Indian waters again; perhaps I read that out to you already.

LOUISE: (*mechanically.*) Good heavens. And what does an animal like that live on?

THEOBALD: The experts can't agree. I find the news of such odd things repulsive. Literally repulsive.

CURTAIN

THE SNOB

A Comedy in Three Acts

Translated by J. M. Ritchie and J. D. Stowell

THE SNOB

Characters

THEOBALD MASKE
LOUISE, *his wife*
CHRISTIAN MASKE, *his son*
COUNT ALOYSIUS PALEN
MARIANNE PALEN, *his daughter*
SYBIL HULL
A MAID
A SERVANT

ACT I

CHRISTIAN MASKE's *furnished rooms.*

SCENE 1

CHRISTIAN: (*opening a letter.*) This is grotesque! (At *the door.*) Come out here, Sybil.

SYBIL: (*enters.*) Is it something important?

CHRISTIAN: My father has treated himself to a bastard at the age of sixty. In this fix he now writes asking for 'reimbursement of the obligations incurred by him for obstetical assistance.' What do you say to that?

SYBIL: Nothing, except that I should like to be the same way by you, as that woman is by your sire.

CHRISTIAN: Don't be an idiot. This is the absolute limit, but he's going to get a shock when he hears from me. By the way —there's something I want to talk to *you* about.

SYBIL: I have to run.

CHRISTIAN: Yesterday was a turning-point in my life. In the four years of our relationship you've seen me come nearer and nearer my goal.

SYBIL: You've worked like a black.

CHRISTIAN: The African mines I helped establish are now prospering, there is no doubt the suggestion made at the Board of Directors yesterday that I should be made Managing Director of the Company will be confirmed by the shareholders.

SYBIL: What a triumph!

CHRISTIAN: I have secretly acquired one fifth of the shares, which I bought when nobody wanted them. Now I have the whip hand, I foresee for myself possibilities of wealth and social position which are really quite something.

SYBIL: Who was it who first pointed out your business acumen

148

and made you stop wasting your time as a miserable Arts student at the University?

CHRISTIAN: You did. You raised me from deepest misery, taught me to wear clothes properly, taught me, as far as was in your power, how to behave in society.

SYBIL: What a sight you used to be in your half-mast trousers and frayed cuffs.

CHRISTIAN: You gave yourself—and money too occasionally.

SYBIL: First things last! I gave myself—but—that's the way I live.

CHRISTIAN: Once and for all I should like to say how deeply I am indebted to you; on a decisive day such as this, to look back and ...

SYBIL: Now don't be silly, my sweet.

CHRISTIAN: ... with gratitude, compare myself then and now —and forget it for ever.

SYBIL: That would be very convenient.

CHRISTIAN: I never enter a new period of my life without clearing up any debts from the previous one. In this little book I have recorded, to the best of my knowledge, any expenses incurred by you on my behalf. I have of course added 5 per cent interest.

SYBIL: Christian!

CHRISTIAN: Chances you missed as a result of your association with me have also been taken into consideration and I arrive at the sum of 24,000 Marks I owe you. You will receive my cheque today.

SYBIL: (after a pause.) If one may be permitted to mention finer feelings ...

CHRISTIAN: Something you taught me to get rid of in all matters of any consequence, swept out of me with a broom of steel. Today we settle the reckoning. No mistake in addition and calculations. Our relationship in the past is explained by and large by my economic dependence. I could not permit such an explanation in my own mind in the future. To have the necessary faith in the reality of my new position, everything around me must change accordingly. Either you take the rational course ...

SYBIL: Which is?

CHRISTIAN: How shall I put it? Simply more *distance* in future. The sum mentioned and an agreed allowance ought to take care of it.

SYBIL: You are tearing my feelings to shreds.

CHRISTIAN: You know I'm right according to your own maxims. It just hurts to see them applied to yourself. I'm about to cut a figure in public life. There can be no mistakes in the calculation.

SYBIL: The world permits you a paid ...

CHRISTIAN: (*puts his hand over her mouth.*) Etcetera.

SYBIL: Am I the only source of potential trouble for your future life? Apart from me and our previous relationship, is there nothing else which might hinder you even more in your drive to gain public esteem?

CHRISTIAN: You know there is ...

SYBIL: If you want to do this thing consistently ...

CHRISTIAN: I make no secret of the fact. What I am, appearance and mental attitudes, I can vouch for before the world. But my parents, as you know, are simple people.

SYBIL: If you should move up in the world ...

CHRISTIAN: No! Let me think this out for myself. You know I can. Simple people. My good mother especially.

SYBIL: They could not teach you even the most primitive requirements of society.

CHRISTIAN: I'm making my own way in the world—one which is particularly unusual because of my birth. It would be folly to stress the gulf between my origins and the position I have achieved by dragging my parents into the public gaze. That is clear. It would be more than foolish, it would be lacking in good taste.

SYBIL: And as you now worship good taste above all else ...

CHRISTIAN: Don't think you can hide your bad conscience about your own past by making ironic comments on mine. What does anybody know of *your* parents? You simply suppressed them, quietly murdered them. Maybe your father was a convict? Was his name really Hull? (*He laughs.*) Never mind, nothing could take away that charm which is your stock-in-trade. In any event, the glory of such a daughter speaks well for his good points. But you interrupted me. The difference in potential between heritage and present hopes has now been sufficiently clarified. But one must add: the awareness of being beholden to anyone for anything at all, even life, is a weak point in my strategy. Everything in my world sprang from me alone, just as I defer to myself alone, hope and fear for myself alone, so I must be free from having to consider others if I am to continue to forge ahead. That's why I'm afraid of my own father and mother.

SYBIL: What will you do? Offer them a sum of money to stay away?

CHRISTIAN: Well, father is not shy; here he is already asking for it.

SYBIL: You have learned how to handle money.

CHRISTIAN: I have learned a lot.

SYBIL: And as you are so logically consistent, anyone who loves you must agree with you—though perhaps with a heavy heart.

CHRISTIAN: I hope my parents will see things as clearly. We are agreed?

SYBIL: I am still trying to grasp this new order: to regard you now from a certain distance—with just a trace of servility.

CHRISTIAN: Things don't become truer by speaking them or doing them.

SYBIL: No, but clearer.

CHRISTIAN: Clever girl.

SYBIL: I love you, Christian. You are the one miscalculation in my life. I'd still give up the 24,000 to keep you.

CHRISTIAN: Then you deserve to die in misery and wretchedness. Take this kiss for nothing.—Now you've spoiled my cravat.

SYBIL: It was dreadfully askew anyway.

CHRISTIAN: In all I learned from you that was the only thing I never grasped. How to make a tie sit perfectly. Show me for the hundredth time.

SYBIL: (ties a cravat round the neck of a large vase.) First, simply cross over. Fold. Pull through other end.

CHRISTIAN: If a bit sticks out at the right . . .

SYBIL: Cut it off with the scissors.

CHRISTIAN: Costs a new tie every time you tie one.

SYBIL: But is noted and appreciated by the initiated.

CHRISTIAN: Which is always what counts.

SYBIL: (*deep curtsey.*) Your humble servant, Mr. Managing Director.

CHRISTIAN: I'm not joking, Sybil.

SYBIL: I quite understand.

(*Exit* SYBIL.)

SCENE 2

CHRISTIAN: Charming girl, all in all. (*At his desk.*) Now to collect my thoughts. (*He writes.*) Revered Count Palen, I have much pleasure in accepting your invitation for 26th inst. With humble thanks. Humble thanks? We'll see. Regards to the Countess. Too familiar. At once too humble and too familiar. Above all he mustn't see how pleased I am to come. The paper's wrong. Be better on a sheet with business heading. 'Head Office of the Monambo Mining Company. My dear Count von Palen. How great a distance that inserted *von* makes! As the first communication in black and white to go from me to their circles, the thing must be absolutely correct and yet full of significance. What does he say himself? 'Dear Mr. Maske, will you eat with us on the evening of the 26th *en tout petit comité*? Yours . . .' Cheap and simple paper. That strikes the note of friendly but superficial familiarity. 'Eat', 'evening',— yes—divine! Let's stay one degree more formal, but in such a way that nevertheless—I'd like to work in a Latin tag, to make it sound virile. What four or five syllables can make me seem important for a moment to minds like theirs? That is the real question and it must be solved. A word of five syllables with a lot of vowels and a rolling rhythm for a start. (*He walks up and down.*) *Dum* da da *dum* da. Unsolicited. For my ear the third syllable is longer than the first. Wrong beat. *Praenumerando*—that's the kind of thing; doesn't make sense unfortunately. *Dum* da da *dum* da. I must find it.

THEOBALD: (*enters.*) Well, here's the bad penny in person. Mother's waiting down below.

CHRISTIAN: Father!

THEOBALD: Look, Christian, that little mishap came along against my will. You know how I dislike melodrama. But with women it's always the same: no sense of proportion. Now we just have to face up to it.

CHRISTIAN: Since you retired you've turned on a similar surprise every year.

THEOBALD: I should never have got out of my usual routine. You pensioned me off too soon. My powers are by no means exhausted and so they go popping off in all directions in multiplicity. I'll just have to find some 'modus vivendi' with her.

CHRISTIAN: Before we discuss anything, I'll call mother up.

THEOBALD: There's this little business of ours first.

CHRISTIAN: I'll arrange that along with everything else, without anybody being any the wiser.

THEOBALD: Eh?

CHRISTIAN: In the course of our conversation a figure will be named.

THEOBALD: How so? What are you up to?

CHRISTIAN: A figure, I say, of several thousands. If in our discussions, agreement is reached in all other respects, you may privately add a thousand for your own little embarrassment.

THEOBALD: You're making conditions?

CHRISTIAN: I'm making conditions.

THEOBALD: Well, this I am curious to see.

CHRISTIAN: (*at the window.*) There she is. (*He waves.*) She's seen me—is coming up—God, what a ghastly get-up! Earlier on you said a word which struck me.

THEOBALD: In what connection?

CHRISTIAN: It had a different rhythm; but it had an impressive sound about it! Remind me later ...

THEOBALD: A thousand, you said?

CHRISTIAN: Provided we're otherwise agreed. (*Exit.*)

THEOBALD: I can hardly wait.

SCENE 4

CHRISTIAN *and* LOUISE MASKE *enter.*

THEOBALD: Put your hat on straight, Louise. You look like a schoolboy in a boater with it perched over your forehead like that. We're thinking of joining you here in the big city. There'll be something or other for me here to keep the inner man alive.

LOUISE: That's just one of father's ideas, you know.

CHRISTIAN: At this time, when all my attention is focused on the goal before me, I wouldn't be able to find a spare moment for you.

LOUISE: Oh, well, in that case—yes, it's just as I thought.

THEOBALD: We're used to that of late, you never seem to have much time for us. What is this goal?

CHRISTIAN: I have prospects of becoming Managing Director of the Company I work for.

LOUISE: Managing!

THEOBALD: (*roars at her.*) Director!

CHRISTIAN: If I am to bring off something exceptional then you must be considerate, and this will require, above all ...

THEOBALD: Just a minute ... we slaved twenty years for you, gave you an education to be proud of. Did without Sunday joints. All because we worshipped you like a little idol.

LOUISE: (*quietly to herself.*) Managing Director.

CHRISTIAN: *Dum* da da ...

THEOBALD: We went without so that you could get on in the world. We've grown old and now we are at the stage where, if we want to see anything of you, we're going to have to hurry.

CHRISTIAN: Let me remove one serious error immediately: since I was sixteen I can recall not one single sacrifice you made for my sake.

THEOBALD: That's going too far.

LOUISE: Father!

154

CHRISTIAN: But I remember you all right, you always took up four-fifths of the room in the house, every thought revolved round you. Even while I was still at school I kept myself by giving lessons, I paid for my own studies at the University and was independent from then on. And who was it who forced his seventeen-year-old son to take his lunch standing to attention in his father's presence ...

THEOBALD: Like a little idol I worshipped you. No one could have wished for a sweeter boy. Isn't that so, mother?

LOUISE: (gestures.) Such a tiny little chap.

CHRISTIAN: You were pre-occupied entirely with yourself, and have never considered my existence for one moment up to the present day. Of late you've possibly been struck by a significant change: my more expansive way of life.

THEOBALD: Let's not go over all that again. In short,—what are you driving at?

CHRISTIAN: You have found me on a day when I am balancing the books of my previous existence. I carry over no bad debts.

LOUISE: What does he mean?

THEOBALD: You'll soon hear.

CHRISTIAN: (takes a ledger out of the safe.) The expenses actually incurred for me I have, to the best of my memory, entered in this book. Interest at 5 per cent has been added to the total.

THEOBALD: So you want to settle up?

CHRISTIAN: Precisely.

THEOBALD: Let's have a look at it. (He puts on his spectacles.)

LOUISE: What do you mean?

CHRISTIAN: You'll soon see, mother.

THEOBALD: (reads.) Upkeep from first till sixteenth year at 600 per annum. 600 including doctor and chemist is not exactly liberal.

CHRISTIAN: I was never ill.

THEOBALD: Even without trying I can think of measles and sniffles. I can still see your permanently snotty little nose before me. We used to rinse it out with camomile.

LOUISE: One morning you had a temperature of 104, I thought my heart had stopped beating ...

CHRISTIAN: The sum entered is adequate.

LOUISE: Big round red blotches all over your teeny body.

THEOBALD: 16 times 600 is 9,600. Now look at this! 'In non-recurring expenses'. How can you possibly remember all the individual expenses incurred over 16 years. They are legion. The whole entry is doubtful from the start.

CHRISTIAN: On the other hand you'll find that my allowances to you, especially recent ones, have not been entered on the debit side.

THEOBALD: That would be the last straw.

CHRISTIAN: (to himself.) I'd give a lot for that word. (He stares at the letter on his desk.)

LOUISE: (shyly to him.) And there was that boil on the back of your neck.

CHRISTIAN: Quite correct, mother.

THEOBALD: Half-a-dozen shirts of best shirting with collars, two pairs of boots, when I went up to the University—50. One gold ring—that's the limit. So she slipped the puppy that ring. And I turned everything upside down to find it.

CHRISTIAN: It was mother's property and her life's talisman.

THEOBALD: 100 Marks would just about cover it.

LOUISE: Do you still wear it?

CHRISTIAN: (shows it on his finger.) Even though it gets tighter every day.

THEOBALD: Still, I must say—an extraordinary business and typical Louise. Final total a round 11,000. With interest 11,800.

CHRISTIAN: (stressing it.) 11,000. (Clears his throat significantly.)

THEOBALD: I see—which you will pay.

CHRISTIAN: Which I owe you.

THEOBALD: You wish to rid yourself of this debt?

CHRISTIAN: I shall pay.

LOUISE: (holding his hand between hers.) We could always have it made bigger.

THEOBALD: Well, what do you know! I call that a very decent action of a dear, good boy. Quite original, the way you've got the whole thing worked out. (Embraces him.) There's something dashing about it, and we know how to appreciate that. So we are in complete agreement.

CHRISTIAN: You expressed the intention of moving to this town. That I do not wish.

THEOBALD: Are you laying down the law?

CHRISTIAN: I do you a favour by paying the money and I expect one in return.

THEOBALD: I'd set my heart on it.

LOUISE: The boy must have his reasons.

THEOBALD: This woman will drive me out of my wits. Can't have a reasonable discussion in her presence.

CHRISTIAN: (*accompanies* LOUISE *to the door.*) Would you like to have a look at the rest of my apartment, mother?

LOUISE: (*quietly.*) Don't worry. Everything will be done just as you wish. (*Exit.*)

CHRISTIAN: Your presence here would dissipate my energies when I need every ounce of them.

THEOBALD: And that's a condition for the 11,800 etc?

CHRISTIAN: An absolute pre-requisite.

THEOBALD: Must give it some thought; after all, where's the advantage for us? Leaving family ties aside for the moment, one must not forget all about security. What kind of income would that sum yield?

CHRISTIAN: 600 from industrial bonds.

THEOBALD: Are you out of your mind! My money goes into the savings bank.

CHRISTIAN: A good 500 then.

THEOBALD: That's not milk and honey—11,000 sounds good. 500 is chicken-feed, and for that you want me to give up my freedom of movement, the only thing a humble man possesses? That will require considerable thought; weigh up the arguments and counter-arguments. No—supposing I give you my word of honour, to stay where we are …

CHRISTIAN: But I don't want that.

THEOBALD: 'But I don't want that'—don't want this, don't want the other! By God, I'd like to know what's supposed to be going on here?

CHRISTIAN: The way you burst in here today shows I would not be safe from your visits in the future either.

THEOBALD: Burst in—why, that's . . .

CHRISTIAN: I'm speaking, of course, in the present context. My life is about to take a completely new turn. In the immediate future I must be free from family considerations.

THEOBALD: This is without parallel in the whole history of mankind! And we who scraped the butter off our bread for your sake, brought one sacrifice after another, no matter what you say? Can you think of parents who do not make sacrifices? Does not every breath drawn by any little brat mean a reduction of some pleasure for the parents? Don't the little beasts interfere with one's sleep, one's meals, one's every comfort? Don't they always have some defect, which must be patched up at great trouble and expense? They're always getting blocked up at one end or the other. Then the whole ridiculous rigmarole of birthdays and so on, that you have to bother with. And what's the result? (*To* CHRISTIAN, *who sits silently in his armchair; loud.*) Fine filial affection! (*Striking the table with clenched fist.*) Fine filial affection!

LOUISE: (*sticks her head round the door and makes soothing signs to* CHRISTIAN *unobserved by* THEOBALD.) I'll see everything's all right.

THEOBALD: Well? (*When* CHRISTIAN *remains silent, he throws himself into the furthest chair, and says calmly.*) If I'd known that, you'd have drowned in your first bath. (*Pause.*) As it is, we're more than 100 miles apart. That's the famous filial affection everybody talks about. Yes, yes. (*Bursts out laughing.*) Ha! But let's be practical! How do you see your wonderful idea working out in practice? If we can only just manage now on my pension plus the 500, no-one can expect us to take upon ourselves the inconvenience of moving, the difficulties of finding a new home without some compensation.

CHRISTIAN: No-one will expect that of you.

THEOBALD: Without considerable compensation. Who's going to pay that?

CHRISTIAN: Possibly I will.

THEOBALD: Well, well . . .

CHRISTIAN: Right here in Europe we have a whole host of cities remarkable for their natural charms and economic advantages; unless of course you'd be prepared to consider America from the start?

THEOBALD: America!

CHRISTIAN: All right, all right. (*He has picked up a large atlas and a Baedeker.*) Brussels, for instance, might be suitable. (*Reads from the book.*) 'Brussels, capital of the kingdom of Belgium, with 800,000 inhabitants. The city is situated in fertile regions on the banks of the Senne, a tributary of the Schelde. The upper City with the State buildings is the seat of the aristocracy and of elegant society'.

THEOBALD: (*who is seated comfortably, listening religiously.*) Not bad; show me the book. (*He reads aloud.*) 'And of elegant society. Language and customs French'. And you really believe a German born and bred would consider switching to Froggy habits? Not for yours truly: *merci*!

CHRISTIAN: The place I really thought of first was Zürich. An absolutely ideal spot, a little paradise in every respect. And the language is German.

THEOBALD: Let's hear something about it.

CHRISTIAN: (*reads from another volume.*) 'With approximately 200,000 inhabitants, Zürich is the most important city in Switzerland, on the shores of the Lake and the banks of the evergreen Limmat!'

THEOBALD: 'Evergreen' is for Christmas trees, not rivers.

CHRISTIAN: 'On the west side flows the river Sihl, which in spring roars along ...'

THEOBALD: That's enough water, thanks. Pity I can't swim.

CHRISTIAN: (*reads.*) 'The city is magnificently situated on the crystal-clear lake, whose gently rising banks are sprinkled with tall houses, orchards and vineyards'.

THEOBALD: Very nice—pretty.

CHRISTIAN: (*reads.*) 'In the background the snow-covered Alps, on the left the mighty slopes of the Glärnisch send their greeting'. (*Shows it on the atlas.*) That white bit there.

THEOBALD: The devil you say!

CHRISTIAN: (*reads.*) 'Local cuisine good. Population rough diamonds'.

THEOBALD: To coin a phrase.

CHRISTIAN: 'In addition, excursions may be made into the wonderful environs'.

THEOBALD: The promised land itself, a veritable Canaan.

CHRISTIAN: Interlaken and Lucerne, the whole sweep of the Alps becomes immediately accessible, in a sense belongs to you alone. Can you imagine what the Alpine sunset is like?

THEOBALD: All right—tell me!

CHRISTIAN: A natural phenomenon of fulminating splendour, a *nonpareil*. With you in Zürich on condition that you leave me in peace for the next few years, I could round off your income to an adequate amount.

THEOBALD: (*after a pause.*) I still have reservations of a purely personal kind.

CHRISTIAN: Not a word more.

THEOBALD: We really should discuss this from all aspects.

CHRISTIAN: For a man like me life consists of facts. You're holding me up with your talk. Something of far greater importance awaits me.

THEOBALD: I'm sixty today. Your mother nearly as old. Life has not been particularly kind to us. We have not much longer to be in this world with you.

CHRISTIAN: Don't you realise that this tone is useless in the face of mightier things. There will be a time for discussing details later. At present things are happening fast. I'll add 2,400 Swiss francs a year on to your income. In three weeks you'll be at your new address. Quick, father. I'm on fire with ambition. The struggle for a place in the sun is fierce, the competition enormous. If I yield an inch of ground, a whole legion will have a foot in the door.

THEOBALD: I'm dumbfounded. Never met such a creature. How am I to digest all these new attitudes? When am I to see the higher significance of all this for me?

CHRISTIAN: Here and now. You've got five minutes.

THEOBALD: Then I accept hesitantly. But I'll be completely out of my depth and lost.

CHRISTIAN: Have confidence!

THEOBALD: But where's the higher significance in all this for me?

CHRISTIAN: Later, later. Shall we shake on it, father?

THEOBALD: Hell and damnation! My whole world has been turned topsy-turvy.

CHRISTIAN: 2,400 francs equal 1,900 marks in cash.

THEOBALD: Plus 500 together with what I've got—that makes something like 5,600 marks.

CHRISTIAN: 7,000 in francs. (At the door.) Mother!

THEOBALD: On the banks of the Limmat? You could knock me down with a feather.

CHRISTIAN: (hands him the atlas and travel books.) See for yourself.

LOUISE: (enters, quietly to CHRISTIAN.) I'll see that he agrees to everything. This scarf on your bedside table and all that lingerie, lace and fine linen—oh, Christy, be careful with women. Temptation to pleasure—I know it comes to all of us sometime. But when one has children and is made Managing Director and can say proudly before God: my Mother was a pure woman ...!!

THEOBALD: (shattered.) Among the Tyroleans!

LOUISE: That is something too, you know, a fine reward.

CHRISTIAN: Of course it is, mother. (Embraces her.)

LOUISE: (leaving.) My little Christy.

(CHRISTIAN and THEOBALD exeunt.)

SCENE 6

CHRISTIAN: (comes back quickly.) Damn, I nearly had the word at one point. (He stares at the letter.) He said it in connection with retirement being too early, and that all his powers were being dissipated. How? In—multiplicity? That's it! (He writes.) 'Multiplicity of affairs, dear Count Palen, unfortunately makes it impossible for me to accept your very kind invitation.' Now it's turned into a refusal; still—who knows, that may turn out to be more useful than an acceptance.

Doorbell rings. He goes to answer it.

CHRISTIAN *and* COUNT PALEN *enter together.*

COUNT: I have come in person to discuss with you the question already broached, namely, your nomination. Before finally proposing you to the share-holders, the Board must know down to the very last detail what the company may expect of you ... I am myself an enemy of business discussions and so I asked Baron Rohrschach to undertake this visit, but it was felt more fitting for me to attend to the matter, as my relationship with you is more—shall we say—intimate.

CHRISTIAN: Thank you, Count.

COUNT: The Monambo Mines are an undertaking of a small group of men who share the same convictions. While there is no direct connection between business and social outlook it is clear we want a man at the head of the concern who is one of us with his whole being. (CHRISTIAN *bows.*) We believe we have found that man in you—a man who combines efficiency with that rarer gift, that feeling for the values of finer tastes, achieved only by careful cultivation, something particularly appropriate where the brutal truth of figures demands a significant counter-balance. (CHRISTIAN *bows.*) In questions of life you have often expressed yourself to me in a manner which corresponds entirely with the opinions of our circles, indeed you almost surpass them in sharpness of formulation. Using the vocabulary of the progressives, I should characterise them as aristocrat-reactionary. (*He laughs.*) And indeed what impressed me most, the intensity of your discourse, seemed to indicate that it came from the heart. Am I right?

CHRISTIAN: Quite so.

COUNT: You touch me to the core. Extraordinary. This gives considerable food for thought. You are obviously well-bred, your manners are perfect even in the sense that you recognised on the basis of certain of our inherited peculiarities, now part and parcel of our nature, that the inconspicuously uniform is the correct thing. One can observe this in certain gestures, but even in the set of a tie. In short, the only thing now lacking is some firm assurance from you, a crystallisation into one binding sentence, which we can put before the shareholders as the essence of your beliefs.

CHRISTIAN: Quite, quite.

COUNT: In the case of a Rohrschach, the 'Baron' before the name provides the sort of assurance we are now asking from you, assuming of course the man is not *déclassé*. Certain guarantees in certain directions. In middle-class families, however, distinguished deeds by forebears offer such guarantees under —certain conditions.

CHRISTIAN: There can be no question of that in my case.

COUNT: Which judgment, of course, implies no blame. Even in families which have attained high bourgeois standing, one is content for this standing to spread its effulgence over all individuals concerned. It will be quite sufficient if you distil from the essence of the social superiority accumulated over the years by your forefathers, the phrase I seek. I do not have the pleasure of knowing your father, your parents; in short, your . . .

CHRISTIAN: Dead. All dead.

COUNT: Then I am very pleased to be able to say that you entirely suffice as representative of the family. Do I see you moved?

CHRISTIAN: I am, Count, at this moment when I must express what has moved my heart since childhood, when I must say this: I have known no longing other than to be like those who not only bear the stamp of the nobility of the deeds of their forefathers, but also bear it externally visible in a cachet of nobility—to stand at their side, accepted by them as helpmeet, to be permitted to bring to fulfilment those principles whose historical representatives they are. It is not for me to enumerate the sacrifices I have already offered for this ideal, but I am prepared to swear to you on oath, my mortal life is dedicated to this alone.,

COUNT: You are an excellent fellow. In this moment you have convinced me. I thank you. Believe I can vouch for your nomination. Do you mind if I smoke? You'll accept my invitation for Friday?

CHRISTIAN: Well...

COUNT: Yes?

CHRISTIAN: Well then, despite the multiplicity of my affairs.

COUNT: I am quite sure you have work to do. In my daughter Marianne you'll find someone who appreciates a character like yours.

CHRISTIAN: I have heard a great deal about the remarkable talents of the Countess.

COUNT: *Enchanté*, my dear Maske.

CHRISTIAN: Please accept my thanks, dear Count.

COUNT: Dear Count—so you have a sense for the nuance.

CHRISTIAN: On the assumption of uniformity in all other things.

COUNT: Witty and very charming, dear friend. (*Exit.*)

CHRISTIAN: (*who has accompanied him to the door, returns, looks quickly into the mirror and starts to tie a tie round a vase.*) First of all a simple cross-over, then one end under, pull the other through. And now scissors. (*He cuts.*) Whatsoever offendeth you, your left eye, cast it out! This tie sits perfectly. So we've done it. We've done it!

CURTAIN

ACT II

SCENE 1

Drawing-room at CHRISTIAN MASKE's. *Two years later.*

COUNT: According to the butler he should be back at any moment.

MARIANNE: We were ten minutes early.—Ah, there is the Corot.

COUNT: Which provides the pretext for our visit.

MARIANNE: A beautiful picture. What bliss to be able to live among such things!

COUNT: It can be yours.

MARIANNE: As his wife? Are you serious, father?

164

COUNT: Serious, Marianne. Haven't we both been obsessed with the same idea for weeks, though we never mentioned it? The man's behaviour has become so pressing of late . . .

MARIANNE: Papa, is he in love with me?

COUNT: Shouldn't we put the question another way? Would you take him even if he did not possess the wealth which can save us from a series of rather difficult circumstances?

MARIANNE: I cannot answer that question. The first times you brought him I scarcely knew who he was, knew nothing of his situation. My emotions were able to decide quite freely. I feel how everything he directs his will to must finally surrender with that same bliss one experiences when one yields to any elemental force.

COUNT: *Tiens!*

MARIANNE: Yes, Papa, this is the decisive encounter for your daughter Marianne.

COUNT: I had assumed you would have to conquer various points of resistance within yourself.

MARIANNE: They are still none of them conquered. We have never yet really come close to each other, our conversation has never left the conventional, yet I felt, whenever he approached and my whole being reared up in challenge, how he and he alone could subjugate me completely.

COUNT: I get a funny feeling with him.

MARIANNE: Why? Do you know of one single feature about him not utterly correct?

COUNT: No.

MARIANNE: Does he live by our rules?

COUNT: Completely. Yet in the end that is the very thing my senses rebel against. I have been observing him for two years. What touched me at first nearly horrifies me now. If this bourgeois is really following his nature in living our life, what difference is there between him and us? You know, I consider nobility a product of breeding towards values which have their essence in time; that is, values which are not attainable in one generation. The Duke of Devonshire was envied the splendour of his lawns by a *parvenu* who asked his advice on how to achieve the same. He answered—'All you have to do is mow

the lawn vigorously every morning—for a few centuries!'
Voilà. In my life I have never attempted to accomplish anything exceptional, I was just a nobleman with an awareness
of hereditary peculiarities. Should this man reveal it is not
necessary to have had ancestors in order to possess certain
inestimable values, I am denied justification in my own eyes.

MARIANNE: Cannot the sum of that which is peculiar to us be
grasped by an extraordinary intelligence: cannot intensity
of will catch up with the slow ennobling process of generations?

COUNT: Possession of whatever kind comes from the confidence
of possessing. If this characteristic is lacking, it is merely
borrowed and the moment comes when some unfavourable
lighting, some *faux pas*, uncovers the pretence. That is the
moment I am waiting for with this man.

MARIANNE: But in the meantime you have attached your star
to his.

COUNT: Yet not to let myself be conquered by him, but to show
up the gaping wound, which will cast him down. Yes, even
if need be to inflict it on him myself.

MARIANNE: So Fate might bring it about that I might be
ranged against you.

COUNT: Heaven forbid!

MARIANNE: No, you forbid it! This man gives me the first
complete sensation of my life. It is still nebulous and un-
defined and resistance is mixed with pleasure. A blissful secret
which can reveal itself in the course of time, but will not allow
itself to be led.

COUNT: Supposing he discloses a failing before our very eyes?

MARIANNE: Never! On the contrary he will become more and
more inscrutable and surprising. The few clues I have to his
person give me this certainty, he is extraordinary and stands
beyond our comprehension.

COUNT: Marianne!

MARIANNE: This I believe and I feel, father. But whatever may
come to pass, you have given me a wonderful youth. Twenty-
five happy years have been mine through your goodness.

COUNT: I have been too indulgent.

MARIANNE: And will continue to be so in the future.

COUNT: But not beyond the bounds of possibility.

MARIANNE: (*emphatically*.) Love sets his boundaries wide.

SCENE 2

CHRISTIAN: (*enters quickly in riding habit*.) My dear Countess —Count. I can at least claim in my defence that it was the Minister of Culture who delayed me, seeking my advice.

COUNT: He is full of your praises, wishes to present you to the President soon.

CHRISTIAN: Would have needed genius beyond my reach to resolve his question. (*With pathos*.) In matters which concern the weal of the state the enormous weight of responsibility saps the strength of any opinion which does not have at its base an awareness of God.

COUNT: *Magnifique!* What were you riding today?

CHRISTIAN: A colt by Charmant out of Miss Gorse—do you like the picture, Countess?

MARIANNE: I have not sufficient judgment in such things— but it moves me.

CHRISTIAN: It is not one of Corot's masterpieces, but the values and tonality are unique.

MARIANNE: Can you tell that kind of thing?

CHRISTIAN: In the course of my life I have seen two or three— hundred pictures by the master.

COUNT: How can you spare the time?

CHRISTIAN: Actually I spare very little. It needed hardly more than the spark of recognition to flash across to me from the first canvas. It caught fire and I was alive to the rest. (*To* MARIANNE.) That's how I am with everything.

COUNT: We must be off. (*To* MARIANNE.) You said you'd call on the Friessens at half-past eleven.

CHRISTIAN: (*to* COUNT.) Will you be going with the Countess, or may I have a few minutes of your time?

COUNT: (*to* MARIANNE.) Do you need me?

MARIANNE: Do stay.

CHRISTIAN: (*to* MARIANNE.) I'll see you to your carriage.

(MARIANNE *and* CHRISTIAN *exeunt.*)

SCENE 3

COUNT: (*picks up a book from the table.*) The Almanac de Gotha: 'Who's Who in Nobility'. He has been checking his sources. (*Turns to page and reads.*) 'Palen—Ancient Westphalian nobility, historical record begins with Roger Palen in 1220. Augustus Aloysius married Elisabeth, Countess of Fürstenbusch, deceased at Ernegg, 16th July, 1901'. My dear Liz. Children: Frederick Matthew, last scion of our line, and Marianne Josephine, now to marry a Mr. Maske.

SCENE 4

CHRISTIAN: (*enters.*) The Countess hopes to pick you up about twelve on her way home. Count Augustus von Palen, I ask you for the hand of your daughter in marriage.

COUNT: Since you put the proposal so resolutely, I must assume you have weighed the matter maturely, from every aspect.

CHRISTIAN: As maturely, Count, as you and your daughter have weighed the answer.

COUNT: Not so. I do not unconditionally know the Countess's decision.

CHRISTIAN: How does it sound conditionally? I beg your pardon; first your own opinion.

COUNT: I myself am against the liaison. But my opinion is merely listened to, and remains without decisive influence. Were you counting on my approval?

CHRISTIAN: I sensed the strongest resistance on your part.

COUNT: I find my admiration for your talents has persistently forced me to distance myself from you. The Countess on the other hand seems, truth to tell, rather *emballée* with you.

CHRISTIAN: Shall I give a more detailed account of my material circumstances?

168

COUNT: I know your career from personal observation, all the amazing successes, both financial and social. About your future, I entertain no doubts whatsoever.

CHRISTIAN: Has my character given grounds for reservations?

COUNT: It offered no point of attack.

CHRISTIAN: May I ask then ...?

COUNT: To be quite frank: class prejudice.

CHRISTIAN: Thank you. That must be so. This very inner exclusiveness is a feature of the circles I esteem. Only if it had been directed against my person would I have been more deeply offended.

COUNT: But you cannot admire and attack a principle at one and the same time.

CHRISTIAN: I love your daughter.

COUNT: You would marry her even if she were not Countess Palen?

CHRISTIAN: That I don't know: as attraction she is indivisible.

COUNT: Assuming the Countess accepted your proposal ...

(CHRISTIAN makes an involuntary gesture which betrays his emotion.)

COUNT: Till a moment ago I thought I knew you. Now that there is the possibility of finding you more closely attached to me I see how much of a stranger you still are.

CHRISTIAN: With people like us there are no means of finding out from a book what kind of stud one comes from. It's a case of groping in the dark.

COUNT: Quite true—with few exceptions the bourgeois name leaves its bearer anonymous and unobserved in his actions. We who are recorded in this book act out our lives before the eyes of our kind and being deprived of a free life among the nameless mass gives us the privilege of seeing our merits noted and rewarded.

CHRISTIAN: Without question. Yet for the man who possesses the inflexible will to bear the consequences of such views, entry into the circle should be open.

COUNT: Such inflexibility is revealed only by time, measured in generations.

CHRISTIAN: The same disposition can be observed in middle-class ancestors.

COUNT: Your parents? Grandparents?

CHRISTIAN: Civil Servants. Serving an apprenticeship to higher honours by the awareness of serving the state. My father ...

COUNT: Such simple origins make personal merit stand out all the more, as the Emperor, our Supreme Leader, reminded us again recently. The case of our Minister of Post and Telegraphs, who comes from a background similar to yours, is the most revealing example.

CHRISTIAN: (*laughs out loud.*) In fact poor but cleanly-dressed parents are beginning to pop up all over the place.

COUNT: Indeed yes. I think we now see each other's views. But the decision is not ours—let us wait. But I must add—my daughter brings no dowry into the marriage. You became rich, we lost our fortune except for a few remnants and we have to cut down, in order to provide my son with the extras his regiment demands.

CHRISTIAN: (*bows.*) Not a word need be lost on that account.

BUTLER: (*enters.*) The Countess's coach is at the door, sir.

COUNT: (*exit.*) I shall let you have her decision.

SCENE 5

CHRISTIAN: I could have said it there and then: 'They are alive and in Zürich'. Prepared for it and already embarrassed by the confession of his own lack of means, he would have had to swallow it and there they were officially presented. Now I must be ready to seize the first opportunity; but I sense she is completely in my power. Why wait? They must come here. Immediately! When the moment comes—present them personally—'*mediam in figuram*' to all of them. Then we'll see. How happy the old people will be! (*He writes and reads.*) 'Come by first train. Most pleasant surprise awaits you here'. (*He rings.*) Everything, from the carriage I send to fetch them from the station, to the private bath in their rooms, must be one big surprise. (*Servant enters.*) Send this telegram off immediately. (*Servant exit.*) Mustn't forget Mother's special pillow and as she falls asleep thinking back over what she and I dreamed my future would be and how everything has turned out so much better, she must feel her life has reached fulfilment. They'll soon adjust. They'll soon learn better manners, and tailor and dressmaker will add the finishing touches.

SCENE 6

SYBIL *enters.*

CHRISTIAN: I'm so happy, my sweet, do you know who's coming?

SYBIL: Your parents.

CHRISTIAN: Who told you?

SYBIL: Necessity. For two years since their departure you have been wriggling on the hook of longing for them. I knew who you were thinking of as you fell asleep and why, when you talked of great profits, your eyes were sparkling. Once the physical separation was assured you became besotted about those two. In the end you could not talk of anything without bringing in one of them somehow or other.

CHRISTIAN: I have missed them badly.

SYBIL: You've managed to convince yourself that you do.

CHRISTIAN: Mother and I were as one—always. She knew nothing beyond me. I was like a little king for her. She approved my great future in advance. We only needed to look at each other with that idea in mind and we would laugh— and father was like the double-bass accompaniment.

SYBIL: Didn't you find I had the same unconditional faith in you?

CHRISTIAN: Yes, but you wanted gratitude. She was a person who expected no thanks, who was happy merely because I existed.

SYBIL: Don't forget how shamelessly your father behaved towards you: firmly convinced that the very sight of him terrified you, he blackmailed you time and time again for the various sums he required.

CHRISTIAN: All in all, not much more than a few thousand.

SYBIL: If he had had any idea of your changed circumstances he would have set to more vigorously. He would really have had a spree, if he had seen how the land lay.

CHRISTIAN: He shall. It is my only wish. That's the fatal thing about families whose roots are still too close to the surface. The whole body of the family has no unity of feeling, does not breathe and move as one in answer to the command from the nerve centre. While some members squander, others live in squalor. However, once the idea takes life that we are all sprung from the same stock, attached to the parent-stem by the finest veins, our well-being is dependent on the health of the organism and every good fortune that befalls any branch of it rejoices us all.

SYBIL: But that idea is positively medieval, has no validity in this day and age.

CHRISTIAN: Can you really claim that, my girl? Do you think because your ears are filled with the empty slogans of a Socialism which preaches the rights of even the most wretched, that you know more about the upheavals of the age than I do?

SYBIL: I know the reality. Millions who, to appease their hunger for bread, will crush any who stand in their path.

CHRISTIAN: The struggle for existence, I've been through all that, too, and the turmoil taught me a lot. Impelled by an insatiable impulse, I waded right through the pap of the commonplace because I had learned that life really only begins when you are through and out the other side. But you saw how I got there, how I 'arrived', how I tore strips of living flesh from my own body and wore them, twisted into an elegant cravat, round my own neck. Little by little I approached that form which the superior being must assume among his peers.

SYBIL: Don't think the battle is over. On every step, even the very highest, the stronger, deadlier enemy stands, whom you must vanquish or he destroys you.

CHRISTIAN: You're talking like a proletarian. You have generations to run before you'll even get an inkling of the truth.

SYBIL: And to think it was I who taught him ...

CHRISTIAN: Not to eat fish with my knife, or pick my teeth in public! You have never got beyond externals. Your dress is that of the enlightened woman of the world. But how far has it become an integral part of your nature, since you first put it on?

SYBIL: That was not my goal.

CHRISTIAN: Sour grapes!

SYBIL: And you, because you conceived the vanity of fetching back your parents ...

CHRISTIAN: Whom I love.

SYBIL: Ever since other examples of simple parents have cropped up.

CHRISTIAN: Idolise!

SYBIL: (laughs.) Because it's becoming the smart thing. A loving son would never permit ...

CHRISTIAN: Not another word!

SYBIL: So your new friends can go into ecstasies over your mother's famous straw bonnet, your father's dubbined boots. The first action you took protected them from debasement and you from humiliation. That was most considerate tenderness on your part, and clever too, as your success shows.

CHRISTIAN: I have made money and need no longer flee the exigencies of life. At last I can pause to consider earthly goods. The first luxury the rich man indulges in is his family.

SYBIL: Your mother and father are not objects of luxury. If you really love them indulge the cult in private. But don't sacrifice them to vanity, just because with you everything has to be just as bon ton dictates. You want to marry the Countess. Do so. But don't give her in your parents the equation to judge you by. For her you must stay aloof and mysterious. You have so much that nobody but you possesses, you don't have to have parents too.

CHRISTIAN: It's no use, I'm set on the idea. I shall strain my entire capital, all my influence to the utmost, to gain my father the respect due to him. Don't contradict me! It is my will! These are things for which you lack every fundamental feeling; everything about you was chance from your birth on.

SYBIL: You'd like to tear open a chasm between us.

CHRISTIAN: I don't need to—it's been there a long time already. In thought and deed. We are strangers. Now, get out!

SYBIL: Really so strange, my lad? Aren't you the same person who used to come to me for money?

CHRISTIAN: You are dreaming. I'm the person who paid you and who is now terminating your services. Save your breath.

SYBIL: Oh for a word—I'd give my life to find it—one word to put a name to you and express how base I find you.

CHRISTIAN: Find it at home. If you distort me in your own mind with suspicions like those you just uttered, you destroy the memory of your one great passion. But that's your affair. If you dare to express these suspicions in public, then expect no consideration from me. I'll have you prosecuted.

(SYBIL *stands facing him, stares at him, then rushes out.*)

SCENE 7

CHRISTIAN: At last. The last thread severed to a past that no longer binds me. Attempts by a mere embryo with the gift of words to make you an enemy to your own nature and rational logic. (*He has taken up a fencing foil and goes through the motions of fencing.*) But as you know the cast of your temperament exactly, don't go pale at yourself, create a picture, a juicy image of yourself and don't give a thought to the judgment of the gallery. (*There is repeated ringing at the bell and he goes to open the door.*) Who can that be? (*After a moment one hears his exclamation outside.*) Mother!

SCENE 8

THEOBALD MASKE *in mourning, and* CHRISTIAN.

THEOBALD: (*after a pause, during which* CHRISTIAN *stands leaning against the door, sobbing.*) It's got to come to all of us, you know. We just have to face up to it. If it hadn't come like a bolt from the blue I should have prepared you. But she always was a great one for surprises and her own death was no exception.

CHRISTIAN: We must have her brought here and buried with appropriate ceremony.

THEOBALD: It was already too late for that yesterday.

CHRISTIAN: And you didn't let me know even that!

THEOBALD: Why should I put you to any trouble? And besides, I wasn't to know if it suited your book. A funeral is an official occasion, after all. During the whole quick catastrophe, the second it dawned upon her what this meant for her, she whispered 'Don't let Christian hear of it'. So it was all according to her wish. Feeling chilly? (CHRISTIAN *exit.*) Made an impression on him, anyway. Well, well, what do you know?

CHRISTIAN: (*comes back, a mourning suit over his arm. He changes during the following, partly behind a screen.*) I am ready now to hear all.

THEOBALD: It's soon told. She was sitting outside on her favourite bench drinking coffee, the way she always did, with a piece of sugar between her teeth. She felt hot, she said, and collapsed.

CHRISTIAN: (*sobs carefully.*) No illness beforehand, no suffering?

THEOBALD: Nothing.

CHRISTIAN: How were her last days? Was she happy?

THEOBALD: She always gave the same impression—she was just Louise.

CHRISTIAN: How did you get on with her after your last little mishap?

THEOBALD: I never carried things too far. Regular but not too often was the rule, and she knew nothing of it.

CHRISTIAN: You did not break with that woman, then?

THEOBALD: She was too fantastical for that. I preferred to put it off. So it remained, not exaggerated, unimportant, just running along calmly. Your mother had quiet days with me towards the end.

CHRISTIAN: I shall make arrangements immediately with an architect and a sculptor for a worthy monument. I cannot tell how much she meant to me. Perhaps the artist will find the means of expressing it.

THEOBALD: Perhaps.

(*Pause, during which* CHRISTIAN *gives further signs of his grief and completes his change into mourning.*)

CHRISTIAN: What an unfortunate chain of circumstances! To-day you would have found at your home the telegram which was to call you here for the happiest disclosures.

THEOBALD: You sent us a telegram?

CHRISTIAN: I was awaiting you with impatience.

THEOBALD: What's happened here that's so important?

CHRISTIAN: If you had come a few hours later you would have found your son engaged.

THEOBALD: Well, well! Is she pretty?

CHRISTIAN: She is—a Countess.

THEOBALD: Christian! Where do you get the nerve?

CHRISTIAN: Does it need nerve?

THEOBALD: Every man to his own style; but I think you've got a little if mine—you have taken a mighty leap.

CHRISTIAN: Away over all of us, father.

THEOBALD: It beats everything. And the other woman?

CHRISTIAN: That is all you have to say about it?

THEOBALD: To someone like me, it's a bit of a surprise turn.

CHRISTIAN: Logical outcome of a completely natural development.

THEOBALD: Me a low-grade clerk, your mother a tailor's daughter: there is an element of violence about it. And the father a count, all the relations—laddie, you are out of your mind!

CHRISTIAN: Nonsense, what do you mean?

THEOBALD: This is crazier than all the comedies in the world. You make a man ridiculous. Have you no consideration left for others? I have never even seen a count in the flesh in my life. Do you have to turn the world upside down every time anybody visits you? I tell you, I'm a retired clerk, living on a pension.

CHRISTIAN: That's all so much clap-trap.

THEOBALD: It's a disgrace! How can you have the nerve to do a thing like that to me? People will be pointing me out in the streets.

CHRISTIAN: (*abashed.*) But . . .

THEOBALD: The Seyfferts! Your mother had some funny enough ideas already. I'm going out of my mind. That time we had our difficulties before did not get me so excited, the death of my own wife did not get me so excited as I am over this.

CHRISTIAN: But father . . .

THEOBALD: (*more and more excited.*) You want to match a mouse with a giraffe, to do a tight-rope balancing act. You're bordering on the abnormal. Your mother dies on me at sixty, just when I'm accustomed to her; it was a blow, but after all one must accept—the nature of things. But the Maskes, me Theobald Maske here, known everywhere, and a whole count's family! It is enough to send me out of my wits. (CHRISTIAN *resignedly has taken up the fencing foil.* THEOBALD, *quite beside himself.*) Perhaps you want to murder me? I would rather stay where I am, an ordinary clerk, than play the clown for everbody's amusement. Have you no memory of your childhood left? Our tiny rooms and the canary; don't you remember how we scuffled along the street and how you at our side had to greet the Civil Service superintendent with due respect? What's a Civil Service superintendent compared with a count?

CHRISTIAN: (*anxiously.*) Just listen a moment, would you?

THEOBALD: So where does that mean we belong now? Oh, my God Almighty! . . .

CHRISTIAN: I fail to understand your terrible frenzy.

THEOBALD: And the things that might happen. Have none of the inevitable hair-raising consequences occurred to you, things any child can see? When you pushed us—two old people—abroad, I was foaming at the mouth with rage; gradually, however, I did see, with Louise's help, some cruel reason in it, did glimpse the deeper significance of it, for you if not for me. And as you saw to it that we lacked for nothing, and, well, let the other half live, I swallowed my pride. (*He leaps up*.) And now you dare propose such a ...

CHRISTIAN: I must interrupt. Even before there was any thought of this marriage, I was torn by a longing which from the moment of our separation became stronger and stronger within me. From now on it was my intention to share my life with the two of you, or as it has been decided otherwise, with you alone—in the closest harmony. I wanted to ask you to move —here, for good.

THEOBALD: (*collapses into a chair*.) That is just perfect!

CHRISTIAN: You ...

THEOBALD: You're not serious?

CHRISTIAN: Entirely. I could not foresee it would arouse in you such opposition.

THEOBALD: You *are* serious, then?

CHRISTIAN: I don't understand you.

THEOBALD: (*going right up to him*.) What?

CHRISTIAN: Don't understand. (*Retreats involuntarily*.)

THEOBALD: You still don't?

CHRISTIAN: That is, I do see what you mean, of course, but consider your reservations irrelevant—partly.

THEOBALD: Irrelevant?

CHRISTIAN: (*intimidated*.) On the other hand, natural—if you really mean it. Oh, God, I suppose I have to give up my dearest wish, though with heavy heart. I still insist on your presence at the wedding, no matter what happens.

THEOBALD: Now, look here: either you are making this suggestion naively without thinking, in which case I say this: it is immoral to want to see your father playing the part of the clown in this farce. To run the gauntlet through the church in my get-up with a countess on my arm and later to sit at the table like a—silly bumpkin ... as 'the simple man of the people' ...

CHRISTIAN: Father!

THEOBALD: No, thanks! Or maybe you want to take a petty revenge on me, by humiliating my self-esteem before the whole world, because I once caused you to feel my paternal authority in your youth, or maybe the invitation is supposed to be a consolation for mother's death. No, Christian, for God's sake, no! Do for me what you have done up till now and I am content—and if you want to do more, then take a second look at your intentions. But remember this: you must include me as a certain potential in your life-scheme: one who will have nothing to do with such things, yet who will not under any circumstances cause the slightest trouble. That's why I came up the back stairway earlier. Now I want to buy myself some clothes while I'm here.

CHRISTIAN: My tailor, my suppliers, will naturally . . .

THEOBALD: They do not cater for people like me. I have other sources. And in the evening I'll be off home again. (*Takes his hat and stick.*)

CHRISTIAN: (*anxiously.*) You must stay a few days at least.

THEOBALD: I must not! Stop this fiddle-de-dee. Why don't you adopt your usual reasonable tone with me? Unseen I came; unseen I shall depart. I don't need your assistance: I'll eat in the first place I come to. And if you should be passing through sometime to see her grave, I'll be quite happy. Apart from this silly marriage idea, you are quite a good fellow: you let a chap live.

SCENE 9

SERVANT: (*enters.*) Count Palen!

COUNT: (*follows immediately.*) With lovely impulsiveness Marianne *would* tell you first what her decision was—she was very happy—inwardly radiant—(THEOBALD *has been trying to disappear.*) Do introduce me.

CHRISTIAN: (*most confused.*) My father—yes—well.

COUNT: *Tiens!* But that's—! I mean—how very nice! Count Palen. Delighted to meet you. (*Gives* THEOBALD *both hands.*) And I was sure you were—how could I have thought—considered our friend an orphan— (*he laughs.*) No, it's true. This makes it all the more pleasant. *Charmant.*

CHRISTIAN: My father has just come from Zürich where he lives, with the news of my mother's death. So I gain Marianne just at the right moment. (*He falls on the* COUNT'S *breast.*)

179

COUNT: My deepest sympathy. (*To* THEOBALD.) To you too, my dear sir.

THEOBALD: (*bows.*) Thank you, Mr. Count.

COUNT: I can give you no better advice than—hurry to your fiancée. In the meantime the old fogeys can stay together. (*To* THEOBALD.) Have you had lunch yet? No? Well, off we go! I can offer no substitute for a wife, a bride, but what a good meal can do ...

CHRISTIAN: My father was intending to go home immediately.

COUNT: That would be asking too much of him.

THEOBALD: Never go without your lunch is what I say.

COUNT: I insist on doing the honours. The time will pass very quickly with condolences and congratulations. Your son has kept you shut away long enough: we can sniff each other out over a bottle of Burgundy.

THEOBALD: 'Sniff', eh? Ah, that's a good one.

COUNT: Isn't that what one says?

THEOBALD: (*laughs.*) I should say sniff, Mr. Count.

CHRISTIAN: (*hissing into* THEOBALD's *ear.*) Just 'Count'. (*To the* COUNT.) My father absolutely insists on catching the midday train.

COUNT: (*vigorously.*) Will you stop! The old gentleman must have a good meal first. Everything else can be settled afterwards. Come along! (COUNT *and* THEOBALD *exeunt.*)

SCENE 10

CHRISTIAN: Why did he change tone like that? Have I made a blunder? (*To the window.*) He is letting him climb into the coach first. What elaborate courtesy! I *have* made a blunder. He noticed my indecision, my embarrassment because of him. Am I blushing, am I pale? (*He rushes to the mirror.*) I'm shaking like an aspen leaf. (*He leaps into a chair at the window.*) He's offering him a cigar. Both laughing away like ninnies. What about? Me? Oh, God! I've made a terrible blunder. Wasn't I going to play him as a trump card, did I not swear five minutes ago I would boast about him, be so proud of him.

It was the one right instinct. And now he will babble to Marianne, to the whole family, that I wanted to deny my own father. Can he not claim I once said he was dead? I shall deny the whole thing straight to his face. A counter-attack! Quick! But what? (*He rings. Servant comes in.*) Prepare the guest rooms. My father has arrived. See that he receives the most careful attention. (*Servant exit.* CHRISTIAN *follows him to the door.*) Hold on! Wouldn't it be better to wait and see? Perhaps he could be got rid of without too much fuss. No, no, no, once and for all! I knew it this morning and it has since been proved! I must present him with a grand gesture as something exceptional. Right, now to set the stage. Lay my plans carefully. And this must take in the whole family. If it isn't already a catastrophe. (*He runs round the room.*) Wonder what they are doing over their wine? What will he get out of the old man if one of them gets drunk? Why in God's name didn't I join them? (*Beside himself.*) For God's sake! Yes, for God's sake! (*He howls out loud.*) Why didn't I obey my simple child-like instinct? I could kick myself!

CURTAIN

ACT III

Reception room in a hotel, lavishly adorned with flowers. Broad curtains in the background.

SCENE 1

CHRISTIAN *and* MARIANNE *enter.* CHRISTIAN *in evening coat over tails complete with decorations,* MARIANNE *with cloak over wedding-gown.*

CHRISTIAN: Breathing-space at last.
MARIANNE: These flowers! (*Examines one bouquet.*) Father's. (*Picks up a card and reads.*) 'For my lost angel Marianne'. And here—what heavenly orchids. (*Reads.*) 'From an unknown lady'.

181

CHRISTIAN: Really? How sentimental. What did he keep talking to my father about at table? Did you hear them?

MARIANNE: Who do you mean?

CHRISTIAN: Didn't you notice? Ignored their ladies at the table. The fat duchess ...

MARIANNE: Aunt Ursula is practically deaf and dropped almost half her meal into her lap.

CHRISTIAN: Who was it sitting two places to the right of her? The Knight of St. John?

MARIANNE: That was mother's cousin, Albert Thüngen.

CHRISTIAN: The fellow kept staring at me the whole time as if I were an apparition—he couldn't eat for staring.

MARIANNE: He has a real frog face; that's why he's called Froggy.

CHRISTIAN: Some rare decorations at table. Are you as intimate with the Princess as her behaviour towards you suggested?

MARIANNE: We were brought up together for seven years.

CHRISTIAN: Seven years. You're on christian-name terms, then.

MARIANNE: But we're also related through our great-grandmother.

CHRISTIAN: The Archduchess?

MAID: (*enters.*) Would your Grace like to change?

MARIANNE: Not 'Your Grace', now, Anna, just plain 'Madame'.

MAID: Very well, Your Grace.

MARIANNE: We've finished with 'Your Grace' and such silly nonsense. I demand respect!

MAID: (*sobs.*) Yes, Madame.

MARIANNE: What's the matter?

MAID: (*bows over* MARIANNE's *hand.*) It is all so moving, Madame does not belong to us any more.

MARIANNE: Nor to myself. It's every girl's fate. Yours too. (*Both off through curtain.*)

SCENE 2

CHRISTIAN: (*leaps to the curtain and listens.*) That Anna— she's got the face of a real informer! The things such a servant baggage picks up from keyholes and passes on ...

MAID: (*off-stage.*) ... looked divine. The minister was crying ...

MARIANNE: (*off-stage.*) ... old Jansen ... nonsense!

MAID: ... Genuine Brussels lace .. no, Brussels lace lavishly draped ... Rose-bud!

MARIANNE: ... Elsie Zeitlow ... bright blue satin with her blonde hair.

MAID: Everybody could see she was—(*stage whisper.*)—showing her bosom on purpose.

MARIANNE: For Heaven's sake! (*Giggling, then whispering.*)

CHRISTIAN: (*bending closer.*) Ah, whispering—always the same, everywhere. Wherever I appear, they're struck dumb; whispers and eyes on the floor.

(*Burst of laughter.*)

MAID: ... tips of his moustache!

CHRISTIAN: That's me! Oh, that day was my Waterloo!

MAID: ... rather ridiculous.

MARIANNE: Be quiet!

CHRISTIAN: *Canaille!* But I heard, Marianne. And this very evening I'll penetrate to the temple of your heart and find out just what you know. (*More laughter.*) Go on, then, laugh! Out, malicious delight! Open all the valves to her bloodstream, you viper. Because afterwards I'll cleanse my wife of your poison down to the very last drop.

MAID: It was too funny.

CHRISTIAN: But not the way you think, you female baboon. It's not settled yet. My counter-charges are loaded. When I let them off, the sound will drown out everything heard before. (*It is now quiet behind the curtain.*) Quiet? What are they up to? (*He kneels on the floor and tries to look under the curtain.*) Underclothes, bare flesh and gestures. I need but one word, a confession of how much the world has gossiped to you, from your father down to that louse Anna there. I have laid such a formidable plan to squeeze it out of you that you'll have difficulty in keeping one tittle to yourself. You will not cross the threshold of my name, woman, until you regard it with awe and emotion.

MAID: (*enters.*) May I fetch something from Madame's case? (*She does so and disappears again behind the curtain.*)

CHRISTIAN: They kept you from me until now, shrouded you in their own reserve. But today you are delivered to me for examination. With finesse I shall reconnoitre in your family to find where my deadliest enemy lies. He and all his trickery must be dragged into the open, evein if I have to strain your conscience to do so. (*He peers into the case.*) What have they stuffed into your luggage? What kind of books are there in this case? Abusive pamphlets? (*He pulls a book out of the case.*) The New Testament. Hmmm. Wonder what there is stored up against me deep down in her heart of hearts? We'll tear all that out too, when the time comes.

SCENE 3

THEOBALD *in morning-coat pokes his head round the door.*

CHRISTIAN: This is going too far.

THEOBALD: Just for a minute.

CHRISTIAN: What now?

THEOBALD: Affection.

CHRISTIAN: You're drunk.

THEOBALD: Partly. But I am also affectionate. Wanted to blow you a kiss all evening but I couldn't catch you. Don't try to talk your way out of it, boy. You are stupendous and I am proud of you through and through. You have stripped all the reservations from my soul, like so many paper shirts. You have conquered over all my prejudices and principles. All my life I have lived by proverbs: 'Cobbler, stick to your last', and so on. But you are a law unto yourself alone. How you handled these people today! Not only as equals, but almost condescendingly; they stared at you with an astonishment full of bottomless respect, and the way you fetch a noble little bird into your bed—that makes my bourgeois blood roar. You've mellowed me: I embrace you. (*Embraces him.*)

CHRISTIAN: Softly, softly, she's in there. You're not drunk?

THEOBALD: Just a bit. But what I say is true just the same. At table

184

when all were aglitter with their dazzling orders of chivalry and decorations, it was your proud little head ...

CHRISTIAN: Father!

THEOBALD: I repeat: proud little head, my beloved boy. Your mother should have been there: dawn, dawn was my feeling: can it be possible?

CHRISTIAN: Please, father.

THEOBALD: In you the name of the Maskes is notched a few holes higher. I can see it now, rattling up the ladder of fame. You have all of me in you: no, no, don't speak. Now comes my confession—a very serious matter. Normally, a father does not say this to his son: I am superfluous, a puff of smoke, and I disappear down the trapdoor. My ties with the world, the higher significance of my own existence: you are it. You wanted to get rid of me. Always had it in mind. To me it used to seem a hostile act of aggression. But today the arrangement seems pleasurably smooth, giving boundless satisfaction to both parties. 'Johanna departs, never more to return'. Happy departure for Zürich—High Street, No. 16. There lives Maske, the retired Civil Service Superintendent, and turns his joyful gaze upon his son.

CHRISTIAN: Somebody coming!

THEOBALD: Let them. We, we are now one and the same thing. Carry on and no mistakes ... They feel distrust, contempt, hate, etc., but also boundless respect from complete failure to comprehend.

CHRISTIAN: How do you know?

THEOBALD: On the basis of the great general intoxication I crept into their confidence. They took the long service medal for the Iron Cross, and opened their hearts to me completely.

CHRISTIAN: What about the old man? The lapsus of that fatal day?

THEOBALD: He certainly had his suspicions then, and they were probably still lurking about. But at table today, when I finally burst into a bonfire of enthusiasm for you, he caught fire too. Besides the dear little dove in there had already softened up the paternal heart. He capitulated completely.

CHRISTIAN: So they are finished?

THEOBALD: Finished. And now take tighter hold. Don't relax your grip. In my own way I was always convinced of the significance of our line. Could only communicate it to the nearest few.

CHRISTIAN: To me!

THEOBALD: And you are the one to carry us all upwards.

CHRISTIAN: I have bent the bow. The string trembles in my hands.

THEOBALD: The first arrow is aimed at her. Strike deep.

CHRISTIAN: We stick like leeches.

THEOBALD: Right to the marrow.

CHRISTIAN: I play the trump, the ace of trumps!

THEOBALD: (*peeping behind the curtain.*) I take off my hat to you!

CHRISTIAN: Eh?

THEOBALD: Hehe! (*Both giggle and fall into each other's arms.*)

CHRISTIAN: The Maskes for ever!

THEOBALD: I understand you more or less. Con-sang-uinity! (*He skips to the exit, throwing kisses, etc. Exit.*)

CHRISTIAN: Here life has scaled the heights of drama. The goal gained, the enemy crushed, obeisances before the victor, and exit up centre! But something more significant has yet to come. Let us take soundings to see to what extent the immediate vicinity has sunk from sight and then the little countess, my wife, the one that matters above all else, shall on this solemn evening feel and savour boundless awe. She must collapse and sprawl full length at my feet—no less!

SCENE 4

MARIANNE: (*enters in a negligée.*) Do you like me?

CHRISTIAN: (*aside.*) That's not what matters at the moment.

MARIANNE: There's a pretty story about this lace. Mother wore it on the same night of her life.

CHRISTIAN: No comparison whatsoever.

MARIANNE: I—do I not remind you of another woman from your past? Tell me all. You must have no secrets from me.

How many have you had before me, and which was the special
one? Is there still a thought, a breath of another woman in
you?

CHRISTIAN: What language—how shall I ever talk rationally?

MARIANNE: (*her arms round his neck.*) Once I was in love with
an ensign. I was just sixteen. He was pink and white with a
blonde fuzz on his lip; that was all I knew about him.

CHRISTIAN: What do you know about me?

MARIANNE: If I close my eyes, you are big and dark and broad-
limbed, and you swivel your hips as you walk.

CHRISTIAN: Is that true? (*Goes over to the mirror and takes a
few steps in front of it.*) Well, one could certainly call it a
rolling gait. There's rhythm in it.

MARIANNE: (*laughs out loud.*) And how do I walk? (*She raises
her skirts and trips a few steps.*)

CHRISTIAN: And what else? What else do I do?

MARIANNE: Business.

CHRISTIAN: What kind?

MARIANNE: Does it matter?

CHRISTIAN: At thirty-six I am Managing Director of our largest
industrial concern, control one fifth of the national income.

MARIANNE: *Tiens!*

CHRISTIAN: You get that word from your father. Has he discussed my affairs with you?

MARIANNE: He mentioned this and that.

CHRISTIAN: This and that? That can cover a lot.

MARIANNE: I'm tired.

CHRISTIAN: (*aside.*) Invitation to the Dance. (*Loud.*) Too
early. Am I not a complete stranger to you? Has your father
never talked seriously about me—really never? Think back!
Didn't he come home feverishly excited one day? Reflect!

MARIANNE: I never saw him feverishly excited in my life.

CHRISTIAN: So he held his counsel. Don't you think it is meri-
torious in one so young to hold such a post; what would you
say if someone was a general at thirty-six?

MARIANNE: Only a prince can be that. (*She sits on his knee.*)

CHRISTIAN: Or?

MARIANNE: Who?

CHRISTIAN: Guess!

MARIANNE: I don't know.

CHRISTIAN: The man of genius. In the course of this year forty-one companies wanted to announce the issue of new shares to the total value of approximately three-quarters of a billion. But I said I was against it for the following reasons: for these 750 million the public are offered not new mineral wealth, but the product of the exertions of a good half-million extra men which the country is encouraged to produce. The share capital of industrial companies consists in essence and interest entirely of human material and its work product. Do you understand?

MARIANNE: (still on his lap.) I'm trying to.

CHRISTIAN: Pay attention! If there is no work, the masses cut back the procreative process. If new factory chimneys spring up, the valve is quickly opened. So we captains of industry wait and see that the capital does not anticipate the natural human growth, but maintains the balance. Do you understand?

MARIANNE: I think so.

CHRISTIAN: Rather we must try by slowing down the tempo of human procreation to produce higher quality. There you have one small example of the practical part I play in the national economy. (He has pushed her off his lap and walks erectly round the room.) Hey? That's classic, Helmholtz would have said. (He grabs MARIANNE by a button of her dress and shakes her gently backwards and forwards staring fixedly into her eyes as he speaks.) I could quote you another similar stupendous example of my work in the question of lowering the steerage rate in our Steamhip Companies. Men are short-sighted and the economic fate of millions rests in the hands of a few.

MARIANNE: Are you really so rich?

CHRISTIAN: Rich? A term for small traders! I can do anything you like to name and the power to do so comes from the power of the blood. You've seen my father a few times now. A personality! What? Even in him the peculiar qualities of our race were already clearly marked. Nothing in excess, everything completely functional. Did you notice today at table? Of all those present, his hand was the one that showed most vitality in drinking the toasts. Pity you never knew my grandfather. Eccentric as they come—still! All that comes down to me from my forefathers but it has only reached full fruition in me.

MAID: (*enters.*) Would Madame not like to take the jewels into safe keeping? Here in the hotel—sir, perhaps? (CHRISTIAN *takes a diadem shaped like a crown.*)

MAID: Good-night!

CHRISTIAN: Quite a remarkable shape, really.

MARIANNE: A Marquis' Crown from whose inheritance it comes, for the ladies of our family to wear on their wedding day; a Marquise d'Uffés was my mother's great-aunt.

CHRISTIAN: *Bon.* What was I saying?—But I have a surprise for you.

MARIANNE: (*Claps her hands.*) Show me!

CHRISTIAN: Turn round a minute, till I've unpacked it and set it up.

MARIANNE: (*turned away.*) One, two, three—

CHRISTIAN: (*has uncovered a picture which was leaning against the wall wrapped in cloth and has set it up against his own legs.*) Now you can look. Over here. (MARIANNE *looks at a female portrait.*) My mother, Marianne, who would like to meet you face to face on this day. My mother, who dearly loved her son.

MARIANNE: What a striking face!

CHRISTIAN: Isn't it? Painted by Renoir.

MARIANNE: (*flings her arms round* CHRISTIAN's *neck.*) I will love him more even than myself, your son, my Christian.

CHRISTIAN: Gently, take care not to damage such a valuable work of art. (*He has leaned the picture against a table.*)

MARIANNE: Her thick brown hair. Your colour. And such a glorious complexion.

CHRISTIAN: She came of centuries-old peasant stock. Some talk even of Vikings. See the solid family jewels, the red coral at her ear. One of her forebears was a magistrate on Hlar in the

189

Swedish off-shore islands. There's a story of his meeting with Charles XII.

MARIANNE: What marvellous hair!

CHRISTIAN: It reached to the back of her knees when loose. Renoir saw her one day in the Bois de Boulogne. The decision to paint her was said to be instantaneous—but the reason for it—that was the best of all. Now unbutton your little ears, what follows is the most charming thing in the world. Well, then: father and mother walking in the Bois after a sedate *déjeuner* in the cascades. A bottle of Burgundy had not been lacking. Suddenly—the lady stands stock-still as if nailed to the spot, refuses to go a step further. Father, his grey topper jauntily on his head—he has often dramatised the situation for me—calls, beckons, entices—she won't move.

MARIANNE: What was wrong with her? (CHRISTIAN *whispers into her ear.* MARIANNE *laughs out loud.*) Her drawers! But that is delightful! Heavenly!

CHRISTIAN: (*roaring with laughter.*) And then Renoir! You can imagine him, he's often told me—beside himself, but completely beside himself. It must have been a sight for the Gods.

MARIANNE: The enchanting lady standing like that in full daylight.

CHRISTIAN: In short, he procures entry into the youthful *ménage* and with him a French Viscount, who had witnessed the scene at his side.

MARIANNE: How long ago was this?

CHRISTIAN: Oh, it must have been about a year before I was born.

MARIANNE: How the telling of a personal anecdote brings people closer together. I seem to know her better now. The situation can't have been very pleasant for your father.

CHRISTIAN: He always was and still is 'bon garçon' with an appreciation of good clean fun. He adored his young spouse and was also quite captivated by the charm of the spectacle.

MARIANNE: The costume shows excellent taste.

CHRISTIAN: She was a past master when it came to style.

MARIANNE: A charming fashion! How becoming the cape is, and

all the divine ladies who dressed that way are now no more.

CHRISTIAN: I'm going to have a monument erected to her memory in Buchow (*He hangs the picture on the wall.*)

MARIANNE: Did you buy the property?

CHRISTIAN: I'm buying it. For that very purpose really. She was a woman, all in all, so much larger than life that she has the right to such a token of esteem.

MARIANNE: How wrong was the picture I had of your family till now. Only now do I see them properly. You have the gift of bringing people to life.

CHRISTIAN: More correct to call it the ability of creating concepts. What normally comes out of people's mouths are words, mere words.

MARIANNE: I need Anna once more—

CHRISTIAN: Oh, not that girl again!

MARIANNE: I cannot open this dress at the back.

CHRISTIAN: Let me. (*He starts to look for the hooks.*) Words by which no two minds mean the same thing and hence useless for creating full communication between two beings. (MARIANNE *yawns.*) Pure reason brings together groups of similar configurations of the phenomenal or noumenal world into mere expression, which formulates the essential nexus of the complex, and that is a concept.

MARIANNE: (*yawns.*) Ha!

CHRISTIAN: (*unbuttoning.*) Conquest of multiplicity, that's what it is. The petticoat too?

MARIANNE: Please.

CHRISTIAN: In fact, Marianne, and now listen seriously, every act the human spirit performs intends essentially but one thing: it domesticates the enormous area of environment by conquering the multiplicity of phenomena. So Beech, Oak, in whose names their own multiplicity has already been subsumed, are finally seen as forest. (*He has finished with the buttons.*)

MARIANNE: Thanks. (*She puts her feet on a chair and unbuttons her shoes.*)

CHRISTIAN: Only a fool would make the joke—you can't see the wood for the trees. (MARIANNE *goes through the curtain into the bedroom.*) Where are you going? While it should go : you can't see a tree for sheer forest. (*He has followed her and stops at the curtain.*) If you understand that you have the whole theory of cognition in your pocket. (*He comes back front, saying loudly, backwards.*) At any rate you now have an idea how a brain like mine works, eh? (*Rubs hands, aside.*) Ça Marche ce soir! (*Stops in front of the picture and says, deeply moved.*) My darling mother! (*Loud.*) You know, as a girl she took a trip with friends to the United States and came back via the South Sea Islands and Asia. In Honolulu, King Kalakaua fell madly in love with her. (*Behind the curtain one can hear someone going to bed.*) That was 1880 or 1881. (*He has taken off his shoes and only then his coat, so that he suddenly stands there in the glory of all his decorations. He raises his arms and looks round as if expectantly. Pause.*)

MARIANNE's *voice* : What became of the Viscount?

CHRISTIAN : What Viscount?

MARIANNE's *voice* : The one who saw the episode in the Bois de Boulogne and got to know your parents.

CHRISTIAN : Oh, yes, the Viscount! Psh—well—he—(*stands, suddenly rigid, in front of his mother's picture. Pause.*)

MARIANNE's *voice* : Well, what became of him?

CHRISTIAN : (*aside.*) If I only knew what I ... but of course ... great Caesar! This is where I've got you. This will really flatten you, my little Countess! (*He goes to the curtain and whispers.*) Marianne!

MARIANNE : (*excitedly.*) I'm coming! (*She appears with a dressing-gown thrown over her shoulders.*)

CHRISTIAN : I see destiny in your sudden question.

MARIANNE : Why, what did I say?

CHRISTIAN : That Viscount and what became of him—

MARIANNE : Yes!

CHRISTIAN : I should never have opened my lips.

MARIANNE : Christian! Whatever is it?

CHRISTIAN : Impossible! Never!

MARIANNE : Christian! I am your wife—I have a right ...!

CHRISTIAN : But I'm also a son.

MARIANNE : You have certain obligations to me.

CHRISTIAN: But also shame and respectful modesty for my mother.

MARIANNE: That Viscount ...

CHRISTIAN: My tongue will utter no word more ...

MARIANNE: She—the Viscount was your ... fa ...

CHRISTIAN: (*strongly*.) And I forbid you for the rest of our life ever to touch upon this again! Ever to let anyone, even me, guess what you suspect, what you suppose. My name is Maske, and that's all there is to it.

MARIANNE: (*shattered*.) Son of Heaven! Of course, I'll be silent. But the way I regard you from now on is my affair. (*Gently*.) And I feel as if a last barrier between us had been cast down, as if only now I were yielding to you without inhibition. (*With outstretched arms before the picture*.) Sweet mother adultress! (*To* CHRISTIAN, *collapsing slowly at his feet*.) My dear husband and lord! (CHRISTIAN's *smile and grand gesture of relief*.)

CURTAIN

1913

Play in Three Acts

To the memory of Ernst Stadler, the poet

Translated by J. M. Ritchie

Motto—All the world ever needs to save it
Is never very much.

Characters

His Excellency, Baron CHRISTIAN MASKE VON BUCHOW
PHILIPP ERNST
OTTILIE } *his children*
Countess SOFIE VON BEESKOW
Count OTTO VON BEESKOW, *his son-in-law*
HARTWIG, Prince OELS
WILHELM KREY, *secretary*
FRIEDRICH STADLER
EASTON, *a tailor*
CLERGYMAN
BUTLER

The scene throughout is the library at Buchow Castle

ACT I

SCENE 1

WILHELM: (*at the desk.*) Yes, that's it! This letter sums up the whole problem in a few words. (*reads.*) 'I showed you those qualities of our nation given the stamp of approval by history and those additional new abilities the modern German has acquired through the assimilation of annexed races. On the other side of the balance sheet were placed all those faculties whereby success is achieved in the present day and age, and it becomes clear, the characteristic characteristics of a great people, which shall be nameless, still lie dormant. Like everywhere else, there is but one thing stamped on our fevered brains —the international rush for gold'.

Next on the programme, catchy slogans with popular appeal. (*reads.*) 'Bemused though we are, one clarion call leads us straight to the heart of the matter: we abandon the problems of mankind in general, all calls to brotherhood across national frontiers. While it is true we desire to be humane beings, above all we wish to be Germans. Consciously we strive to plumb the depths of our own essential being, and it is the new national idea, embracing every soul in the fatherland with like concern, that we raise far higher than the wishy-washy spirit of the age and while we afford ourselves full honour and enthusiasm, we also feel respect for anything significant from abroad.' (*Stands up.*)

Isn't that wonderful: a sacred, wide-ranging, patriotic brotherhood and wide-ranging German ideas. I owe them all to this house, which chance brought me to. Its crass capitalistic spirit revolted my most vital organs and now every hour carries me nearer and nearer my mighty goal, the act of liberation. Quick, an envelope!

OTTILIE: (*enters.*) Good morning.

(WILHELM bows.)

OTTILIE: (*after silence.*) Is Baron Philipp Ernst coming on the eleven o'clock train?

WILHELM: Your brother's rooms are in readiness for that hour.

OTTILIE: Our father's condition worries him.

WILHELM: His Excellency is more seriously ill than he looks.

OTTILIE: (*whistles a popular song then silence.*) My sister and brother-in-law are bringing Prince and Princess Oels with them on Friday.

WILHELM: Everything is in readiness to receive them.

OTTILIE: Did a book called 'Sex and Character' come?

WILHELM: It came and was placed on the shelf.

OTTILIE: Will you give it to me?

WILHELM: I am not authorised to do so without His Excellency's permission.

OTTILIE: I ordered the book. It's my property.

WILHELM: Would you kindly find it yourself?

OTTILIE: I order you.

WILHELM: I take orders from no-one but His Excellency.

OTTILIE: Where is it?

WILHELM: In the second bookcase, first section from the top, with the W's.

OTTILIE: (*goes up to the bookcase and sees the book is very high.*) Would you be kind enough to help me.

WILHELM: I beg to be excused.

OTTILIE: Why?

WILHELM: I'd rather not answer that question.

OTTILIE: You think the book does not belong in the hands of a young girl, is that it?

WILHELM: I prefer to leave the question unanswered.

OTTILIE: (*runs to the bookcase, places the ladder, climbs up and takes the book.*) Even by your silence you overstep the

199

line to be drawn between an employee and the actions of his employers.

WILHELM (*gets up and goes to the door.*)

OTTILIE: Help me down! I'm feeling faint.

WILHELM (*exit.*)

(OTTILIE *slips, half falls down the ladder and remains lying on the ground.*)

SCENE 3

CHRISTIAN: (*enters.*) Ottilie! (*Lifts her up, puts her in a chair.*) I had a terrible dream; this is it come true.

OTTILIE: I lost balance—reaching for a book.

CHRISTIAN: Hurt?

OTTILIE: No.

CHRISTIAN: The best book learning is no compensation for a broken leg. What were you after?

OTTILIE: The young author of this book shot himself, because he discovered uncharted continents of the spirit of such dimension ...

CHRISTIAN: (*laughs.*) He did the right thing! Uncharted continents of the spirit, indeed! For sixty years I've been Chief of Staff standing out in front of armies of men and I've never managed to figure out more than a few words of command applicable to ancient primitive emotions. That's all I've got but I'm far better off than most of my contemporaries who have absolutely no idea with what kind of appeal they can seize and hold the milling masses. Your author suffered from a nasty delusion. Sixty-five million mouths to feed in Germany over 500 thousand square miles. At this stage of the race one drive becomes dominant: getting enough to eat. Even sex shrivels away. As for uncharted continents of the spirit! You're wasting valuable time.

OTTILIE: I've plenty of time.

CHRISTIAN: From fifteen to twenty-five to mature. One thousand eight hundred days. This tome is hefty. A panacea you'll take five days over. Have you before your soul the three minutes Barras gave Napoleon to decide his whole life with the assumption of the supreme army command? They stared each other out in silence; then Napoleon called out: I'll do it! Do you recall the gesture of the 18th Brumaire?

OTTILIE: I'm no politician.

CHRISTIAN: Everybody should be with every ounce of his being! In the future you'll have to take decisions for 15,000 workers in our factories. You must model yourself on somebody.

OTTILIE: There are three of us.

CHRISTIAN: You have no time for rubbish like that.

OTTILIE: Or playing polo.

CHRISTIAN: Polo is of inestimable value. Sharpens the eye for distances. For the nearness of the adversary! That's what it does! With members of the real Establishment you're not only playing polo you're playing for acceptance. They've been in the public eye for all the thousand years that your forefathers lived a nameless existence. So you have to drive yourself to the utmost to catch up. Isn't my life an example to you?

OTTILIE: A horrible one, Daddy. You burst through the house like a bomb. When you're in the room it's as if the door's been left open.

CHRISTIAN: Life with a goal! It's for my darling I've done what I've done. Enough is not enough! Why? If it's not increasing, it's decreasing. It's time you learned how to master life.

OTTILIE: The world does not obey everybody.

CHRISTIAN: It does the man who has faith in himself. Even in his own weaknesses. Repeat a dozen times for all the world to hear (if it's true) I am greedy—in the end it will be counted one of your good features. But first you must admit to *yourself* with the necessary force that you have this feature.

OTTILIE: You mean a young girl should say she's . . .

CHRISTIAN: As future head of Christian Maske & Co. you can say anything you like about yourself. Only an applicant for a job needs to have good things said about him. What's the matter?

OTTILIE: I'm thinking about what you said.

CHRISTIAN: Is there something else?

OTTILIE: It's a staggering thought. Suppress none of one's secret wishes: abstain from none?

CHRISTIAN: Well, child, what's stirring in the dark depths?

OTTILIE: It's too light here to tell.

CHRISTIAN: Whisper in my ear. I'll keep my eyes closed.

(OTTILIE *leans against him, whispering in his ear.*)

CHRISTIAN: Heady intoxication of power! Rule men—devour. That's it exactly! That's class!

(OTTILIE *runs into a curtain and hides in it.*)

CHRISTIAN: (*pulls her out.*) Out with it! Bring it out into the light! What you really think. More power to your confession and with head held high you'll march over mortals. All I had to start with was supreme self-confidence.

OTTILIE: I have it sometimes. Sofie has it all the time like you. She ought to be your favourite.

CHRISTIAN: When is Philipp Ernst coming?

OTTILIE: At eleven.

CHRISTIAN: She'll crush both of you against the wall. How often have I told you and the boy: you're letting control be wrested from your fingers. Why don't you take an interest? You can't tell a stock from a share. She'll strangle you in spite of all protective legal clauses. You run around the periphery of life; she sits at the centre and weaves her webs. After my death she'll extract the money from your pockets at knife-point.

OTTILIE: Not against my will.

CHRISTIAN: She knows every trick in the book. Look at what she has done for herself when she took my place during the few weeks of my illness. From dawn till dusk she keeps the telegraph wires humming. That woman thinks in explosive discharges, every stroke of her pen means more money for her bank account. One day's absence costs me prestige, power, money. (*Sits down.*) This is how she sits at her desk. She has every ledger entry for every factory in her head, she calculates to the penny. She knows every customer like the back of her hand, knows what his instincts will automatically tell him to do and keeps firing him instructions which he takes for his own wishes. At this very moment—oh, what a creature—how she schemes against me!

OTTILIE: Father!

CHRISTIAN: Has God forsaken me, why am I sitting here giving her free rein to sign agreements of utmost importance?

OTTILIE: You must not get excited.

(The telephone on the desk rings.)

CHRISTIAN: Silence! *(on the phone.)* Who? Witman? The meeting over? What about the Dutch Government's conditions —what? Yes, I'm talking about the arms delivery—accepted by our board? Whaaat? Speak up, Witman! It's a deal, assuming the bill is passed by Parliament in Holland? I see. *(He drops the receiver.)* Great God in Heaven, that vulture! Against my explicit instructions? *(On the phone again.)* You still there? My son-in-law's speech a success throughout the nation? *(He flings down the receiver.)* That's the last straw. I'm a fool. While I'm here tending my decrepit corpse my own daughter is out there smashing my life's work to pieces.

OTTILIE: What's all this about guns for Holland?

CHRISTIAN: And this is the woman you two puppets are going to stand up to? Three days after my death you'll be cut to ribbons. That boy! Didn't I guide his adolescence according to my principles and he turns out a wastrel. Still, you've got the breeding. I've just sounded you out. Come here! *(Takes her by the head and talks into her ear.)* Cast off childish things—shame. World Power—no dream—tangible reality. *(He takes a book from a drawer and opens it on the desk.)* What's that figure?

(OTTILIE stands with eyes closed.)

CHRISTIAN: The figure—read it!

OTTILIE: One hundred and twenty.

CHRISTIAN: Millions! Darling, little Queen. Grow claws, take the Field-Marshal's baton, seize what you want. It is all meant for you, not her.

OTTILIE: I promise—I'll—try—with all my might.

CHRISTIAN: Face up to your most secret, most shattering thoughts. Something flashed in your eyes then. What was it? You have something in mind. Realise it! Now! Just for practice! Blood of my blood. You'll have power in your hands I never had at your age. A bomb, am I? Now we'll make the bomb go off with a bang at just the right place. (*He rings.*) What's the pass-word! *La sensation!* Vital, untrammelled awareness of living. Away!

(OTTILIE *exit.*)

SCENE 4

WILHELM: (*enters.*) Your Excellency?

CHRISTIAN: Private Secretary, child of your time, where have you been hiding? Busy with your own pressing affairs? Following a fiery speech from Count Beeskow, the Board of Directors of our Armaments Branch has accepted the conditions of the Dutch Government for the arms delivery.

WILHELM: Against Your Excellency's wishes?

CHRISTIAN: I expressly forbade it. Why did I do so?

WILHELM: Your Excellency fears we ourselves may be at war in the near future, and wishes to keep our works available.

CHRISTIAN: And to have our competitors tied up with deliveries to Holland. Besides, the prices finally agreed upon are below the profit margin. How can we describe the behaviour of my son-in-law, led on the end of a rope by my own daughter? Palace Revolution. Why didn't you let me go to Berlin? Convalescing, am I? What's the use of a well-tended corpse when they're out there wiping out all I stand for.

WILHELM: Who would ever have expected so much initiative from the Countess?

CHRISTIAN: Me. For the last two years I've been trying to make you realise what my daughter is like.

WILHELM: It is Your Excellency's pleasure to portray the

Countess as an example of a modern being motivated solely by the lust for power, while my feelings do not permit ...

CHRISTIAN: What do your feelings not permit?

WILHELM: If I give offence, Your Excellency, I shall say no more.

CHRISTIAN: Speak!

WILHELM: All the thousandfold turbulent emotions inside one human being cannot be re ...

CHRISTIAN: Fool! Sixty-five million on 500 thousand square miles. Belly hunger for the poor. Power hunger for the rich. Basta.

WILHELM: No, Your Excellency!

CHRISTIAN: Yes!

(WILHELM *is silent.*)

CHRISTIAN: (*roars.*) It is! It is! Do me a favour and look around you in the world. Soar up high, take the bird's eye view, look at the globe or at Germany by itself if you like. Is it still all the fault of the Jews? Be honest, my boy, tell the truth! When will you finally fight your way through to the one big ugly fact and place it firmly before your eyes: belly hunger of the plebs, power hunger of the rich. That's the whole truth. Get me the Stock Exchange quotations. Armaments?

WILHELM: (*reads.*) 264. 6 points up.

CHRISTIAN: Idiots! Should be 6 points down, if that lot had any sense. Get me Berlin. Direct.

(WILHELM *puts the call through.*)

CHRISTIAN; The doctor after lunch. I go this evening—must know how they set about doing our competitors out of the contract.

WILHELM: Something Your Excellency does not like?

CHRISTIAN: In the eyes of the world she's pulled off a great coup. I'm dying to know her overall strategy, I assure you she has made her mighty leap to push me out once and for all.

WILHELM: I'm sure the Countess's name is never publicly mentioned.

CHRISTIAN: No. The glory goes to her clown of a husband. But she fathered the scheme. She knows it and that's all she needs. (*Loudly.*) The clown, he can't even get her with child, to perpetuate the dynasty.

WILHELM: The more insignificant Count Beeskow is in reality, the more human and touching that makes all the Countess's efforts to show him in a good light.

CHRISTIAN: Too simple a solution. There's more to that woman than meets the eye. (*The telephone rings.*)

WILHELM: (*at the receiver.*) Mr. Witman? His Excellency would like to speak with you.

CHRISTIAN: A poor spy, this fellow Witman. If he does not know every single detail, he's out on his ear. (*Takes the phone.*) Where the hell did you get to? Now—the factors governing the Dutch Government's decision? Ah—ah—ahah! (*He drops the receiver.*) God help me! (*He picks up the receiver.*) Yes—yes—I see! (*He replaces the instrument slowly, almost ceremoniously, then goes to an armchair in which he sits silently; finally he utters a groan.*)

(WILHELM *stands in silence.*)

CHRISTIAN: (*gets up, without looking at* WILHELM, *he says.*) God help me, I will not be thrown on the scrap-heap. I still have another thirty years in me. My work is everything, I am the creator, my will decides when I go. Such a measly little female—but what vast potential. I see her plans are more far-reaching than I thought. This means a fight to the death. Right. (*To* WILHELM.) How was it done? According to Witman, round about the time when the news of the Dutch orders broke, she began to lay a lot of stress in her private life on her Protestantism. Visited charitable gatherings, endowed crèches. When a few days ago the final decision was in the balance she made a significant donation to the church which the newspapers made it their business to proclaim with all due pomp. Some of us here just couldn't see what she was up to. Then she used a go-between in The Hague to insinuate the idea that it would strike people as peculiar if an out-and-out Protestant country like Holland were to give Catholic firms (in other words our competitors) orders worth millions.

This from a woman who never gave a damn about her faith.

WILHELM: That is unbelievably despicable.

CHRISTIAN: My young friend, it is genius, pure and simple.

WILHELM: Proves how right your verdict of the Countess was.

CHRISTIAN: Genius. That is my verdict now. No two ways about it.

WILHELM: Have I Your Excellency's permission to reply?

CHRISTIAN: No.

WILHELM: I must.

CHRISTIAN: Silence! Did she or did she not act logically?

WILHELM: On the assumption that life on earth consists entirely in the acquisition of material goods . . .

CHRISTIAN: On that assumption.

WILHELM: She is a genius.

CHRISTIAN: The rest, old fellow-me-lad, you can keep to yourself. Or do you want to show moral indignation, cough up some crap about the rudiments of good up-bringing?

WILHELM: I should prefer not to make myself appear ridiculous.

CHRISTIAN: Back to our topic. The instincts of this genius are directed against me, against my personal prestige. To make everybody from director to share-holder realise that I am now expendable. Do you see what she's up to?

WILHELM: Of course.

CHRISTIAN: Incidentally, what did you mean, you don't want to appear ridiculous? In whose eyes?

WILHELM: In Your Excellency's eyes, naturally.

CHRISTIAN: You're keeping something back; but that's your business. In short: what happened in Berlin means cards on the table.

WILHELM: Your Excellency will play the trump.

CHRISTIAN: My dear fellow, I shall open just a little the floodgates of my ideas, and this Semiramis in miniature will be swept aside. I shall not go to Berlin, I'll await her arrival here instead, then I'll skin her alive so completely that . . .

WILHELM: The Countess will come prepared.

CHRISTIAN: She lacks experience. For forty years I've been at the centre of things. Every possible move has been used in the past. I've fought over scraps with Bismarck till the sparks flew. The Dutch deal will be stopped by Parliament at the last minute. I swear it! This religion gimmick is a miserable flicker of light. All I need is a walk in the woods and the necessary brainwave will come to snuff it out; and the support of all concerned, indeed of the whole political world, will feed my flame again. Seventy years old, my friend: but the flame has not diminished.

WILHELM: Your Excellency is enjoying the battle already.

CHRISTIAN: The wheels are beginning to turn.

WILHELM: And if all else fails there's still the celebration for your seventieth birthday on 1st July.

CHRISTIAN: Wrong way round; perhaps the fireworks of the birthday party will suffice to dazzle the world anew with my brilliance. If not, I'll unleash my full radiance. In any event: plenty of life ahead in the immediate future and (*pinches his ear.*) masses of newspaper-cuttings. Your task is to attach the two younger children more closely to me. Forget your reserve. Give the boy and girl too a fat chunk of real life to bite into. Into the waste-paper basket once and for all with all fossilised childish amusements and flirtations with mere ideas. All I need is a walk in the woods ... (*Exit laughing.*)

WILHELM: (*goes back to the desk, writes.*) An envelope! Quick! To the Executive Committee of the Patriotic National Youth League, Berlin. Off it goes! (*Stands up.*)

SCENE 5

PHILIPP ERNST: (*enters.*) Good day, Dr. Krey, isn't my father here?

WILHELM: His Excellency took a walk to think over an unexpected occurrence.

PHILIPP ERNST: Let's leave him to it. D'you know, for me an unexpected occurrence is the most frightful thing in the world, because it always occurs as something unpleasant between two pleasant sort of *choses*?

WILHELM: It can be the other way round too.

PHILIPP ERNST: How?

WILHELM: Can't it come as a pleasant interruption in an unpleasant situation?

PHILIPP ERNST: In a well-tempered existence an unexpected occurrence is the only unpleasant situation imaginable. Oh, dear Dr. Krey, is there any news of my sister's arrival?

WILHELM: Friday evening. Their Highnesses Prince and Princess Oels will be in the Countess's party.

PHILIPP ERNST: You mustn't say Prince and Princess. They are not married. Brother and sister. The Princess is a charming widow. The brother twenty, a young blade.

WILHELM: I did not know.

PHILIPP ERNST: Auburn hair and freckles and a ruddy complexion. *The* Merry Widow, Doctor. She was the one involved in that incident with Count Chamel. Chamel the sportsman. Deauville. You know. Fireworks *à la digue*, at night. Casino and all that. Where are we all sleeping?

WILHELM: For you the usual appartment, Baron.

PHILIPP ERNST: Have the bath taps been seen to? Always made an infernal din. They say the widow is dressing better. Used to go in for artistic, loud checks. Very distinguished checks —but still ghastly.

WILHELM: Baron, could you possibly spare me an hour to go over some of the business correspondence you ...

PHILIPP ERNST: That is a stroke of luck. Just what I wanted to ask you; I've been lugging a sheaf of papers around for months, settlements, balance in your favour, etc., etc. You know; that's to say, one never knows in whose favour it is; net, gross— it's all double Dutch.

WILHELM: Here's a page from a ledger. Would you like to take a look?

PHILIPP ERNST: Doctor—you may think me *bebête*—but I swear I can't, I get all choked up. Funny that way. Can't stand fowl anywhere near me either. Same sort of *chose*.

WILHELM: It's all so simple. A matter of three or four basic concepts.

PHILIPP ERNST: (*beside himself.*) I beg you, *c'est plus fort que moi.* Net, gross, debit, credit. (*He shudders.*) Voyons.

O

WILHELM: (*laughs.*) You'll be taken advantage of.

PHILIPP ERNST: I live by other tricks.

WILHELM: May I beg to be excused?

PHILIPP ERNST: You will look at the papers I'll send you?

WILHELM: Gladly. (*Bows, exit.*)

SCENE 6

(PHILIPP ERNST *shudders.*)

OTTILIE: (*enters by the gallery and rushes down when she sees her brother.*) Philipippin!

PHILIPP ERNST: Diddledumpling! (*Embrace.*) How you've grown!

OTTILIE: How handsome you've grown!

PHILIPP ERNST: Oh, I haven't!

OTTILIE: How divine you look *sans barbe.* Slimmer too.

PHILIPP ERNST: 26 in. waist measurement. Easton will be stunned by my measurements.

OTTILIE: And your hair; crew cut. Show your teeth.

(PHILIPP ERNST *does so.*)

OTTILIE: Marvellous!

PHILIPP ERNST: Now yours?

(OTTILIE *shows them.*)

PHILIPP ERNST: Splendid. Colgate?

OTTILIE: Gibbs' Dentifrice. What have you brought me?

PHILIPP ERNST: Bath salts Morny. Primavera in your bathwater. The Rustle of Spring. You splash about *au dessus de tout.* Also Houbigant's *Mon Délice* and the *Gazette du Bon Ton.*

OTTILIE: (*pirouettes in front of him.*) How do I look on the whole?

PHILIPP ERNST: Comfy. 130 lbs.

OTTILIE: Shame! 126 net.

PHILIPP ERNST: You mean, stripped—i.e. gross. Oh, Diddledumpling, isn't life wonderful. (*He puts his arm around her.*)

OTTILIE: Yours is. Life with father is something else again. I fear, Philipp Ernst, there are serious things in life. Business.

PHILIPP ERNST: Sofie is cut out for that.

OTTILIE: It's something we have power over.

PHILIPP ERNST: O *là là*. I have power over something else.

OTTILIE: Over women?

PHILIPP ERNST: It does me. I'm sorry for you because you can never experience one thing—the full charm of women.

OTTILIE: Lilie Oels is coming. Have you got your eye on her?

PHILIPP ERNST: I never have my eye deliberately on anyone. I'm just always around, *voyons*.

OTTILIE: You have the will, the knack.

PHILIPP ERNST: My little tricks.

OTTILIE: Oh, I wish I knew them! Poor fellow, I think your visit is not going to be so cosy as you hope.

PHILIPP ERNST: How so?

OTTILIE: Father is in a state of indescribable excitement as a result of his enforced leisure.

PHILIPP ERNST: I never under any circumstances expose myself to attacks on my peace of mind.

OTTILIE: It looks as if serious times are almost upon us. There is talk of war.

PHILIPP ERNST: I'm exempt, I'll go to a spa, take a trip round the world, (*Excitedly.*) Unpleasantnesses of whatever kind, no matter where they come from, I decline on principle!

SCENE 7

CHRISTIAN: (*enters.*) Seven trunks—that can only mean my first-born. (*Embrace.*) You've been in London? What news from Hadfield & Co.? Have you seen the electric hoists at Fowlers? These fellows are building up to a capacity of 50,000 h.p.

PHILIPP ERNST: Marvellous!

CHRISTIAN: What happened to your whiskers?

PHILIPP ERNST: Shaved off.

CHRISTIAN: What are they saying about us? Any rumours about our pneumatic wheels? Unbeatable. What about the British balance of payments?

PHILIPP ERNST: Greetings from Alshot, and other assorted English aristocracy.

CHRISTIAN: (*studying him.*) Is this the latest fashion? Now, listen closely! I've talked with your sister: my health is in a bad way.

PHILIPP ERNST: You look fine.

OTTILIE: The specialist was quite pleased today.

CHRISTIAN: Couldn't be worse. Tomorrow you might be faced with dividing up my estate. You are not the heirs of any Tom, Dick or Harry. Your estate consists of fourteen concerns, which constitute a major part of the national economy. Room for all three of you—and your families. I've sown the seeds. You can gather the most heavenly harvests. But till today you have slouched, you especially, Philipp Ernst, in the conviction that I will do all that's necessary for your future. This is done. By legal settlements, binding as far as possible, after my death.

PHILIPP ERNST: Thank God!

CHRISTIAN: But the most cunning legal settlements in the world are nothing against the will of a single-minded person.

PHILIPP ERNST: The law, *cher père.*

(WILHELM *enters.*)

CHRISTIAN: There's always a strictly legal way of fixing things, without ever invoking any law. It's impossible to explain when you have no grasp of the most fundamental concepts. In short, after some time the figure on your fortune won't have changed, but the value of it will, since you are incapable of testing the real value of what you are offered.

PHILIPP ERNST: What average heir ever would be?

CHRISTIAN: That's why it is so easy for other people to live off his money. It's not the few millions one possesses one-self, it's the enormous sums which the public entrusts to a handful of men and which they can use as they will that gives them the incomparable power.

WILHELM: I beg your pardon, Your Excellency!

CHRISTIAN: Without a twinge of feeling, your sister will leave you with nothing but what you stand up in, in record time.

PHILIPP ERNST: Doctor Krey, *cher père*!

CHRISTIAN: (*beside himself.*) Because you are criminally careless with your possessions, and pay more heed to your toe-nails than to your money. Don't try to tell me that nine-tenths of the propertied classes do exactly the same as you. In time you will all be reduced to paupers, and you deserve it. From her point of view it's no sin, logical consequence of her superioority, she makes short shrift of *imbéciles*.

PHILIPP ERNST: Doctor Krey, Papa!

CHRISTIAN: (*to* WILHELM.) Come here! Knock some sense into their heads. The girl is willing. Her life is at a turning-point. One jolt could drive her to decision. (*to* PHILIPP.) I've let you go your own way for a long time. Now I demand some sense. I demand it! You hear! Silence! Luckily for you, in a fit of megalomania our little bird has had the idea of leading me a little dance. I'm game for her, and I'll show her it's all right to take on minors, if need be even equals, but sheer bravado to take on a superior. But if I break her neck just before my demise it is only to your advantage if you know what to do next. So, forwards! (*to* WILHELM) I'm on the move. The outline of the plan is still vague; but I'm beginning to have an inkling of something on a horrific scale. (*Exit.*)

SCENE 8

Silence.

WILHELM: Baron?

PHILIPP ERNST: Dearest Krey, you behold me absolutely shattered.

OTTILIE: What needs to be known, we shall acquaint ourselves with. And what needs to be done.

PHILIPP ERNST: Later, please, not now.

OTTILIE: We have the determination. Come. (*They disappear up the stairs.*)

WILHELM: Such cynicism is the limit. So fraud is legally perpetrated. The nation legally plundered by the handful of men who manage its fortunes? So I was right to start with something practical: using my writings to make the poor aware of the risks their money is exposed to, and once fear for their possessions has roused the people I can make a more fundamental appeal: all the national values of conscience and love are in danger! Never was I so completely free from the influence of your enchanting, abominable attributes—

(OTTILIE *who has followed his words, towards the end hanging over the gallery, climbs the balustrade.*)

WILHELM: What are you doing?
OTTILIE: I'm going to jump!
WILHELM: For Heaven's sake!
OTTILIE: I'm jumping!
WILHELM: Stop! (*He rushes up the steps and grabs her.*)
OTTILIE: (*with a look of triumph.*) Don't hold me so tight!

CURTAIN

ACT II

SCENE 1

The same room. WILHELM *and* FRIEDRICH STADLER *enter.*

FRIEDRICH: First your hand, Wilhelm! My hand on behalf of all of us. Your last letters fanned the embers to flames; the majesty of your concepts conjured up a Fatherland of which till then we were only dimly aware. The fire of your resolution created a national future which had more than mere human appeal; it appealed to us as men!

WILHELM: Friedrich.

FRIEDRICH: You should have seen the vows we made, the tears young men shed; some leapt onto the table, your magic brought forth songs, and it became clear no political mind since time immemorial has been so liberated and liberating.

WILHELM: (*embracing him.*) Friedrich!

FRIEDRICH: Your profile is remarkably like Mirabeau's! To business! Above all my mission: tomorrow our unanimous vote of confidence will make you President of our League. I rushed here headlong with the news.

WILHELM: How is this possible? I've done nothing to merit it.

FRIEDRICH: Nothing? Everything. You found the formula, using the worn-out words of our everyday speech you found the formula to send spheres spinning through space anew, forced youth up on its feet, ready to march shoulder to shoulder with you.

WILHELM: What an enormous responsibility!

FRIEDRICH: Who could bear it but you; who the fame ensuing from it?

WILHELM: I consider myself a member of the rank-and-file ...

FRIEDRICH: Since all opposing factions unite in answer to your call, you are the Leader. This you are by virtue of your national concept, which for the first time brings together all who in this day and age live on German soil and are sworn to oppose the speculations of international finance.—You lanced the abscess of the age, out of the fever clouds of stock market hysteria you led us back purified to the crystal streams of our forests. In the meantime we have done something practical! The most compelling items from your writings have already been circulated to all the universities and technical colleges.

WILHELM: Really?

FRIEDRICH: You are already the great white hope of the younger generation; because of this they are pouring money into the fund for the propagation of your intentions which has been established.

WILHELM: Surprise upon surprise!

FRIEDRICH: I myself donate my own private fortune.

WILHELM: But, Friedrich! That's impossible ...

FRIEDRICH: Giving it up will bind me tighter to our goal.

(WILHELM *embraces him.*)

FRIEDRICH: You see the effect you have.

Brothers, though it cost one's blood, one's all,

Merit must be crowned,

The lying brood must fall.

To be young and not to have to indulge in experiments about your purpose in life, but to see, thanks to the genius of a living hero, a living goal before one's eyes to which one can devote oneself entirely out of the fullness of one's blood, how many generations enjoy that privilege? And we owe it to you! And now, come with me. In view of your new office this summons is the real reason for my presence here on behalf of all of us.

WILHELM: I'll come.

FRIEDRICH: We leave today.

WILHELM: Today! That is—willingly as I would sever my connections with this house I can't just up and leave. I'm free, no-one will try to stop me. It's just that exceptional things are entrusted to me, which just at this moment I alone survey. To hand the whole lot back to the boss ...

FRIEDRICH: How many days?

WILHELM: A week!

FRIEDRICH: Too long for our impatience. I can't stand your being here. My love for you, the appreciation of the unique, exceptional natural force you embody, dangers which the spirit of this house constantly threaten to ...

WILHELM: (*laughs.*) Afraid, when you know not a soul here has the slightest hold over me?

FRIEDRICH: Uneasy. Try to get things tied up today—fix your departure definitely for tomorrow.

WILHELM: I'll try.

FRIEDRICH: In that case I'll stay and we'll leave together. Can you put me up for the night? But in such a way that I am spared the sight of everybody else. Even thinking about the inhabitants of this house I find unbearable.

WILHELM: That can be easily arranged. Come. (*Both exeunt.*)

SCENE 2

OTTILIE: (*enters, goes to the desk, takes a piece of paper from the waste-paper basket and reads.*) 'There is but one topic of the day: property. The rich scream to have their property protected, the poor want the privileges that ensure a life of comfort. Obsessed with material possessions the nation seems incapable of any higher flight'. (*She flings the sheet back into the basket and takes out other scraps of paper and reads.*) 'Decadent pleasures. Corruption. Moral economy. Passionate patriotism. United front against a world up in arms'.

SCENE 3

WILHELM *enters.*

OTTILIE: (*leaving, both meet in the middle of the room.*) Why are you avoiding me!

(WILHELM *looks her straight in the eye.*)

OTTILIE: You're a coward.
WILHELM: Shouldn't you be more careful?
OTTILIE: I don't need to be.
WILHELM: I do.
OTTILIE: Afraid for your job?
WILHELM: For my life.
OTTILIE: Do I do something to you?
WILHELM: No.
OTTILIE: (*points.*) What about up there?
WILHELM: Just pity.
OTTILIE: Nothing more?
WILHELM: Hardly.

217

OTTILIE: That's not true. You're driving me ...
WILHELM: To sensations.

OTTILIE (*exit.*)

SCENE 4

WILHELM: You underestimate the intellect which walks beside you, my good girl. Use me for your whim of the moment, that's what you'd like, meanwhile these splendid lads so full of enthusiasm offer me power over their lives and their initiative. One, whom you still see in a position of subservience, soars far higher than the plane of your existence: by virtue of the incorruptibility of his freely expressed viewpoint he makes an heroically significant impression on his age which for this reason acclaims him as immortal. Immortal—Ottilie! Meanwhile you and your money remain in nameless obscurity. The day will come when I shall repay the impertinence of your puny efforts with the revelation of the *real* line to be drawn between us.

SCENE 5

CHRISTIAN: (*enters.*) You're invisible during the day and in in the evenings. Every chance you get you disappear into your room. What's so pressing? You writing poetry?
WILHELM: I'm writing down my thoughts on international capitalism.
CHRISTIAN: Devastating critique, I presume. If you had any real grasp, you could be a new Beaumarchais for the nation.
WILHELM: Two years at Your Excellency's side ...
CHRISTIAN: If I were more often as communicative as the other day ...
WILHELM: Perhaps your few disclosures suffice for a grasp of fundamentals; from there on it's a case of putting two and two together.

CHRISTIAN: Perhaps. Do you think I'm afraid?

WILHELM: Why afraid, your Excellency?

CHRISTIAN: My boy! The irresistible pen of a master-mind could certainly expo—Never mind. Do your best, light the fuse under the powder-keg. If a new régime arises I'm ready to start from scratch. Corporal or General—as long as I'm right in the thick of it.

WILHELM: Would Your Excellency's magnanimity extend to giving me a few hints where I fail to do justice to the problem on this or that point?

CHRISTIAN: (pinches his ear.) That is up to you, friend. Show me the draft. If it is unsatisfactory, which is what I expect, never. Anybody guilty of mere breach of the peace deserves to be lynched. If I see a genius is about to appear on the scene —what better should I do than associate myself with him right from the start?

WILHELM: I knew it. That alone ultimately made it possible for me to stay any length of time in this house.

CHRISTIAN: Getting a bit ambitious again? Career?

WILHELM: In view of unforeseen events of some importance I should like Your Excellency to accept my resignation immediately.

CHRISTIAN: Ours is a gentleman's agreement—you are free at any time. Although in view of the particular business in hand just at the moment you would be sadly missed. Sadly. In three or four days it would be all over. On my day of glory I could release you into, what we hope will be, a life of glory. Can't you be tempted, aren't you superstitious? Then do it as a favour for me.

WILHELM: I shouldn't like to be ungrateful.

CHRISTIAN: And witness a situation which you won't forget for the rest of your life. Only three more days. Is it a deal?

WILHELM: Your Excellency, may I leave it till this evening to submit my decision, which does not depend on me alone?

CHRISTIAN: How do you get along with my son?

WILHELM: It is very difficult to get close to Baron Philipp Ernst.

CHRISTIAN: This is another point where I'd like results from you. So—I can still depend on you for a short spell. Yesterday evening it was too late to get hold of our little red-headed rabbit. Can't expect her and her husband to appear before eleven o'clock this morning. Time to take the waters as prescribed, unless I decide not ...

WILHELM: Dr. Brunner, your personal physician, left strictest instructions.

CHRISTIAN: In the letter to Witman add this—what was the last paragraph?

WILHELM: (reads from the letter.) 'In particular His Excellency's name should be stressed in conversation with employees at all levels from the office boy to members of the board. All those who indicate by word or gesture that they do not share the conviction that now as always every decision rests with His Excellency are to be reported. For his imminent seventieth birthday His Excellency would welcome the most emphatic manifestation of this awareness.'

CHRISTIAN: 'Of this awareness. For the rest, as soon as his recovery is complete, which can only be a matter of a few days, he will come roaring back like a ...'

WILHELM: Wouldn't Your Excellency be well advised to practice a little moderation in the next few days?

CHRISTIAN: In the next few days I must win my Waterloo or give up the ghost. Take this down—'come roaring back like a hurricane through the Sodom and Gomorrah into which he has gained insight during his illness'. See that the Countess has a copy right away, in time for lunch. The opening bars of our altercations have just been played.

(BUTLER enters and reports something to CHRISTIAN.)

CHRISTIAN: Here already? I'm coming.

(BUTLER exit.)

WILHELM: Your Excellency changes colour. What is it?

CHRISTIAN: Haven't you noticed anything about the same time these last few days? I told you: just three more times twenty-four hours. And even if she had the devil for an ally, I've got God Almighty Himself flashing His lightning behind the scenes. (Exit.)

WILHELM: Now, what does that mean?

(MAID SERVANT *enters, gives* WILHELM *a letter. Exit.*)

WILHELM: Who's this? (*Opens the letter.*) From her! Why, it's a declaration of love! How can she be so brazen? I repulsed her unequivocally and she comes back fearlessly and humbles herself. What extraordinary behaviour. A trick? But there are other ways of luring me, she doesn't need to lay herself wide open with a letter. Whatever happens: from now on these lines are in my possession for all eventualities. (*He reads.*) 'For a long time I have been aware of what I owe you, the uplift of your mere presence; but only now today do I stand free of all extraneous influences, filled with the irresistible desire to be enlightened by you about myself and life'. Is it possible? No whim? No trick? (*He thinks it over.*) No. A genuine, passionate decision. Where is she?

SCENE 6

COUNTESS SOFIE *and* COUNT OTTO *von* BEESKOW *enter dressed in jodhpurs.*

SOFIE: Have you any idea who is with my father, Krey?
WILHELM: None, Countess.
SOFIE: You don't know either? He's not well. His physician, Dr. Brunner, complains particularly that in spite of everything he will not rest. Shouldn't it be your duty to strain every nerve to make him?
WILHELM: The Countess knows His Excellency's temperament.
OTTO: How true.
WILHELM: Countess, His Excellency has instructed me to see that you receive a copy of this letter to Mr. Witman.
SOFIE: Business communications go to the Count.
WILHELM: Where should the document be delivered?
OTTO: Give it to me at lunch. No business in the forenoon.
WILHELM: Gladly. Will you excuse me? (*Exit.*)

SOFIE: How the house has changed.

OTTO: The old man at death's door.

SOFIE: I wonder who is with him?

OTTO: You coming riding or not?

SOFIE: Where is Ottilie hiding?

OTTO: Cheerio, then!

SOFIE: A couple of minutes, Otto. How he dragged his feet about the garden—who would have expected the collapse to come so quickly!

OTTO: Seventy is a ripe old age. He has had your superiority too long on his mind.

SOFIE: Anticipating the facts again.

OTTO: A blind man can see he's finished.

SOFIE: If he really feels he's finished he'll be determined to go to any lengths against us, once he has found the most effecttive point of attack: he knows our prestige in the eyes of the firm and the world is closely tied up with the implementation of the Dutch deal, and we are totally identified with it. So he will do everything in his power to sabotage it.

OTTO: Too late. You know how decisive your trick was in The Hague.

SOFIE: The way he is, he cannot let us get away with that triumph, he's stuffed to the gills with rage at me. A nature like his, which is so self-obsessed, cannot stand anything significant alongside itself and *coûte que coûte*, will crush us. The approaching end will give him ten times his normal strength.

OTTO: You're seeing ghosts. A decrepit old ...

SOFIE: When will you begin to have an inkling of the power of the blood in this family? We go right into a thing tooth and claw and stand or fall with it inextricably.

OTTO: Mad lot. *Parvenus*, when you get right down to it.

SOFIE: Fresh blood full of new life, when you get right down to it.

OTTO: Settle your differences among yourselves and don't go too far.

SOFIE: This time there'll be no quarter, for after this it's curtains. If you're scared take a trip. I must have my hands completely free.

OTTO: I want you to keep out of it, understand?

SOFIE: It's all for you, Otto, for your prestige, your position after he's gone. Your striking success and his ignominious exit must be seen to coincide. If he dies leaving you behind defeated by his brilliance, you will be an empty husk walking in his shadow for the rest of your days.

OTTO: We really did start something.

SOFIE: And you want to admit defeat when victory is so near?

OTTO: All right. Up and at him. But keep cool!

SOFIE: The two children need to be given a warning. We know that he has pumped some courage into them by legally binding arrangements for after his death. So we must make them realise the kind of people they're dealing with. I'm not worried about Philipp Ernst.

OTTO: The watch-chain I brought will paralyse him. A simple string from the button-hole to the watch will send him into fits of rapture for a long time to come.

SOFIE: That character always creeping around here has his eye on Ottilie.

OTTO: Great Scot, what gives you that idea.

SOFIE: Would be a miracle if he hadn't. Educated paupers like him are always secretly dying to climb into our league.

OTTO: And she is just a blank cartridge.

SOFIE: She's a babe in arms dazzled by some crazy appeal the fellow has.

OTTO: So he is included for incidental elimination.

SOFIE: You see to the children and give me a clear field.

OTTO: What do I do about Ottilie?

SOFIE: Oels.

OTTO: Pair them off?

SOFIE: For a start. He is stupid. Give him a few pointers.

OTTO: I'll put him in the picture.

SOFIE: Who on earth can be with him?

OTTO: You've got me worried.

SOFIE: I'm sure that's the key. Forget about riding, keep him under observation.

OTTO: Then there's this damned seventieth birthday into the bargain, which he will certainly exploit for a celebration.

SOFIE: For an overwhelming demonstration if he has his way. You will immediately dash off a letter to Witman to the effect that the old man forbids any mention of it in view of his state of health. The press must also be instructed.

OTTO: You're on fire. Don't let yourself get carried away.

SOFIE: All the way, to keep up with him.

OTTO: He will use every weapon.

SOFIE: I'll outflank him by saying I'm pregnant.

OTTO: That'll really make him mad.

SOFIE: (*round his neck.*) I'm mad as it is. At least mad enough to worship you.

OTTO: (*kisses her.*) My pet.

SOFIE: (*in total surrender.*) My Jesus!

SCENE 8

CHRISTIAN: (*enters.*) Greetings, my dears! (*Embrace.*) Charming of you to come. Everything alright? Sofie looks dazzling. No news? When I'm going to be a grandfather, I mean. (*He laughs.*) Plenty of time. Our muscle-man—(*He pats* OTTO *on the shoulder.*) will attend to that. Seen the children?

SOFIE: How are you, father?

CHRISTIAN: Great, weigh four pounds more than I did a month ago, just starting to live.

SOFIE: That's wonderful.

CHRISTIAN: Yes, isn't it wonderful? Why aren't you two off riding?

SOFIE: We're looking for the brats.

OTTO: Has Prince Oels said hullo yet?

CHRISTIAN: He's running around the garden with Ottilie. Why didn't the Princess come?

OTTO: Coming the day after tomorrow.

CHRISTIAN: Want to show you my new stallion. By Hannibal out of Mistral.

OTTO: Hannibal never mated with Mistral.

CHRISTIAN: What am I saying—Minehaha.

OTTO: That's different.

CHRISTIAN: Fighting cock, our Otto. Always proper. (*Exeunt.*)

SCENE 9

PHILIPP ERNST *and* PRINCE OELS *and* BUTLER *enter.*

PHILIPP ERNST: We can't go up to my room. One of the bath taps wasn't working and now the whole apartment is under water. (*to the* BUTLER.) Ask the gentleman to step this way.

(BUTLER *exit.*)

OELS: You have your tailor come all the way from London?

PHILIPP ERNST: For Heaven's sake, *petit prince*, don't say tailor. Easton will go off his head, if he hears you. He is a gentleman. Works in Germany for a *clientèle* of two. Prince Taxis and myself.

OELS: I'd like to try on a morning coat. This jacket is ghastly.

PHILIPP ERNST: Easton is very tactful, he won't notice the— thing.

OELS: It's the best there is in Berlin.

PHILIPP ERNST: Having suits made in Berlin—one might just as well have oneself fitted with a ring through one's nose.

OELS: As an officer ...

PHILIPP ERNST: Don't say that word in front of Easton. For him you're a gentleman or you don't exist at all.

OELS: My heart is going pit-a-pat.

PHILIPP ERNST: So it should.

OELS: How does one talk with him?

PHILIPP ERNST: Correct social behaviour is to avoid any sug- gestion whatsoever of intellectual leanings. Needless to say, he oozes social graces and *savoir-faire*.

225

P

SCENE 10

BUTLER *ushers in* MR. EASTON *and places two elegant leather cases beside him. Exit.*

PHILIPP ERNST: *Guten Morgen,* Mr. Easton.

EASTON: *Guten Morgen,* Sir, how do you do?

PHILIPP ERNST: (*introduces.*) Prince Oels.

EASTON: *Guten Morgen,* Sir.

PHILIPP ERNST: But we must speak English. Easton babbles English divinely. Now show us your surprises.

EASTON: May I show some *caleçons?* Underpants, Siamese design, *dernier cri?*

PHILIPP ERNST: Later. Above all, have you got the new *redingote?*

EASTON: Certainly, sir, and the *gilet.*

PHILIPP ERNST: (*to* OELS.) *Gris perle.* Any other *couleur* is criminal.

(EASTON *helps* PHILIPP ERNST *into waistcoat and jacket.*)

OELS: Enchanting. Absolutely first-class.

PHILIPP ERNST: (*to* EASTON.) Just a touch higher and closer to the collar.

EASTON: (*marks.*) Certainly.

PHILIPP ERNST: I'm revamping the *redingote.* Gentlemen, there has been an attempt in recent years to make us adopt a substitute ...

OELS: The so-called tail-coat.

PHILIPP ERNST: From which Heaven protect us.

SCENE 11

OTTO: (*enters.*) *Guten Morgen,* Philipp Ernst. Morning Mr. Easton.

EASTON: Morning, sir.

OTTO: Gorgeous coat!

(BUTLER *enters*.)

PHILIPP ERNST: Whisky, soda!

(BUTLER *exit*.)

PHILIPP ERNST: The characteristic feature of the age of democracy is the short coat which one can observe in the sports jacket, for example, or the dinner jacket. Hence the morning-coat is the only thing that distinguishes the *homme du monde*. For it must be worn properly. None but the svelte, athletic gentleman shows off its cut to good effect.

OTTO: Hear, hear!

PHILIPP ERNST: (*to* EASTON.) Drop the shoulders a fraction.

(EASTON *marks*.)

PHILIPP ERNST: When the picture is completed with waistcoat in *gris perle*, tie in the same colour, and top hat, it deserves the title 'Royal Coat of the Male'.

OELS: Proof.

PHILIPP ERNST: A tail coat at close quarters will make in six hours a conquest that would take a sports jacket two days.

OELS: Prove it!

PHILIPP ERNST: Bets?

OELS: Who, where?

PHILIPP ERNST: A kingdom for a woman!

OELS: My sister the day after tomorrow.

OTTO: (*hums*.) 'Toreador', etc.

PHILIPP ERNST: The proof will be absolutely conclusive.

(BUTLER *brings whisky and syphon of soda. Exit.*)

EASTON: All right, sir.

(PHILIPP ERNST *takes off coat and waistcoat.*)

OELS: May I try it on? (*Puts on waistcoat and coat.*)

SCENE 12

OTTILIE *appears above on the gallery and stands hidden behind a pillar.*

OTTO: That has a certain *cachet*.

PHILIPP ERNST: Great Scot, *petit prince*. Beau Brummel! (*Kisses him on the brow.*) Irresistible.

EASTON: Beautiful.

PHILIPP ERNST: If you had presented yourself to Ottilie in this royal coat instead of appearing dressed as a Tyrolean peasant your most secret wish would have met with fulfilment.

OELS: D'you really think so?

PHILIPP ERNST: Look at yourself in the mirror! The girl could not fail to be enraptured. *Petit prince*, what a divine thorax you have!

OTTO: You look enchanting.

PHILIPP ERNST: With your complexion *je pourrais m'imaginer le gilet en ecossais gris mauve*. Divine!

EASTON: Indeed.

OELS: I'll give anything—you must let me have the coat!

PHILIPP ERNST: Hardly, *petit prince*, *voyons*.

OELS: I must have it, my life depends on it. Gentlemen, support my claim.

PHILIPP ERNST: Should we help?

OTTO: All for one.

PHILIPP ERNST: *Bon*. Now then, Easton, out with your rarest treasures. The quarry is a woman! What have you got? (*He plunges into the cases and scatters on the floor.*) Neckties, shirts, *bretelles*, handkerchiefs, socks. There we are, *petit prince*, *jaune indien* and pumps to match. When you cross your legs always allow just one hand's breadth of sock to be seen. A dozen, Easton, and this *robe de chambre*. *Robe de chambre* reminds me—not so long ago we were all wearing pyjamas like gypsy barons or sleeping-car attendants. How ghastly!

EASTON: Would you like to look at another model *avec le col Robespierre et des manches pagodes*?

PHILIPP ERNST: Try it on!

OTTO: Out with it!

PHILIPP ERNST: Slip your pants off!

(*All are busy with* OELS *and dress him in the pyjama suit.*)

WILHELM *has appeared on the gallery and stays there without noticing* OTTILIE *or being noticed by her or the others.*

PHILIPP ERNST: Apollo Belvedere! Just a touch of *Houbigant* and let's see you walk.

(OELS *walks about the room.*)

EASTON: Splendid, sir.

OTTO: Lucky girl!

PHILIPP ERNST: She'll flop at your feet like a poodle. You're a beauty, Hartwig!

EASTON: Indeed.

PHILIPP ERNST: Brother-in-law! Welcome to the family!

OTTO: No trouble at all!

OELS: With force, if need be!

OTTO *and* PHILIPP ERNST: Bravo!

EASTON: Indeed.

OTTILIE: (*standing in the middle of the stairs above them.*) Bravissimo! (*She storms down the steps into their midst.*)

PHILIPP ERNST: Surprise attack! *Sauve qui peut!*

(OELS *has fled behind a chair.*)

OTTILIE: Gentlemen, take me as one of your own. What was the password?

OTTO: Oels!

OTTILIE: Oels! *Voilà.* Tataratata!

PHILIPP ERNST: Out you come, my little prince! She is one of us all the way. (*He pulls him out; to* OTTILIE.) What does the connoisseur say to this apparition?

OTTILIE: Absolutely spiffing.

PHILIPP ERNST: What a figure! Such harmony, such immaculate masculinity. Can you imagine anything more handsome?

OTTILIE: Have you nothing for me, Easton?

EASTON: Certainly, *mademoiselle.*

PHILIPP ERNST: How do you fancy these? (*Lifts up a pair of panties.*) Siamese embroidery. (*He takes a pair of full-length stockings and holds them against* OTTILIE.) How about this for my diddledumpling?

EASTON: (*extracts a large shawl embroidered with silk flowers.*) Voilà!

(*All gather round it with exclamations of admiration. Then* PHILIPP ERNST *drapes it round his sister.*)

PHILIPP ERNST: And now: La Furlana! Avanti! (*Mouths the music of the dance.*) Partners, Princey! (OTTILIE *and* OELS *dance the Furlana extremely gracefully, the others joining in with music and shouts.*)

OTTO: (*at the window.*) The old man!

OTTILIE: Ooh! ooh!

(*All scatter head over heels.* OTTILIE *takes* OELS *by the hand and disappears with him,* EASTON *has stuffed everything into his cases, with* PHILIPP ERNST *helping him. Then the cases are kicked under the sofa and both exeunt.* OTTO *is the last to leave.*)

OTTO: No danger from these two. They're both harmless.

SCENE 14

The scene remains empty for a few minutes.

WILHELM: (*above.*) Shameless hussy! (*He comes down the steps quickly, takes* OTTILIE's *letter from his pocket, tears it up and throws the pieces into the waste paper basket.*) All lies and deceit of your class, depravity now as always. Snippets of seven or eight foreign languages, grimaces of unbridled licentiousness; all for the sensation of the moment. Leaving me the little secretary in the dark suit! (*He sees a pair of panties on the ground, lifts them up a little with the point of his shoe, and immediately kicks them aside.*) And her haughty glance falls on my clothes and clumsy footwear. Not in silken raiment, as other men, does the apostle go; but he it is who shall cause the springs of the land to flow again, set life free from your stupid ecstasies. Beware! This was the deciding moment. Almighty God, you have given me a visible sign which I interpret aright and leave this house this very day.

SCENE 15

OTTILIE: (*enters; she is still wearing the white shawl.*) I must say a few words by way of explanation.

WILHELM: What I saw with my own eyes from up there says more than enough.

OTTILIE: My little joke with the boys.

WILHELM: Once and for all I shall have nothing to do with such jokes, with this sort of world.

OTTILIE: I beg of you!

WILHELM: Let me pass!

(OTTILIE *steps to one side.*)

WILHELM: (*furious.*) What do you want with me?

OTTILIE: If somebody asks you for enlightenment, aren't you obliged to give it?

WILHELM: To you least of all.

OTTILIE: I've done nothing to deserve such severity. If I was sometimes a bit forward it was from embarrassment. I can't talk to you simply. Because I revere you, I am embarrassed.

(WILHELM *goes to the door.*)

OTTILIE: I know you have a goal high above that of other men.

WILHELM: And I know: you are the smooth type found in your circles, you do not differ from them in any way.

OTTILIE: That used to be true. Since I know of your great plans, however ...

WILHELM: You? (*laughs*) of my—

OTTILIE: Since I have seen you rouse in us a wave of patriotic feeling, since I know the range of your ideas—regarding the reawakened German of our day and how you are revered by ...

231

WILHELM: But how do you come by such . . .?

OTTILIE: For instance, that in order to arrive at some form of moral economy, we should not every time before we strike a match—is this expenditure really necessary?

WILHELM: How can you know this?

OTTILIE: We should aim at real values instead of the production of trash. Have I understood correctly?

WILHELM: How is this possible?

OTTILIE: One who produces miracles wants miracles everywhere. You shall receive this proof from a girl's enthusiasm. I feel myself close to binding decisions; please believe in my fidelity just a few more days till the decisive deed. (*Before he can stop it, she has bent over his hand, kissed it and left the room.*)

WILHELM: What a victory, what a great moral victory in the middle of the enemy's camp. (*He runs up the steps.*) I'm coming, Friedrich! Quick, this is the moment to pen the fiery address to our friends for tomorrow. A truly national document. (*Looks at himself in the mirror.*) Mirabeau! Why not!

ACT III

SCENE 1

The same room.

Before the beginning of the act the Eichendorff-Schumann 'Mondnacht' sung by OTTILIE *to a piano accompaniment can be heard through the closed curtain.*

'It was as if heaven
Had softly kissed the earth,
So that earth with its shining blossoms,
Must dream only of heaven'.

'The breeze passed through the fields
The corn swayed gently
The woods rustled softly
The night was bright with stars'.

232

The curtain goes up. The local CLERGYMAN *is at the piano playing the accompaniment.* OTTILIE *is singing;* CHRISTIAN, WILHELM, PHILIPP ERNST, OELS, OTTO *and* SOFIE *provide the audience in the room.*

OTTILIE:

'And my soul spread
Wide its wings
And flew through the silent land
As if it were flying home.'

CHRISTIAN: Divine composer, Schumann!

CLERGYMAN: Great poet, Eichendorff!

CHRISTIAN: Especially: And my soul . . . (*Hums the next bit.*)

OTTILIE: (*looking at* WILHELM, *hums.*) As if it were flying homewards.

CLERGYMAN: Mendelssohn, Schubert, Schumann—an evening filled with delights. But it is terribly late. I must bid you goodnight, Your Excellency.

CHRISTIAN: (*accompanies him to the rear.*) Good-night and many thanks for everything.

CLERGYMAN: A pleasure, Your Excellency. (*Exit.*)

PHILIPP ERNST: (*to* OELS.) Is your sister coming soon? ... What a bore, all this music. A waste of my new coat.

OELS: Ottilie was not favourably disposed today. Do you still believe in my chances?

PHILIPP ERNST: You have two gentlemen's guarantees. Pity about the coat.

OELS: (*points to* WILHELM.) Who is the black—thing?

PHILIPP ERNST: Secretary.

OELS: A *peu près domestique?*

PHILIPP ERNST: *Je ne suis pas sûr.*

OTTILIE: You look wretched, Father.

CHRISTIAN: What were you so excited about all day?

OTTILIE: My mind is made up about you know what.

CHRISTIAN: Against her?

OTTILIE: I shall not be the underdog.

CHRISTIAN: Bravo! (*to* WILHELM.) My first batch of telegrams has produced a considerable reaction at The Hague. But today's the day for the bomb to go off there, who knows maybe right at this very moment.

SOFIE: (to OTTO.) I'm uneasy. The deal should have gone through by this time. Something's wrong at The Hague.

OTTO: What a mummy! Looks as if he'll drop down dead in a heap any minute.

SOFIE: I'm terribly uneasy.

CHRISTIAN: (to SOFIE.) *Tu as ton beau jour.* We must have a little chat afterwards.

SOFIE: Gladly. (to OTTO.) This is it. Leave me alone with him later.

OTTO: Remember! Self-control!

SOFIE: God help me!

PHILIPP ERNST: You've got me all confused about Father, it can't really be so serious.

SOFIE: One must be prepared for any eventuality. In the event ...

PHILIPP ERNST: Of an accident ... (*Mops his brow.*) No calculations, please.

SOFIE: It's all agreed: you leave us your share in mortgage form, which guarantees you an income at an interest rate of four per cent.

PHILIPP ERNST: What does that mean for me?

SOFIE: At least five times as much as you get at present.

PHILIPP ERNST: *Charmant.* And no net and gross?

SOFIE: All payable in advance.

PHILIPP ERNST: *Charmant.*

OTTO: (*joins them.*) Absolutely fantastic: know what he was going to wear for a watch-chain—a piece of string.

PHILIPP ERNST: String? How d'you mean?

OELS: For a watch-chain?

SOFIE: Who?

OTTO: Our late friend Siekermann.

PHILIPP ERNST: Smart fellow.

CHRISTIAN: (*who is sitting at the back with* OTTILIE *and* WILHELM.) What are you up to with Philipp Ernst?

OTTO: We're talking about a watch-chain.

PHILIPP ERNST: But how d'you mean, string?

OTTO: Two platinum fasteners, one at each end—between them a simple string was to stretch from the watch pocket to the button hole. Siekermann's death brought the realisation to nought.

PHILIPP ERNST: String?

OTTO: With a dress-coat.

PHILIPP ERNST: The devil!

OELS: *C'est épatant.*

PHILIPP ERNST: Otto, promise me, Sofie and I have had a chat and—in short I have waived certain claims.

SOFIE: Please!

PHILIPP ERNST: I know: no calculations. Still—as a quid pro quo: don't mention the string to anybody else. Oels, this is mine! I let you have the *redingote,* and I'll fix Ottilie for you once and for all. She hasn't a chance.

SOFIE: (*to* OELS.) You have intentions, Prince?

OELS: May I count on your support, Countess?

SOFIE: We'll see.

PHILIPP ERNST: Let me have the string, you lot. Agreed? And seriously: mum's the word to everybody. I'll be eternally grateful. (*He shakes hands with each of them individually and goes to the back.*) Whatever will Easton say?

CHRISTIAN: When a system has reached its peak there is always the possibility of change.

WILHELM: Your Excellency sees things historically. Materialistic ages are followed by idealistic ones. Satiation . . .

CHRISTIAN: . . . demands variation.

WILHELM: But I maintain: Germany's better, spiritual part is filled with such boundless hatred for the tyranny of money and the power which follows from its use that it can only be pacified by the extermination of the principle.

SOFIE: A purely theoretical demand.

WILHELM: Theory will do for a start.

SOFIE: Who will reduce it to a sufficiently significant formula? Whose voice raised in moral indictment will be so penetrating as to be heard by all?

CHRISTIAN: That is the crux of the matter. If the people were once to follow a resounding cry—who knows? But where is the brain, *the* self-awareness, and *the* conscience.

WILHELM: They'll be there when the time comes, just as what's needed always has appeared at the right time.

OTTILIE: Definitely. (*Exchanges a glance with* WILHELM.)

SOFIE: Other way round. Once the man is there the age follows.

CHRISTIAN: Krey has a feeling he is not far off.

WILHELM: There is every likelihood.

SOFIE: And then?

WILHELM: No quarter, Countess.

SOFIE: (*laughs.*) A la guerre comme à la guerre.

WILHELM: Tabula rasa.

SOFIE: Messiahs and sermons don't scare us. What's needed is ...

WILHELM: (*strongly.*) Fire and brimstone! We're agreed, Countess. (*He gets up.*)

CHRISTIAN: (*laughs.*) The devil!

SOFIE: Il est fou.

PHILIPP ERNST: War?

CHRISTIAN: Revolution, Philipp Ernst.

PHILIPP ERNST: I'll retreat to a spa. (To OELS.) All this talk of war and so on. Hope nothing happens before my watch-chain ... ça c'était bête. I'm going to bed. Goodnight all.

CHRISTIAN: (*to* WILHELM.) As you see it, Germany's sunk pretty low, poor chap.

WILHELM: Doesn't need much for it to surge up again!

CHRISTIAN: (*to* WILHELM.) Go now. Tomorrow I need you early, as you're only willing to stay another forty-eight hours.

(WILHELM *bows; exit.*)

PHILIPP ERNST *and* OELS (*exeunt.*)

CHRISTIAN: (*to* OTTILIE) He takes it damned seriously—that fellow!

OTTILIE: So he ought.

CHRISTIAN: You are in love?

OTTILIE: Perhaps, father. The tide caught me and I'm being carried along.

CHRISTIAN: Engine ticking over? Then plunge into life! You've got your wings, child. Say farewell to the old ways. You'll get there, wherever it is, with or without him; what's the difference, as long as you can fly? Bye-bye, bye-bye!

OTTILIE: Good night, sleep well, father. (*Embrace, exit.*)

CHRISTIAN: You too, Otto—going up so soon?

OTTO: If you will excuse me, Your Excellency! (*Exit.*)

CHRISTIAN: Fighting cock, our Otto. Always on the ball.

(*All lights are out except for one lamp.*)

SCENE 2

SOFIE: Why do you encourage that loafer's platonic drivel?

CHRISTIAN: Krey puts some life into it, he has the kind of drive which has always made me feel good.

SOFIE: He doesn't look the kind of man to shake nations to the core.

CHRISTIAN: He has some very worthwhile ideas. And he's very near to hitting the bull's eye—it's not only the bones of the masses that are filled with dread, even the initiated quake at the roaring from the mountains of gold amassed over our heads, which now threaten to engulf us. How would you react to a consumer's strike?

SOFIE: Caused by what?

CHRISTIAN: By moral demand. Suppose every consumer saved on something small, just one shoe-lace, one nail, one piece of paper ...

SOFIE: Why should he when production costs get cheaper and cheaper?

CHRISTIAN: Because he's sick of the mass-produced rubbish we impose on him, because maybe he'd like to get his hands on something decent again, because the mass consumption of all the goods in his daily life has brainwashed him till he is not aware of any individual value in anything and he consumes and discards feelings, judgments and even himself just like everything else and is incapable of imparting any quality to them. Because in the end the whole trend sickens him to the

237

depths of his soul. I've told you time and again, as well as the frantic pursuit of methods for doubling and trebling the production of certain articles you should also have all factories and laboratories working on means to improve quality.

SOFIE: It is impossible to operate with two conflicting principles. We stress standardisation, made for masses, not made to measure.

CHRISTIAN: Exactly, you fools. In the glass factories the light bulb of inferior glass stamped out in tens of millions triumphs while the quality of the microscopes is abominable. I have always resisted this trend.

SOFIE: On the contrary, such ideas are quite new for you; perhaps the fruits of Krey's teaching already, and the first stirrings of anxiety. Who was it who amassed capital, increasingly formed monopolies and mergers? Who was it who again and again conjured millions out of his imagination and vision, which now have to show dividends. Where from, for heaven's sake? Our generation took over the manufacturing state from you ready-made and totally rejects any responsibility for having created it. You bequeathed us every recipe together with the main ingredient of every recipe: namely, total lack of scruples. We expand just as you did, only with more foresight and business acumen, without, it is true, knowing what it is all leading to.

CHRISTIAN: What about an unsuccessful war?

SOFIE: We'll see. I'm not afraid.

CHRISTIAN: *Après nous le déluge!* We are ripe. If only our little friend knew as much as we do.

SOFIE: All the world ever needs to save it is never very much. Incidentally such sentiments from you are really astonishing.

CHRISTIAN: I've never entirely lost them. What better can one have in place of feelings?

SOFIE: Will power.

CHRISTIAN: Has it stood the iron test? I started in a small way, my parents had three rooms, a maid, and a canary. At first I sneaked, pushed and copied; I was an adventurer and a snob. Got there in the end, with no preconceived ideas left. Only things salvaged were a few sentiments.

SOFIE: One might get the impression things were going badly for you.

CHRISTIAN: Things are going badly. I'm balancing my books and feel possessed more by general human emotions than by personal ones. I feel: if only someone or other would succeed in destroying brick by brick the structure we created.

SOFIE: That is bankruptcy. Same thing happens to firms that go bust—with your permission I personally will quite emphatically withdraw my business from you.

CHRISTIAN: You have quite emphatically already done so. But what I just confided to you is a family secret, more like a message from the Beyond. As far as my earthly existence is concerned, I demand for reasons of prestige that in future you pay more attention to the orders of the boss of our organisation than you have done recently.

SOFIE: It is impossible to make great decisions as accurately from the sick-room, as one can at the focal point of affairs.

CHRISTIAN: That focal point is still here! (*Points to his forehead.*) Where the tiniest cog of the minutest machine was first conceived and set in motion. I appointed you my accountant.

SOFIE: Like you, I too now have insight into the remotest cog in the economic machine. I have demonstrated that my apprenticeship days are over.

CHRISTIAN: You mean your issues of shares for a project that will not be operational for another five years?

SOFIE: What's unusual about that?

CHRISTIAN: It's stupid, because it's so criminal even the stupidest fool can see through it and whoever started it is bound to be a laughing stock for life.

SOFIE: (*hands him a telegram.*) The share capital is oversubscribed.

CHRISTIAN: 150 million. Interest to be received in five years 40 million marks profit. Liabilities?

SOFIE: The board has the right to pay the shareholders a dividend of four per cent.

CHRISTIAN: (*laughs out loud.*) Has the right—that's wonderful!

SOFIE: The formulation is mine. The only thing is—the share-holders have no right to demand it. (*Laughs.*)

CHRISTIAN: If only Krey could see with my eyes the tragic aspect of such behaviour for the world—and the humour of it.

SOFIE: These characters who find fault with our systems—what can they offer to compare with such inventions?

CHRISTIAN: Only a pure heart at most. What a laugh! All right, well done. I like the 40 stolen millions. You are the *canaille* I took you for.

SOFIE: Thank you.

CHRISTIAN: Your brainwaves are small scale compared with mine, but we'll let that pass. But where do you get the nerve to countermand my orders?

SOFIE: In the matter of the arms delivery it seemed to me, and to others, my policy was superior.

CHRISTIAN: What seemed to you— (*Shouts.*) What right have you to undermine my subordinates' faith in my infallibility?

SOFIE: I must reinforce their faith in mine, or rather that of my husband.

CHRISTIAN: That gelding!

SOFIE: I'm pregnant!

CHRISTIAN: You lie!

SOFIE: May God be my witness!

CHRISTIAN: A Beeskow brood to foul my nest? That can't possibly be the will of heaven as my reward! Rob my son and Ottilie of their inheritance, would you, and dictate wisdom from my chair using my authority, would you, my little dove? Right, you'll see the fiery opposition of my will to stop your maneuvres.

SOFIE: The Dutch Government accepts our offer.

CHRISTIAN: Accepts it? Have we got the contract? All right, little girl, out with the telegram confirming it! Why do you hesitate?

SOFIE: It should be here any minute.

CHRISTIAN: Should it! Why? Because we've come up with a bobby dazzler. Long live Calvin, long live the Reformation! Divine! But how does Daddy counter that all of a sudden?

God damn it, what does old *hors de combat* Daddio do then?

(*He does a few entrechats.*)

SOFIE: Control yourself!

CHRISTIAN: May the seed rot in your womb! What does this genius, (*Seizes her by the arms and pulls her close*) this genuine genius of a Maske father do? What master stroke does the magnificent old bird come up with in the end and flatten the gelding brood and their crafty scheme. (*He spins around hopping on one foot.*) Haven't you seen—he—

(SOFIE *has run out.*)

CHRISTIAN: Where are you, I want to enjoy my triumph, see you smashed! (*He staggers out after her in a frenzy.*)

SCENE 3

WILHELM: (*appears on the gallery. He is wearing an old overcoat over grey drawers. He peers over the railing and finding the room empty he comes down. He speaks to someone above.*) I just want to fetch my papers. (*Takes a bundle of papers out of the desk.*) That's all there is. How happy the dear fellow is that I'm coming with him right away just like that. But who could resist his entreaties any longer. (*He goes back to the stairs humming.*) 'And my soul spread wide its wings ...' At the same time I'm doing something for the girl's imagination. The inflexibility of her moral will is still not to be trusted. That's why my flight tonight is bound to imprint a certain image of me on her memory. (*He has stepped to the window; looks up and out.*) Farewell! For I realise better than you what an abyss separates us, and so I depart. Because I know you must fill the social gulf between us with unquenchable longing. But first, pride will haul you back one thousand times into yourself and your own sphere, again and again irresistible longing for the Unknown, the Strange, must first conquer concepts etched on your brain. Just as you yourself move only in the most well-bred manner, wear only silks and

241

Q

lace, of the kind you are now taking off—there! Her shadow! Sleep well, Ottilie—sweet dreams!—So you too have your cast-iron concept of male appearance, male apparel and naturally anything different appears incomprehensible, painful, ridiculous to you. (*He has come nearer the sofa and Easton's cases and kicks out one of them with his toe.*) As if it were in any way to one's credit to wear such frippery if one has the means. No credit, to her mind it's not just to one's credit, it's essential. (*He has lifted up a gaily coloured, very elegant pyjama suit consisting of very loose trousers and a jacket like a waistcoat with sleeves.*) This is more like it in your eyes. This is how you'd expect to see me in leisure wear. In your wildest dreams, even when I appear as the loftiest of heroes, your Parcival purest of fools, it's in trousers like these, (*laughing he has pulled on the trousers,*) in a jacket like this. (*He puts it on.*) That's how you see me in your mind's eye. All it needs is the watch and chain and the turban, only then is the proper image of the real man complete, quite apart from any consideration of inner qualities. (*In front of the mirror.*) Not that it's all that bad ... (*Hums.*) 'My soul spread wide its wings ...' One is immediately set apart from the broad mass of the hoi-poloi.—Shoot the cuffs; really, with all this and the appropriate *savoir faire* one could feel more at ease when confronting the very circles one is fighting to the death. Show just a corner of handkerchief ...

SCENE 4

CHRISTIAN: (*rushes in.*) She's nowhere to be found. Denying me my last pleasure. Where is she? Who's that? Come here all of you and listen! Stage lights! Lights up in front! (*He screams out.*) The Good Friday stunt at The Hague is all washed up! (*He grabs* WILHELM.) Dear friend, is she there? Hold me up—I told you, your eyes would still behold the glory. I just have to open my mouth ...

(OTTILIE *enters in nightdress and stops on the threshold.*)

CHRISTIAN: (*goes towards her.*) There's Sofie—the one who wanted to take the wind out of the proud frigate's sails. Sofie, you foundering tub. I die—a Catholic—your game is killed off stone cold and Holland turns away in horror. Krey, is she broken, can you see it in her eyes? Catholic, phone all the newspapers—Christian Maske & Co.—turned Catholic today! Flash of brilliance! (*He falls dead on the threshold at* OTTILIE's *feet.*)

OTTILIE: (*screams.*) Father!

SCENE 5

The occupants of the house enter through all the doors in night attire, servants quickly remove the body from the room. There is a great deal of coming and going between the room into which the corpse has been taken and the scene.—A servant puts on the lights. Now the fashionably exaggerated splendour of the night attire, in particular that of PHILIPP ERNST *and* PRINCE OELS, *both of whom like* WILHELM *are wearing a kind of turban, can be seen, as well as the general similarity between* WILHELM's *outfit and theirs.* WILHELM *pressed in embarrassment into one corner of the proscenium stands with both hands before his face as if trying to crawl away inside himself to hide. All present exchange commiserations with each other, shaking hands and embracing.*

OELS: (to PHILIPP ERNST.) My poor chap!

PHILIPP ERNST: A terrible—

(WILHELM *staggers towards the steps*).

PHILIPP ERNST: (*to him.*) Horrible thing to happen. Thank you, thank you! (*Gives him both hands. Exit with* OELS.)

(WILHELM *stops at the steps and utters a great sob.* OTTILIE *stands before him.* WILHELM *hides his face in his hands anew.*)

OTTILIE: I am all alone. I need you to lean on. (*She embraces him.*)

243

SCENE 6

FRIEDRICH *appears on the gallery, hat in hand. He hurries down the stairs, stands close in front of the couple.* OTTILIE *frees herself from* WILHELM. FRIEDRICH, *who only now sees* WILHELM, *makes a gesture of shocked horror and raises his hand to strike* WILHELM.

WILHELM: (*beside himself.*) Hear me first!

(FRIEDRICH *looks* OTTILIE's, *then* WILHELM's *outfit up and down with an indescribable expression, drops his fist and makes a grand gesture of farewell.* WILHELM *hangs his head and escapes from the room at top speed.* OTTILIE *follows after she has looked* FRIEDRICH *coldly up and down.* FRIEDRICH *puts on his hat.*)

SCENE 7

An old butler appears.

FRIEDRICH: The way out, please?

BUTLER: Through the hall—won't you be staying till morning, sir?

FRIEDRICH: No!

BUTLER: May I order a carriage? At night it's ...

FRIEDRICH: I'll find my way.

BUTLER: It's very dark. A light, perhaps?

FRIEDRICH: A light must be found! God willing—light the way to the great goal. (*Exit through door centre.*)

(BUTLER *puts out all the lights, opens the window. The wind blows the curtains into the room.*)

CURTAIN

THE FOSSIL

Drama in Three Acts

'There are still men like Tellheim.'

Translated by J. M. Ritchie

THE FOSSIL

Characters

Ex-Cavalry General TRAUGOTT VON BEESKOW
HIS WIFE
HIS DAUGHTER URSULA
HIS SON OTTO
SOFIE née VON MASKE, *Otto's wife*
ULRIKE ⎫
        ⎬ *their children*
ACHIM ⎭
AGO VON BOHNA
FRÄULEIN VON RAUCH, *governess*
FÖHRKOLB, *the chauffeur*

Prussia 1923—in the country.

ACT I

SCENE 1

TRAUGOTT VON BEESKOW: (*in battledress.*) I'm dead in the eyes of the world, it's stone dead in mine! Don't come to me with questions and plans of campaign! Neutral ground between Here and Hereafter. Here we're not father and son, I'm no Prussian ex-cavalry brass-hat, you're no captain of industry. Astrologer up in the observatory—that's me. Alchemist down in the cellar—that's you. Basta!

OTTO VON BEESKOW: I'm not seeking contact.

TRAUGOTT: We've given our word of honour! This old gun-turret gazebo in the gardens is no office, no club-room; it's a mausoleum which allows us to see each other from time to time for what we are—monuments, gigantic statues of better days: me the victor of St. Gaillard, you the inventor of the deadly YT Gas that reduces reinforced concrete to rubble. I've decided I don't fit any more. I'm unfit for human society. A mere formula, put on ice, living off shares.

OTTO: All right! This is no plan of campaign, no question. This is a warning!

TRAUGOTT: Warning—to a cavalry general?

OTTO: Ago von Bohna has suddenly come back from Moscow!

TRAUGOTT: Christ, sealing wax and arse-holes!

OTTO: Powerful reaction. You're not such a fossil.

TRAUGOTT: That was a belch of psychological acidity. (*Roars.*) No chemical double-talk with me! Logic! Fundamentals!

OTTO: I eschewed verbs and attributes. Simply mentioned the name: Ago!

TRAUGOTT: Damnation!

OTTO: You see! No need for action to blast you out of your stupor.

TRAUGOTT: Crisis and catastrophe are synonymous with that name.

OTTO: All I said was: Ago. Full stop.

TRAUGOTT: That full stop has the force of a shell from a Fifty Pounder! (*He stamps his foot.*) Boom! I know my explosives.

OTTO: All I did was put the two together—Ago and Moscow.

TRAUGOTT: Moscow is havoc, Ago cataclysm. The formula A + B = End of the World.

OTTO: (*goes to the steps leading down.*) That was all.

TRAUGOTT: Halt! Now that you've broken the armistice and opened fire.

OTTO: No more to tell.

TRAUGOTT: Are you trying to tell me communication needs sentence structure? Doesn't the substantive by itself give the clearest, overall picture? Are we journalistic nincompoops? We communicate in short-hand. The truth! Out with it! Since you've broken your oath and made me functional again, turn the handle some more.

OTTO: These are the first words between us in three years. All 1919, 1920 and 1921 you were as mute as a fish.

TRAUGOTT: What was there left for a Prussian General to say after Versailles? He had to lose the power of speech, hold his trap.

OTTO: Nothing for the German munitions manufacturer to add either. Our silence was right and proper, historical necessity. Tactfully your wife and mine and your daughter joined in the quintet of silence.

TRAUGOTT: (*roars at him.*) Bah!

OTTO: Exactly. Now it appears we were in wireless contact with the world after all.

TRAUGOTT: Scoundrel!

OTTO: The scoundrel you idolised, whom mother adored and Ursula—words fail me. That selfsame Ago reappears like a ghost after five years' captivity in Russia and Siberia, after seven years' absence in all.

TRAUGOTT: What do you want me to do? Rush to the phone: 'Beeskow here—who're you?'

OTTO: I've a feeling there's current running through you. You're plugged in.

TRAUGOTT: You swindler, liar, cheat! It's your business training. You can't help it. You're suppressing one vital item. That last letter I had!

OTTO: I don't know what was in it.

TRAUGOTT: You lie. You just don't know the actual wording.

OTTO: I saw how you raised your eyebrows after you read it.

TRAUGOTT: You've known what that means since the first time I belted you over this rocking-horse of yours. You know what was in the letter.

OTTO: Guessed perhaps.

TRAUGOTT: You can read my eyebrows like a book.

OTTO: Ago caught some infection—over there?

TRAUGOTT: Exactly! Worse than syphilis! At least that can be cured with Salvarsan and mercury. (*Rushes up the stairs.*)

SCENE 2

URSULA *enters, exchanges looks and gestures with* OTTO, *comes down the steps.*

TRAUGOTT: (*appears at the top of the stairs.*) There's a machine gun right here. Anybody who comes within a hundred yards of this emplacement and fails to stop when challenged will end up looking like a sieve. Nosey parkers have been warned! I've got a Zeiss telescope which can see right through you and your intrigues. I'm a fossil, but I've still got my finger on the trigger to blast you from a great height.

OTTO: Absolutely no reason for us to fight, Papa; you carry on looking at Sagittarius and Aquarius. I'll carry on peering into my retorts with Ursula. (*He climbs down the steps to the cellar.*)

TRAUGOTT: (*dashes down the steps.*) Still on the line? Rung off! Bit sudden! Boom boom!

URSULA: (*comes up the steps from below.*) Good morning, Papa! (*Kisses his hand.*)

TRAUGOTT: You in the picture, Ursula?

URSULA: Think so.

TRAUGOTT: You're a Beeskow! Feudal aristocracy! First recorded mention 550 A.D. when the Hohenzollerns were still swinging from trees. That's really something!

URSULA: Which I value now as always.

TRAUGOTT: You're the last of the race with real breeding. Your brother's a gelding.

URSULA: I'm a Beeskow. At your command.

TRAUGOTT: What's water?

URSULA: H_2O.

TRAUGOTT: Exactly! The fact that it can be made into mineral water is completely irrelevant. Pure accident!

URSULA: Beeskow for ever! Papa.

TRAUGOTT: Don't throw yourself away. You've survived the flood that's the main thing. Still a Beeskow even *après le déluge*.

URSULA: Always to the fore!

TRAUGOTT: You are my plus quantity.

URSULA: And yet you retreat because of Ago's coming?

TRAUGOTT: Him? Coming here?

URSULA: Definitely!

TRAUGOTT: (*beside himself.*) How do you know?

URSULA: Telegram! (*Hands him it.*)

(OTTO's *head has appeared in the stairs.*)

TRAUGOTT: You hadn't the guts to tell me!

OTTO: Your eyebrows!

TRAUGOTT: (*reads.*) Arrive ... (*Crumples the telegram and flings it away.*) Ha!

URSULA: So you are going to retreat, father? Going to pretend you've died, gone away?

TRAUGOTT: I just don't fit. Stuffed dummy.

URSULA: Draw a parallel! Between yourself and him! The Bohnas have been there alongside the Beeskows acre by acre, fate by fate for centuries. You've told me yourself a hundred times.

OTTO: That's right.

TRAUGOTT: What's that, you degenerate wretch? You dare—?

OTTO: I'm thinking of you.

TRAUGOTT: A model, a standard, yes! But I'm no parallel. I'm nearly seventy—he's not half that.

URSULA: Don't be an old fossil.

TRAUGOTT: (going for her.) Daughter!

OTTO: She's right.

URSULA: Enough sudden retreats! Either—or!

OTTO: A bas le silence!

URSULA: Show a little enlightenment, father! A man who tackles the stars ...

OTTO: Need fear neither Moscow nor the Devil himself.

TRAUGOTT: (bends down for the telegram, flattens and reads it.) Tomorrow maybe—or even today already?

URSULA: Act as quickly as possible, naturally!

TRAUGOTT: Good! My mind is made up! But tactics, strategy must be bang on.

URSULA: But of course.

OTTO: We're all under your command.

TRAUGOTT: Blood beginning to run high. Action stations! (To OTTO.) You shoot across! To the advanced positions! Put out patrols! He shall not take me by surprise!

OTTO: Sirrr! (Off.)

TRAUGOTT: Battle: The old excitement is bubbling up again. I mass my infantry then—boom! The big gun. Are you on fire like me?

URSULA: We burn with one flame—a fight to the finish!

TRAUGOTT: When things start to happen rise above them. Sail into the skirmish in your petticoats—you'll do a damned sight more damage than your bourgeois contaminated renegade brother. Use your charms to the utmost and deliver the enemy up to me.

URSULA: Your faith in me shall not be misplaced!

TRAUGOTT: And then I attack—boom—boom—and finish him off—with infantry, artillery and massed cavalry reserves! Tataratah!! (He imitates loud bugle calls.—The scene goes quickly dark and lights up again.)

SOFIE, OTTO *and* AGO *enter.*

AGO : Is that—?

SOFIE : The stronghold. Also called the Grail Castle.

OTTOH Fossil Fortress. Armour plated. Battle-ship. Abstract.

SOFIE : Not so loud. You never know whether he's up there or not.

AGO : Why don't you call him!

OTTO : He can't be called. He's a *deus ex machina*—comes on without cue. A kind of Fortinbras.

AGO : So funny the way you're afraid of him.

SOFIE : In his eyes we are the epitome of human depravity.

AGO : His tactics are to avoid meeting me face to face. He makes me out an enemy, though there's absolutely no need.

SOFIE : You *are* one, you know!

AGO : I'm not here as my usual self. Haven't come home for fights and pointless altercations. I'm simply coming back after five years to people who loved me and whom I loved.

OTTO : Quite simply—from Moscow—marvellous!—(*Points.*) Observatory upstairs, laboratory downstairs. We deal with elements which are never afraid of smashing into each other. So no question here of special considerations or beating about the bush. Marrow gets extracted, essence die-stamped, reduced to a formula.

SOFIE : In the same way, we too, son and daughter-in-law, re-ceive no special consideration, he calls us bourgeois. Not for a second can you be anything but deadly dangerous acid in his view, to be called by name at loudest pitch.

OTTO : If not louder! And the sooner the better.

AGO : Is this just an act, or does he just panic easily?

OTTO : An act? He would consider any other kind of reaction mere frivolity.

SOFIE : If you want to establish contact with him, shoot on sight. If you don't he will.

OTTO: Dead on target!

SOFIE: Life or death! Take me for instance. I'm corroded by his exhalations and it's only bourgeois thick skin that keeps me alive.

OTTO: It's the acid test around here. Here we split atoms.

SOFIE: Will your doctrine withstand every causticity?

AGO: (laughs.) It most certainly will!

OTTO: Then get going!

AGO: What good will it do me to toss him? There are millions to be reached nearer the point of enlightenment.

SOFIE: Depressing strategy.

OTTO: Who do you think is the greatest enemy to the development you envisage? Us? The middle-class, upper or lower?

SOFIE: They're a boom and burst bunch, a miserable lot.

OTTO: The aristocracy now—even in present day Prussian Germany it's still productive.

SOFIE: You can say that again!

OTTO: The decisive battle is between the two of you!

AGO: The two of us? What do you take me for?

SOFIE: A Bolshie?

OTTO: Communist.

AGO: If it has to have a name—close enough!

SOFIE: Colourless characters like us would much rather take you as you are—with reservations.

OTTO: In his eyes I'm bourgeois not just because of my marriage, but because I'm prepared to respond to the sensation of the moment, to changing circumstances.

SOFIE: In his eyes you are either A or B. And A and B signify constants on which he counts for his purposes for all eternity.

OTTO: No calculations. Calculation is bourgeois.

AGO: I understand and always have done. I've known the breed since childhood.—And Ursula?

SOFIE: If a middle-class woman loves you she'll go to bed with you even if you are red. But it's her sentimental condition that makes her, not your political convictions. As far as Ursula is concerned you are a blue-blooded aristocrat and not only on father's orders; you're a von Bohna just as she's a von Beeskow and that's all you ever can mean till death do you part.

AGO: Is feudal Germany still so strict?

OTTO: Marxist Germany too. It's all in-fighting and obeying the word of command. Only we in the middle are adaptable, fluid.

AGO: Why do you call the old man a fossil and not a radical?

SOFIE: Because he prefers what has been to what is coming.

AGO: What has been must be expressed in a formula. But not according to aristocratic needs with plus and minus signs.

OTTO: In his eyes you're a minus quality.

SOFIE: Less than minus, nothing.

AGO: I can't believe him capable of such stupidity. If I'm his enemy he must consider me somebody to be reckoned with.

OTTO: How did you go that way?

SOFIE: When you went off to war you seemed a normal, average, aristocratic Ulan lieutenant.

OTTO: Tailor's dummy. Regulation blue-grey with epaulets and tassles.

AGO: Darling of the Officer's Mess. Drilled to worship the flag and the ceremonial drinking bout.

OTTO: A stalwart at regimental dinners.

SOFIE: Infatuated.

AGO: With Ursula—totally. Had an understanding with her.

OTTO: And with two or three floozies as well.

SOFIE: Quite the traditional ladies man!

AGO: The marriage arranged with an eye to her ability to give birth to and rear thoroughbred Bohnas to take their places as Pride of the Prussian Army.

OTTO: Plain sailing. *Fortiter et constanter per aspera ad astra,* etc, etc.

SOFIE: What happened?

AGO: The very first flesh ripping shell proved that even the most obsessed aristocrat's will to self-perpetuation is madness if a direct hit can rip him to shreds like any Tom, Dick or Harry.

OTTO: When what is human bursts like a soap bubble one begins to analyse things.

AGO: Exactly. And not just externals. As long as the uniform, the flagwaving and chloroform powder held the pieces together, the boil on the outer skin could be stopped from bursting. But in the stinking prison camps, latrines, fever bouts—

OTTO: Plus lots of books and pamphlets—

AGO: No! Even the ones I read masses of later on did not subvert me. Life itself did, with its horrors, starvation, slaughter, suppurating pus day after day. Then in shattered health on wet straw came the question: why go on living in this way?

SOFIE: Whence the conclusion?

AGO: Society always obeyed feudal and bourgeois command whose aim was general slaughter for reasons of profit.

SOFIE: Hear, hear!

AGO: War to the knife between the greedy and the envious.

SOFIE: Oho!

AGO: Your surplus value, the capitalistic exchange value created over necessary consumption is the capitalistic element which bars the way for the dispossessed. Any fool knows that. But my flash of insight was this: it applies not only on the material but on the cultural plane as well. Just as you do not *use* the millions amassed but only exploit the fact that you've got them behind you in order to build up an unbalanced social structure, so too surplus culture also bolsters your ostentatious presence. Every volume of Goethe on your shelves—whose contents are totally unknown to you—shores up this ghastly respect in which you are held.

SOFIE: Rembrandt, Mozart mere fronts for the cultured classes?

AGO: Same as shares, debentures, securities—

OTTO: So capital is not sinful—

AGO: Any intellectual property is inadmissible exploitation of what's dead and gone.

SOFIE: Very neat!

OTTO: So that's what the old man's got to listen to.

AGO: And more if he wants. These are just the initial scraps. I have a complete systematic exposition ready for publication.

OTTO: (*clasps his hands over his head.*) For God's sake, Bohna!

SOFIE: (*after a pause.*) To be blunt, Ago—this is not the kind of thing for a septuagenarian.

OTTO: Especially one like him. Let's about turn and have lunch. Make our getaway as quickly as possible.

SOFIE: Quick! While there's still time.

OTTO: Let's go!

AGO: Does this mean you're afraid for him?

OTTO: Fear of panic. Come on! Quickly!

AGO: As you please. I don't want to be in anybody's way. Just came here for a breather after the crises and catastrophes I've been through.

(*They are about to leave when*)

SCENE 3

URSULA *comes in from outside.*

SOFIE: (*to her.*) You remember—

URSULA: (*going up to* AGO.) Ago! Welcome home.

AGO: (*gives her both hands.*) Ursula!

URSULA: (*to him.*) You've hardly changed.

AGO: Neither have you.

SOFIE: Grown more beautiful?

AGO: Perhaps.

SOFIE: We were just going across for lunch.

URSULA: Isn't Ago going to see father first?

AGO: Is he here?

URSULA: He's just coming.

AGO: Does he know?

URSULA: Naturally. Weren't you ill?

AGO: Dangerously—three times.

URSULA: Improved any?

AGO: In my own way.

URSULA: As a man—much improved!

AGO: As a human being—much improved.

SOFIE: (*points to* URSULA.) What about her?

AGO: As a woman—much improved.

SOFIE: You mean lovelier?

AGO: More mature—I don't know.

URSULA: Let's hope so.

OTTO: She's my assistant. Chemistry is her calling.

AGO: You like analysing things?

URSULA: Synthesizing. We're building a world in test-tubes.

AGO: Re-building!

URSULA: No, I said building. And I know the difference.

SOFIE: All right—come when you're ready—if you absolutely must—talk with father.

URSULA: Has to be!

OTTO: Maybe you'll manage to bring him too—it'll be the first time ever.

AGO: I'll try.

(SOFIE *and* OTTO *exeunt.*)

SCENE 5

AGO: You are transformed, you know. It's obvious now.

URSULA: You too. I feel you're a stranger.

AGO: No wonder! How long ago was it?

URSULA: Seven years.

AGO: And what years! World War and Revolution.

URSULA: What years! You were twenty-eight.

AGO: And you twenty-three. What did we have in common?

URSULA: Feeling.

AGO: We dreamt more than knew what it was all about.

URSULA: I knew your moustache, your teeth.

AGO: And I your blouse with all those frills and things.

URSULA: You were my first taste of what a boy, a young man, was.

AGO: You mine—of a chaste girl. But it was all more a nibble than a meal, savouring the foretaste of what it would be like.

URSULA: Do you believe you know better now, because you've been doing a lot of thinking in the meantime?

AGO: Yes, because I changed my life's direction. Learned to forget about myself. Instead of forming the world after my own image, I naively accept my image and view of it from outside, from the things themselves. The same way I might no longer seek in you virtues traditional for a maiden of noble Prussian family and instead might become captivated by something entirely different, some new element in what you are as a woman.

URSULA: With no particular qualities?

AGO: With nothing the past esteemed; adorned with nothing but what is important here and now.

URSULA: Can't they be one and the same thing?

AGO: They don't have to and it doesn't matter. It's not likely because conditions are constantly changing.

URSULA: Let's wait and see how long you'll remain so modest in your demands of me.

SCENE 6

TRAUGOTT: (*is suddenly standing at the top of the stairs.*) And while you're gawking at the world and not forming it after your own image what are you making of yourself, aren't you telling the most damnable lies?

AGO: Uncle Traugott! A typical cavalry flank attack.

TRAUGOTT: We fossils stand by what's tried and trusted. Where does this technique of contemplating one's own navel leave you?

AGO: Constantly stupefied by multiplicity.

TRAUGOTT: Excuse for laziness and anarchy.

AGO: From the feudal point of view.

TRAUGOTT: Leading article double-talk. Newspaper gobbledygook. The West knows all that guff. Now the East is being infected by it. We in sterner climates are men of action, murderers. A bloody battle-field the Old World.

AGO: It was until now, admittedly. Still at the front, are you?

TRAUGOTT: (*comes down the steps to him.*) Are you a Bohna?

AGO: Bohna! Sirrr! Reporting ready for duty after seven years.

TRAUGOTT: Ready for duty? We'll see.

URSULA: But he requests permission to take a breather before further action, Papa.

TRAUGOTT: What is this, a picnic with beer and skittles? Is this a quiet game of cards? I'm no horse carriage for him to drive about in; you're no umbrella stand for him to let his feelings drip into.

AGO: I'm no redoubt to be taken by storm.

TRAUGOTT: What then?

URSULA: A sponge if you like.

TRAUGOTT: (*beside himself.*) Sponge off!

URSULA: He sucks us up. Fills up on us and then does an about-turn when he feels like it because the conditions are constantly changing. Your old fossil methods are wasted on him. He is the new kind of man.

TRAUGOTT: What kind?

URSULA: Instead of standing fast against change, he is constantly ready to adapt.

AGO: More or less, but there is a difference

URSULA: Little or no roots.

AGO: Little or no encumbrances.

URSULA: Even less responsibility.

AGO: Independent!

TRAUGOTT: In other words—a filthy swine!

AGO: Before you let yourself go with the kind of bad language permissible only in the family circle let me say this—we are as we are, we're not just pretending—so there can be no question of any conflict of ideology between us. It's a question of information, that's all. I know yours already from past experience. Do you want to find out about mine?

URSULA: Right.

AGO: I'm not pushing myself forward, I just ask if anybody wants to hear it. If not, I say hello in passing and disappear for ever without a sound.

TRAUGOTT: The day you are working towards is damnation for the likes of us.

AGO: What right have you to say that? You don't know what it is.

TRAUGOTT: Good God Almighty ...!

AGO: I'd have to be very wrong in what I know about the Prussian Junker if you aren't secretly far more curious than you are angry. So—cards on the table! I'm laying myself open to exhaustive reconnoitering and I'd have to despair of you and of the whole clan if you are too timid to engage in full-scale reconnaisance of the enemy's intentions. (*To the two of them.*) What point would there be in your continued existence if you too distort reality like the bourgeois instead of pinning it down properly?

TRAUGOTT: Who says I'm too timid? But this doesn't mean I let the enemy prescribe my tactics for skirmishing etc.

AGO: Agreed. I am permitted to have my breather while remaining on my guard like you.

URSULA: Agreed.

SCENE 7

OTTO: (*sticks his head round the door.*) What's all this—no corpses, no devastation. Instead I find a cosy family scene.

TRAUGOTT: Nincompoop!

OTTO: Anyway I'll rush the escapees from mutual annihilation off for lunch.

TRAUGOTT: (*heading for the stairs.*) That was lunch enough for me. It turns me up. Take him away and feed the brute!

(*Exit upstairs.*)

AGO: What a character!

OTTO: High explosive! Imagine you still being all in one piece.

AGO: (*to* URSULA.) What about you—can you put up with me for lunch?

URSULA: (*goes half way up the stairs and calls.*) What am I to do—father?

TRAUGOTT: (*roars.*) Double time quick marrch!!

OTTO: Your orders from H.Q. Irreversible. Come what may!

AGO: Must be obeyed.

(URSULA *has come down and he gives her his arm. Exeunt.*)

CURTAIN

ACT II

SCENE 1

The GOVERNESS *is by the door with 15-year-old* ACHIM *and 16-year-old* ULRIKE.

GOVERNESS: You wait here till Grandpapa comes. Mummy insists on your offering him best wishes on the Kaiser's birthday. He'll be expecting it all day.

ACHIM: There is no Kaiser any more. That's all fossilised.

GOVERNESS: Behave, Achim, even if it does go against the grain. Do it for your mother's sake.

ACHIM: All we do all day is do things for the parents' sake. Mummy doesn't care a hoot about the Kaiser and all that rot. The whole thing is your idea!

GOVERNESS: Show some respect, little man. To you I am still Fräulein von Reich. And don't you forget it! (*Goes out and slams the door behind her.*)

ACHIM: So what! I'm so mad I could rape her!

ULI: Achim, please, control yourself!

ACHIM: She's the nail in my coffin. Flirting one minute, impudent the next. Life would be great without her! On the whole the old fogies are quite well behaved. But that bitch with her Goethe and Schiller and now this business with Grandpapa! If something awful happens to her it's her own fault.

ULI: For instance?

ACHIM: What's been getting at you that you're acting like this?

ULI: Leave me alone or I'll tell her what you've been saying about her.

ACHIM: And I'll tell her you've been reading trashy books again, all night, and smoking like a chimney.

ULI: And I that you've been at it again with Lizzie. (*Sings.*) 'Down by the old mill stream'—

ACHIM: And I that you're head over heels in love with Uncle Ago.

ULI: You're crazy!

ACHIM: You're telling me, Uli! Because he's a Bolshie; that really intrigues you.

ULI: Pompous ass! You don't even know what Bolshie means.

ACHIM: That's what you think!

ULI: You are a born bourgeois.

ACHIM: Me bourgeois? Go on!

ULI: Yes, overweight and lecherous, *voilà tout.*

ACHIM: What about you with your fat legs! Mummy's right when she says you're acting the intellectual. *Voilà tout.*

ULI: (*laughs out loud.*) Me acting the intellectual!

ACHIM: All because he's a Bolshie and that's the latest thing.

ULI: (*offers him a bag of sweets.*) Just don't say another word!

ACHIM: (*takes one.*) Any hard centres?

ULI: What do you think, is Ago really in love with Ursula?

ACHIM: Of course he is. Same as she is with him. And maybe more so.

ULI: I don't find her attractive at all.

ACHIM: Bit medieval. But gorgeous legs.

ULI: I don't think my legs are too fat.

ACHIM: Too heavy in the calf. Lizzie's are really lovely.

ULI: Maybe Ago is more interested in things of the mind.

ACHIM: When Old Grandpapa lets him have it. (*Sings Offenbach's 'Grandduchess of Gerolstein'.*)
Then bim, bam, boom
Then ridi, ridi, doom
I'm General Boom-Boom!

(*He laughs.*)

ULI: Ago is not afraid of anybody. He has the younger generation and the Social Democrats behind him. I think he's wonderful. *Voilà tout.*

ACHIM: Would you—?

ULI: Marry him? Of course. But I don't think he believes in marriage; he has moral scruples.

ACHIM: He's in love with Ursula.

ULI: I'm richer than she is. And he hasn't a penny. Has to sell his estate here.

ACHIM: You're not his type. Give me the whole bag and I'll tell you all I know.

ULI: Halves!

ACHIM: All of it!

ULI: You don't know a thing.

ACHIM: What I saw yesterday evening when I peeped through the key-hole.

ULI: (*gives him the bag.*) Take it!

ACHIM: Well, he was standing there in his shirt sleeves and he picked the family photographs off the bureau one by one. Mater, pater, you, me—

ULI: And?

ACHIM: Put them back again, shaking his head.

ULI: What does that signify?

ACHIM: Why, I think—damn all!

ULI: Idiot!

ACHIM: Who, me?

ULI: No, him!

ACHIM: Then he picks up Ursula's picture—solemnly—(*Acts it.*) —with lots of feeling.

ULI: And?

ACHIM: Kisses it.

ULI: Balls!

ACHIM: A smacker. The works! Cub's honour! That's because she has lovely legs.

ULI: They're not in the picture. As for her bust, (*she laughs.*) she has damn all!

ACHIM: All the same.

ULI: I really couldn't care less.

ACHIM: I don't think!

ULI: You can read it in my diary. Quote: 'Uncle Ago is a Bolshie and an idiot'. Unquote.

ACHIM: I think so too. They say they're all the rage.

ULI: They're ten a penny. The place is swarming with them and the new chauffeur is one too—a real beauty.

ACHIM: You seem to feel attracted to them.

ULI: To the chauffeur?

ACHIM: Well, you keep showing him your legs.

ULI: Me—?

ACHIM: And how! Sitting there crossing your legs. I know that game!

ULI: Me cross my legs? Besides that doesn't mean a thing. Mummy does it and so do all the other ladies; a bourgeois like you, naturally—

ACHIM: I'm going to go on the land. Won't give a damn for anything. Basta! And later—watch my smoke! (*Gesture.*)

ULI: If things get too boring and I can't take any more I'm going to go into a nunnery.

ACHIM: You'd have to turn Catholic first, like Grandpa Maske.

ULI: So what!

ACHIM: Well, in the nunnery perhaps your legs won't matter.

ULI: Bah! (*She sings.*)

> 'No need for tears when we must part
> Just round the corner you'll find a new sweetheart'.

(ACHIM *sings the refrain with her again and they dance.*)

SCENE 2

TRAUGOTT *enters like a flash with* URSULA. ULI *utters a scream.*

TRAUGOTT: Now then you howling dervishes? What punishable offence or unprincipled act do I catch you at this time?

ACHIM: On the contrary, Grandpapa. We came to offer you our best wishes on the occasion of the Kaiser's birthday.

TRAUGOTT: I can see the congenital infamy in your eye as you say it.

ULI: We came at Mummy's express wish.

TRAUGOTT: All right, all right. You'll get no sweets out of me.

ACHIM: (*presents him with the bag of sweets.*) We have plenty. Take one!

TRAUGOTT: No thank you. What's to become of you?

ACHIM: Uli says she's going into a nunnery.

TRAUGOTT: Diabolical! The Beeskows are Protestants!

ULI: It's not definite yet.

TRAUGOTT: I can see you in a different place entirely.

ULI: That may well be.

TRAUGOTT: And you—you scoundrel?

ACHIM: Certainly not a Bolshevik like some people.

TRAUGOTT: Aha! I won't say what I think.

ACHIM: Why not? In our family we don't mince matters.

ULI: Don't be cheeky, Achim.

ACHIM: That's not cheek. Do you still ride the old rocking horse, Grandpapa?

TRAUGOTT: (*suddenly pretending he is going to wallop* ULI.) Out, before I do something I'll be sorry for!

(*Children exeunt howling.*)

SCENE 3

TRAUGOTT: Riffraff! Veritable Sodom and Gomorrha, but well out of the way, thank goodness.

URSULA: Products of their background. Depressing examples of the principle of adaptation of the species. In a different setting the boy might develop very well.

TRAUGOTT: Half breeds, that's all they are. (*Changing tone.*) —what about him?

URSULA: What you feared.

TRAUGOTT: No hare-brained schemes?

URSULA: He is as scientific as you or I. Works from facts.

TRAUGOTT: Operational?

URSULA: He has a manuscript in long-hand. I've only seen the outside of it. His comments from it sounded—well-rounded.

TRAUGOTT: And?

URSULA: The blood may rebel—intellectually he will always win.

TRAUGOTT: (*beside himself.*) What is this station anyway? The end of the line?

URSULA: The track governed by signals seems to have run out.

266

From now on we'll have to find our own, blind but happy through thick and thin.

TRAUGOTT: Where to? First we'll cause one hell of a crash. With a roll on the drums we lept onto the world stage back in the year dot. We're not going to shuffle off into the wings without kicking up a bit of a rumpus.

URSULA: For finished articles like us there's nothing for it but to find a bidder.

TRAUGOTT: You women would just go off without any more ado, would you?

URSULA: No, father. We too have character—more than you know—as well as sex! And now don't worry about me like you always do. Or you'll have a chink in your armour which he'll find like a shot. Believe me, ecstasies and sweet compromises are no use to me.

TRAUGOTT: You loved him once.

URSULA: Perhaps.

TRAUGOTT: Still love him?

URSULA: Is that the deciding factor with your kind? Was it ever with you, father? We are class and good breeding first and foremost and as they say nowadays: you have to be somebody.

TRAUGOTT: What you would lose ...

URSULA: I must just keep us alive inside me.

TRAUGOTT: You still remember.

URSULA: (tiredly.) Yes, father!

TRAUGOTT: I love—and admire you, daughter.

URSULA: Your schooling, father!

(Short pause.)

URSULA: (in a different tone.) Now—what's the plan?

TRAUGOTT: First the manuscript, book. With it he's strong—without it—qui vivra, verra!

URSULA: Which one of us?

TRAUGOTT: You! I'll keep in the background.

URSULA: And how? Just so we both know exactly what's happening.

TRAUGOTT: (grasps her by her two hands, whispers.) Go to

it—double time quick march! This time I trust you utterly, even if it were to seem as if all hell were opening up before me. Pretend passion, absolute abandon! It's the only way that will work.

URSULA: It was your *sang froid* that won you victory for the Hohenzollerns. Will you be able to keep cool when it's me that's involved? Your Ursula?

TRAUGOTT: With my faith in you I'll be an iceberg.

URSULA: Think you'll manage?

TRAUGOTT: Iceberg!

URSULA: You know, for a goal like this I need to have my arms free!

TRAUGOTT: You'll do the right thing. I trust you.

URSULA: Then go. He should be here any minute.

TRAUGOTT: (*goes to the steps.*) Kaiser's birthday! Symbolic!

URSULA: No looking or listening.

TRAUGOTT: I swear! (*Up the steps. Disappears.*)

URSULA: How long would love for a woman last in a man who is prepared to jettison his own ancestors and centuries of breeding?

SCENE 4

AGO: (*enters.*) I've come to say goodbye.

URSULA: Already?

AGO: Nobody will miss me. I'm leaving on the night train. Car picking me up at 12.30.

URSULA: I thought the sale of your estate would have taken you longer.

AGO: Agents! Since Otto out of consideration for his father absolutely refuses to do the natural and profitable thing and buy it for himself.

URSULA: So—this is goodbye.

AGO: Yes—much as I'd like to come back to more personal matters.

URSULA: There's too much of the turmoils of our age within us. As long as Tellheim is socially displaced, what in the old

268

days they would have called dishonoured, the fate of Minna von Barnhelm is unimportant.

AGO: There are still men like Tellheim!

URSULA: (*offers him her hand.*) Lessing was a great German dramatist.

AGO: (*takes it.*) The greatest!

URSULA: The one point we agree on.

AGO: The only one?

URSULA: Perhaps.

AGO: Should we try to find out?

URSULA: No declaration of love!

AGO: That is unnecessary. Until we are in agreement about the state of mankind neither of us would give the other a finger on the personal level.

URSULA: You wouldn't either?

AGO: I wouldn't either.

URSULA: So we stay out of it.

AGO: We are out—whether we like it or not. And that is our fate today.

URSULA: And that's how it's always been. You know the old love-song—'They could not be united ...' For some reason or other.

AGO: We are not on the same plane. There are no intrigues keeping us apart, there's no higher force any more to please the poet. It's just that we feel more interested in the fate of mankind than in our own.

URSULA: At any rate you do.

AGO: You too! Make no mistakes about yourself. Never mind about -isms and ideologies—you are still a child of the modern age.

URSULA: I do not deny that I can be roused by matters beyond the purely personal. But only by family, breeding, background —by the past.

AGO: But—!

URSULA: No more about me! Quick before you go—your new ideas in a nutshell for me to remember you by.

AGO: MINE IS A COPERNICAN REVOLUTION! It wasn't so much that he changed astronomy as such, but because he came up with the new idea: we see everything wrongly, from the wrong point of view. Supposing one were to change the perspective! We used to think the earth was motionless— and yet it moves!—I have abandoned the examination of any particular feudal or bourgeois ideals, such perspectives are fundamentally wrong so I have rejected all of them and arrived at a new one.

URSULA: Really? You are—?

AGO: In practice—nothing. Whether the proletariat comes to power by evolution or revolution concerns me but little; engagement and political action even less. I live and work to ensure one thing: if there is another November Revolution in Germany it will not be at a loss and at sea for the lack of its own theoretical foundations.

URSULA: Can you provide them?

AGO: Yes, using pure proletariat philosophy I am attempting to organise the combined forces of the proletariat just as in days gone by a feudal and a bourgeois philosophy mobilised the forces of these respective classes.

URSULA: Have you found the necessary point of departure?

AGO: Yes! The persistent, imperturbable, incomparable class-consciousness of the proletariat!

URSULA: (seriously.) The starting point is good!

AGO: (inflamed.) Magnificent, and you'll see how the whole world will rise up in storm once it knows it is exchanging something antiquated for something brimful of life.

URSULA: Quod esset demonstrandum. That subjunctive means—

AGO: Soon be reality!

URSULA: It's all too simple and impudent. I don't believe it.

AGO: Chapter after chapter goes into it in depth. Each follows the one before in unbreakable chain. By nature and breeding I'm no dreamer. Nothing but stark facts in my book.

URSULA: Where did all the thousands of new facts come from all of a sudden?

AGO: War, Revolution developed them.

URSULA: Name one example.

AGO: In future every child born in or out of wedlock bears the name of the mother! Thereby two historical vices of the average male,—one: infidelity, two: lack of a sense of responsibility—and their barbaric consequences—are rendered innocuous. Humanity sights a new continent of the spirit.

URSULA: So, you're not a Copernicus, you're a second Christopher Columbus.

AGO: You admit that it makes sense?

URSULA: The logic is gripping but the ethic is ghastly. This sees things purely from the man's point of view. Casts us women out of the realm of the mystic and mysterious into stark reality.

AGO: Spares the child the shame of the father's licentiousness. The significance of the sexual act lies not in the sexual pleasure of the male or the female, but in the fate of the child.

URSULA: It's significance lies in the sweet release it offers everyone from all restrictions.

AGO: Such anarchy is called feudalism. *Après nous le déluge.*

URSULA: Long live the sexual impulse!

AGO: You, a lady of the ancient aristocracy, shout that in 1923.

URSULA: Aristocracy is still productive!

AGO: So it's with the aristocracy and not with the defeated bourgeoisie that the man with the social conscience must engage in life and death struggle.

URSULA: We two are the symbols of the conflict.

AGO: I know my opponent!

URSULA: I love my enemy!

AGO: Are you not afraid, exposing yourself like this?

URSULA: When naked a woman is not exposed—she's still in full possession of her arsenal.

AGO: I feel it!

URSULA: Defend yourself as best you can!—I conceal nothing more. I can tell you—I loved you and still love only your appearance as a man, but am horrified at this creature's new concepts.

AGO: Which you fail to grasp.

URSULA: Which I sense are poisonous to a noble, proven and well-rounded world and my special place in it. (*Takes his hand.*) What did you fall in love with? Me, Ursula, incomparable among women, with my special way of looking at you, touching you—till you tremble in all your limbs before me? (*She gazes deeply into his eyes.*)

AGO: (*weakly.*) Ullie!

URSULA: Ullie for you and me only. And if you smash what makes me unique, you render unrecognisable the one you singled out from all other women.

AGO: If I succumb to you, I change the shape of the world as I see it so drastically I should not wish to live, in spite of everything.

URSULA: (*comes still closer to him.*) You wouldn't? (*And summoning up all her female power.*) In spite of—everything?

AGO: (*carried away.*) How delicious this is—(*Leans against her.*)

URSULA: Just delicious or uncommonly delicious?

AGO: (*with a start.*) Now listen, I want you to really understand! All this loveliness, this explosive feminine anarchy of yours—I can take it all in on one go. But it would take some little time before you began to appreciate the ramifications of my creation.

URSULA: All right, bring the book, read it to me!

AGO: When?

URSULA: Later this evening. Here!

AGO: When?

URSULA: When everybody is asleep at our place.

AGO: When?

URSULA: Eleven. Before your train leaves. So that I'm properly informed for the future.

AGO: And you'll surrender and listen?

URSULA: Not to Columbus or Copernicus. Female to male—incorruptibly.

AGO: I'll overwhelm you!

URSULA: Not with words. No matter how impressive they are.

AGO: Actions speak louder than words! (*Tries to draw her to him.*)

URSULA: (*frees herself.*) Away! Before somebody finds us!

AGO: Eleven!

URSULA: Eleven! Here!

(AGO *exit quickly.* URSULA *sways a moment, runs to the window, watches* AGO *hurry away and hiding behind a curtain throws him a kiss of total surrender. Pulls herself together and starts to leave by the stairs. At this moment there enters the* GENERAL'S WIFE, *sixty years old, dressed in black.*)

SCENE 5

URSULA: (*rushes to her without a word and flings her arms round her neck.*) Mother!
GENERAL'S WIFE: What's the matter, child? This is not like you?
URSULA: Nothing, mother.
GENERAL'S WIFE: Has the General—?
URSULA: Tell father—everything is going ahead nicely. I'll fly back and report immediately. Just one moment! (*Hurries off.*)

(GENERAL'S WIFE *climbs the stairs.*)

TRAUGOTT: (*upstairs from the door.*) Where is the child? Where is ...? (*In full dress uniform and decorations.*)
GENERAL'S WIFE: Everything going ahead nicely. Coming back immediately to report. And here's a telegram from the 'League of True Patriots'. (*Hands it over.*)
TRAUGOTT: (*downstairs reads.*) 'Three cheers for our revered Founder and President on this festive occasion.' Thank You! (*He runs to the gramophone and cranks like mad. The 'Hohenfriedberger March' rings out.* TRAUGOTT *roars out the word of command.*) And now: PARRRADE—MOUNT! (*Wearing his plumed helmet he mounts the rocking-horse. Draws his sword, shouts.*) To the front, double time, quick, CHARGE! (*Singing the words and wielding his sabre lustily he rides like mad.*)
GENERAL'S WIFE: (*with a scream of delight.*) Oh! General! General!

CURTAIN

ACT III

SCENE 1

OTTO and FRÄULEIN VON RAUCH *come up from the laboratories.*

OTTO: Here's some money.

RAUCH: That won't go very far—you know a spring bonnet just the teeniest bit frivolous costs twice as much.

OTTO: You got the same the day before yesterday.

RAUCH: What about clothes, shoes, lingerie? You like to see me well turned out.

OTTO: This can't go on till the cows come home.

RAUCH: I shouldn't have to come begging. Bad for the character. After all I am a von Rauch.

OTTO: You've no finer feelings!

RAUCH: Don't you like me any more?

OTTO: Course I do. Haven't I just proved it?

RAUCH: I love you first and foremost—before God!

OTTO: That suits me fine. (*He gives her money.*) There! But keep your eye on young Uli! Watch her closely. That girl is beginning to have eyes and ears where she is not wanted.

RAUCH: She is precocious. She has your temperament. She is after Ago.

OTTO: He'll be gone this evening—once and for all.

RAUCH: Lord be praised, I'm sure!

OTTO: Now move! Watch the step. Pst! (*Pushes her out the door and follows a minute later.*)

SCENE 2

FÖHRKOLB: (*climbs in the pavilion window on the right. Switches on a small electric torch.*) Pst!

ULI: (*sticks her head round the curtain over the alcove.*) Pst! Hullo!

FÖHRKOLB: Here already?

ULI: Just caught the old man red-handed with the governess.

Got eyes where I'm not wanted, have I! Shower! (*She steps forward.*)

FÖHRKOLB: (*giggles.*) Well, well!

ULI: Mum's the word! This is my affair!

FÖHRKOLB: Naturally, you have my word, Miss!

ULI: (*steps up to him.*) Listen, don't get any funny ideas just because I meet you secretly in the middle of the night.

FÖHRKOLB: What kind of ideas?

ULI: All just pure curiosity on my part to see what your type is really up to.

FÖHRKOLB: What do you think I'm up to? Wait with the car to drive people like that bloody white-collar Commie Baron Ago to the station. Half an hour from now.

ULI: I'm not interested in that. What about how you live, think and so on apart from that.

FÖHRKOLB: Nothing special.

ULI: Are *you* a real—Bolshevik!

FÖHRKOLB: Communist Party member. More or less.

ULI: Well then, what do you want with me, a capitalist?

FÖHRKOLB: (*grins.*) You are also a very good-looking girl, Miss!

ULI: I shouldn't give a damn about whether you were good-looking. There are hundreds of people who look all right. What do you think, that makes you different from us—? (*Suddenly.*) Quick! Light out! Achim is after us.

FÖHRKOLB: (*his torch out.*) Impossible! Nobody there! He's got off with Lizzie.

ULI: Suppose you suddenly came to power,—let's take a night like tonight and imagine that your comrades have stormed our castle with torches, hand grenades, etc., and you're at their head doing a Garibaldi and all that—what would you do with me?

FÖHRKOLB: I'll give you just one guess, Miss.

ULI: My guess is what anybody would do under the circumstances. You don't have to be a Commie to do that. You should really find some new and different way to do it.

FÖHRKOLB: Damnation! That's not playing the game.

ULI: It is your duty to be original in all respects.

FÖHRKOLB: No rules laid down to cover that yet.

ULI: Rules? You're joking. If that's the case everything remains the same as before. No thanks! Take another example. Supposing I allowed you to kiss me, etc.—what would your feelings be?

FÖHRKOLB: I'd get excited and I'd enjoy it immensely.

ULI: That all? Anybody would. If I were to start something with a Commie like you, it would have to be something different, like me turning Catholic. Sensational.

FÖHRKOLB: All you've got are certain little attractions. Which are top hole I admit. But there's still only one way of trying them out as it were.

ULI: You're wrong there. I enjoy you in a very special sort of way, because you're far beneath me, a dangerous character, a kind of beast of prey, a monster. If you didn't give me the creeps on account of class distinction and all that, I should not be standing here at this minute. You can take my word.

FÖHRKOLB: You're beginning to give me the creeps too.

ULI: Here, what d'you mean?

FÖHRKOLB: At myself.

ULI: What are you going to do about it?

FÖHRKOLB: Now that I come to think of it ... (*Comes at her.*) My God, you little beast!

ULI: Go on then!

FÖHRKOLB: You're just like all the rest, nothing but a female exploiter!

ULI: So what!

FÖHRKOLB: Profit mad, vultures, that's what.

ULI: What if we are?

FÖHRKOLB: (*excited.*) Bloody impudence!

ULI: C'est la vie, chéri.

FÖHRKOLB: (*beside himself.*) French! That's the last straw.

ULI: Voilà!

FÖHRKOLB: I've a good mind just to belt your pretty little face just a bit out of line!

ULI: (*faces him.*) Go on then!

FÖHRKOLB: You don't mean it, do you?

ULI: I most certainly do, my lad.

FÖHRKOLB: (*hits her.*) Try that!

ULI: (*steps back dumbfounded.*) Good God!

FÖHRKOLB: And here comes number two.

ULI: You really are a dangerous character!

FÖHRKOLB: I'll teach you and your whole clan how to be-have. We, the proletariat, have reached boiling point! (*After a minute in a different tone.*) You're not angry, are you?

ULI: Why?

FÖHRKOLB: Because I hit you?

ULI: You're a sheep, Fritz. You're not straight in your own mind about Bolshevism. I can see that much.

FÖHRKOLB: That'll come. I clouted you one, didn't I?

ULI: You'd never have had the nerve off your own bat; I put the idea into your head.

FÖHRKOLB: You wait and see! I'll work it out.

ULI: You'd much rather be tender.

FÖHRKOLB: You're right there, Miss. (*He beams.*) Very much so! (*Steps closer.*)

ULI: Not now! I've a feeling we'd better disappear. Pst!

FÖHRKOLB: Just one little kiss.

ULI: (*holds up her mouth to him.*) But keep your distance, com-rade! And be quick!

FÖHRKOLB: (*kisses her.*) You're so sweet! I just don't know. Soft and lovely. You know how to handle men, Miss. You're the tops!

ULI: You like me?

FÖHRKOLB: And how!

ULI: (*lifts her skirt.*) Like my legs?

FÖHRKOLB: Super!

ULI: Not too plump?

FÖHRKOLB: Not a bit.

ULI: Right now disintegrate. Comes the dawn!

FÖHRKOLB: And you don't need to be scared of me. (*One leg over the window-sill already.*)

ULI: You're telling me! (*Shouts suddenly.*) Somebody coming!

(FÖHRKOLB *exit by the window.* ULI *undecided runs downstairs.*)

TRAUGOTT *and* URSULA *enter.*

TRAUGOTT: What's that chauffeur fellow flitting about here for? His kind are forbidden to set foot on the premises. Have to set man-traps to catch them.

URSULA: (*still in the doorway.*) What a night!

TRAUGOTT: The whole circle of fixed stars in the northern hemisphere our approving spectators!

URSULA: I never saw them so clearly with the naked eye. Normally they're like diamonds pinned on black velvet; tonight they are light-charged hanging in space.

TRAUGOTT: Remarkable their rigid resistence to change! This is exactly how Copernicus saw them. In the centre the pole-star, depending on him the Little Bear, watched over by the Dragon and Cepheus. Which is your favourite—Arion, Pollux the Giant?

URSULA: Antares in the Scorpio. He has the brightest eye.

TRAUGOTT: (*arm round her shoulder.*) Look! Eagle, Swan, Cassiopeia with the Wagoner in the Milky Way keep shining watch.

URSULA: I envy you your knowledge of well bred constancy.

TRAUGOTT: (*threateningly.*) Which in your heart you no longer have?

URSULA: In the laboratory I chase molecules. Always trying to find out how they can be split. That has some effect on one's soul.

TRAUGOTT: Above all else the heritage of your blood is resistance to change.

URSULA: My profession impresses on me the image of eternal change.

TRAUGOTT: Suddenly I feel your morale is slipping.

URSULA: (*laughs painfully.*) If you could see the two of us, him and me through your telescope, we should be like Leo and Virgo about to smash into each other—horribly.

TRAUGOTT: Why do you laugh, if you don't feel like it? In the heavens there are no collisions.

URSULA: We poor humans—oh!

TRAUGOTT: (*tenderly.*) You hesitate, my little one? Something wrong? Can you not make it? Do you want me just to kick this fellow to the devil before it goes any further, keep quiet and do nothing but look at the stars when the storms gather round us?

URSULA: It is our business as fixed stars to stay where we are. The other way we should be like cast off planets drifting about the firmament.

TRAUGOTT: And to be a guiding light for the Fatherland against the enemy within and without. True patriots! Are we no good? Mistaken about ourselves? Out with it!

URSULA: You—never, God knows. And I—that remains to be seen with him.

TRAUGOTT: You see the consequences clearly? You're quite clear?

URSULA: That I cannot refute the doctrine he proclaims. For he listened to the voice of the age and human conscience; no personal ambition any more for me to censure. If I am to conquer him it must be with charm and the blind intoxication I can lead him into step by step.

TRAUGOTT: Exactly! Step by step! Victory depends on brilliant phasing. Not quickly, not cheaply, not without always repairing any break-through inside you (*Powerfully.*) And never touch reserves. Get over the man and beyond him as quickly as possible! You are engaged in an out-flanking offensive, the whole movement, or even one flank of it must never stop for a minute.

URSULA: Give him no time to come to his senses and act for the good of mankind.

TRAUGOTT: And above all you must not lose your senses and act as a woman! That understood!

URSULA: Understood as always.

TRAUGOTT: In the turmoil of battle hear the thunder of a father's heart-beat and that of a whole way of life. (*He thunders out in song.*) 'In the furious dance of war ...!' (*Snaps to attention, salutes her, then climbs up the steps humming the tune.*)

(URSULA *hurries to the window and peers out.*)

TRAUGOTT: (*from above.*) Well?
URSULA: Nothing.

(*Silence.*)

TRAUGOTT: Well?
URSULA: Not yet.

(*Silence.*)

TRAUGOTT: Think he's not coming?
URSULA: Of course he is.
TRAUGOTT: Know what you've got to do?
URSULA: In my blood.
TRAUGOTT: The book, type-script—reserves? Remember?
URSULA: Everything!
TRAUGOTT: Victory or nothing! (*And tenderly and greatly moved.*) Ursula!
URSULA: The true patriot! Female version. (*Suddenly.*) He's coming.

(TRAUGOTT *exit quickly, upstairs.*)

SCENE 4

Only the bright flames in the fire-place light the room.

AGO: (*enters.*) How did it go?
URSULA: Easy, once they were all asleep. What about you?
AGO: Said my farewells. Car's waiting with my things. I met the young boy as I slipped out the door.
URSULA: The bright night has all life astir.
AGO: Divine stir of nature! Battle-cry of revolutions.
URSULA: Not the Marxist one. That's rationality.
AGO: We stop a long way short of Marx. But go beyond Bakunin in demanding both religion and art. Proletarian, of course! Dreams and where appropriate complete madness. We are less restricted than you are, unbiased; but we want all this to be

not something private, we want it to spring from the common purpose of federalistically-minded human beings.

URSULA: And we wanted it for ourselves?

AGO: It was in the interest of the ruling classes to be pretty harsh on those under them.

URSULA: Aristocrats are also Christians.

AGO: Boundless selfleshness needed a safety valve to reduce the pressure. That's why clemency and compassion were taught and quietly insinuated into the people.—Hear the essence of my doctrine from the beginning of the book. (*He reads.*) 'Happy the man, who totally consumed in work is not too laden with the burden of feudal or bourgeois culture, which make of him a man in the chains of prejudice. And happy the man who sees this: all that is known is knowledge intended for use *against* him by the cultured classes. Throughout the dreadful history of man since Plato, so-called "ideals" have been mobilised against him, are multiplied and kept alive by teachers of philosophy who never accept the reality of things as they are, but who instead out of sheer arrogance want something better, more rational. Thereby horribly distorting the nature of the world into something dependent on thought or belief! —The day of the world as it really is, man as he really is, has not yet dawned.'

URSULA: No half measures for you!

AGO: This welter of intellectual ideals must be countered by proletarian enlightenment which says this: 'only reality, the one and only exists, in which every creature assumes the right to be accepted not on the basis of any preconceived norm, not out of obedience to orders from those who think they know better, but for itself and to be a responsible being as a thing in itself.'

URSULA: Very decisive! To the point!

AGO: But one thing I cannot conceal: right now there is so much awareness in me of the particular beauties of life that sweeter than the longing to set the universe aflame with my fire is the urge to sweep you off your feet as I never managed to before and that this was always at the back of my mind in coming here.

URSULA: How demanding suddenly after such high principles! What you have just been saying was: 'Down with uncontrolled Desire.' But instead of accepting me as I really am (as you do everything else) now you say I'm special, incomparable, and you want to have a special impact upon me. You isolate me for your own pride and pleasure. But I refuse to agree to what is an old fashioned standpoint already rejected by you yourself and demand that you measure me by the new. Doesn't your book, your revelation say: what separates the property owner from the proletariat is that the latter wants no property he is not prepared to part with again quickly. That all material and spiritual goods (bourgeois Ideals and Culture) kept for one's self are a sin against one's fellow men. That all I should mean to you should be ultimate nuance from a dead Capitalistic age is for the girl who understands you the greatest possible insult and lowers you in her esteem.

AGO: No!

URSULA: You above all cannot permit such compromise. Not even woman should be a pretext for ideals; let's put it bluntly, she should be just another thing.

AGO: I don't want to be so exacting.

URSULA: Then you must be.

AGO: I reject pre-rogative but admit of natural pre-eminence.

URSULA: You thought that up right now to suit your case.

AGO: Do you think a whole new world order can be accomplished in one night?

URSULA: That's what I want to know. What you said was War and Revolution had already brought it about. That was a lie!

AGO: Haven't had such a stimulating hour for years, I'm sure.

URSULA: (forcefully.) SO WHY PUBLISH SUCH A BOOK? Who doubts that human insight into the plans of the Invisible is slowly improving? But how can someone who is still slowly adding vital facts to his insight dare set himself up as a prophet who has mastered chaos? Even God hadn't much to boast about before the seventh day.

AGO: (points excitedly to his book.) And yet there is so much that is pregnant here.

URSULA: Not the whole thing. Tragic for you and your kind

that you haven't managed to complete what you are turning over in your mind for mankind. More tragic still for the world if Providence were to find no means of rendering you all incapable of indulging in ill-considered actions.

AGO: And because we have not finished the job, does that mean your kind should be allowed to carry on plundering mankind? Is the horror to continue?

URSULA: It only horrifies you in theory. In practice, as you have shown, even the rebel wants choice things too. But we do not condemn you for this, we simply demand of the new leaders perfection such as we possessed: your total sense of honour and responsibility.

AGO: Since when does the woman in love insist on honour?

URSULA: Since man taught her to. Since when the socialist on gratification of private passion? (*She has stepped up to him, looks him full in the face.*)

AGO: Since woman was created as lovely as you.

URSULA: (*cheers.*) Are you beginning to break out of the closed circle and know that feeling?

AGO: I've a feeling—I love you!

URSULA: You love me—? What does that mean, really?

AGO: (*exploding.*) And lust for you.

URSULA: You mean you want to possess me all for yourself? Tragic lack of logic!

AGO: Flame of blind desire that burns for you—unique woman!

URSULA: Your work is still worthless. Will you finally confess it?

AGO: I'm not very heroic, but the cause is—!

URSULA: Not by a long chalk!

AGO: (*embraces her.*) I love you more than I do mankind.

URSULA: Away with half measures. (*She seizes the book.*) Destroy—!

AGO: (*beside himself.*) No!

URSULA: What comes between us and is useless for greater things. Free us—(*She holds the book aloft in her hand.*)

AGO: (*with a scream.*) Murdress! (*Grabs for the book; but the fire of her eyes forces him to submit.*)

URSULA: (*has flung the book into the glowing embers in the* fireplace where it flares up, rushes arms outstretched into his embrace with great scream of deliverance.) Ago!

(AGO takes her, carries her, almost flings her in an access of love and fury through the curtain.)

SCENE 5

Already during URSULA's last words TRAUGOTT has appeared on the upper stage. He and his mighty shadow have experienced the last outbursts. Now he hangs over the banister in the direction of the two in the closed alcove, so that his shadow falls right across the whole stage; waits for a moment, one great threatening look. Then URSULA's suppressed scream of ecstasy rings out— TRAUGOTT clearly grasps suddenly what is happening—he utters a hoarse croaking shout and roars with giant gesture: Vermin! Shoots off his revolver into the curtain, then rushes down the stairs.

SCENE 6

At the first shot ULI has appeared in the bend in the stair-case and FÖHRKOLB's face has bobbed up at the window right. Now ULI rushes with raised fists and great scream.

ULI: (who has ripped the curtain open and closed.) Both dead! Murderer! Fossil!
TRAUGOTT: (shakes her off as she goes for his throat, whereupon she rushes to the window, the door in screaming fits, shouting.) Help! Help!
FÖHRKOLB: (through the window like lightning, goes for TRAU- GOTT who flings him back. Then to ULI.) I'll drive into town like the wind and let justice deal with the monster.

SCENE 7

OTTO: (has entered quickly, taken in the situation at a glance.) Quick! Take the car and get going! In thirty minutes you can be over the border! Have you your passport and visa on you?

TRAUGOTT: At all times! But don't be so wild—we don't want any more excitement and tragic pathos. (*With clenched fist on his breast and last look towards the alcove.*) They are choked inside me, past! Now—form and breeding to the bitter end. (*Steps up to* FÖHRKOLB.) Our public must be kept in the picture at all costs. You drive me yourself, my lad, and—hand me over to justice.

OTTO: Father—are you—?

TRAUGOTT: What can happen to me in this day and age? Eh, you idiot?! Eh? (*And when* OTTO, *rigid, does not answer, forcefully.*) Well then! (*Then to* FÖHRKOLB *in harsh voice of command.*) By the right—quick—march! Above all there must be order and justice in Germany! Hurrah! (*And goes out erect and bare headed dragging the chauffeur after him by the arm.*)

QUICK CURTAIN